DEADLIER
Than the
Male

: Few actresses caught the perfect combination of abject evil and absolute seductiveness so well as the late Ingrid Pitt, posing here with a beloved 'familiar.'

DEADLIER
Than the
Male

Femme Fatales of 1960s and 1970s Cinema

by Douglas Brode

BearManor Media

2016

Deadlier Than the Male: Femme Fatales in 1960s and 1970s Cinema

For information, address:

BearManor Media
P. O. Box 71426
Albany, GA 31708

bearmanormedia.com

Typesetting and layout by John Teehan

Published in the USA by BearManor Media

ISBN—1-59393-185-9
978-1-59393-185-8

Dedication:
To my own real life life-long dream-girl
Sue Anne Johnson Brode

SIREN'S SONG: Joan Collins spoofed her own bad-girl image with a guest-villain appearance on TV's *Batman*.

Table of Contents

The Lethal Ladies...

Acknowledgments

TO MY SON SHANE JOHNSON BRODE, for his endless hours spent at creating the perfect combination of classic photos; to the various movie studios and distributors who were kind enough to allow me to use these fabulous images for the sake of creating a film history that would honor the memory of the actresses featured here; and to Tony and everyone at the Copy Center on Stone Oak Parkway in San Antonio, TX for their generous contribution of time and work to make certain that the project would all come together.

ANGELA DORIAN'S ALTER EGO: When the popular brunette Playmate of the Year donned a blonde wig, she doffed her name, as well as her clothes, to become Victoria Vetri, seen here in *When Dinosaurs Ruled the Earth*.

Introduction:
"Kiss Me! Kill Me!"
Bad Girls and the Male Imagination

"With an actor, you never know how long your money is going to last until your next film. So you always have to keep working. That's more or less what it's like."
– Barbara Bouchet

"Being considered a cult star is nice, but it doesn't pay the bills."
– Barbara Steele

ONCE UPON A TIME in Hollywood, circa the late 1980s, an East Coast film critic, in Los Angeles for a preview screening of a major release, met an old friend for dinner. At a pleasant if hardly upscale restaurant, they shared memories of their mutual lifelong interest in B-movies—the kind of projects that have never been heralded with an expansive press junket. Diehard junk buffs, the two picked up their conversation at the point where they'd left off years earlier. Each had always been particularly enamored of Femme Fatales from the 1960s and 1970s, a two decade period during which the movie business experienced a radical transformation. When the Sixties, a decade described as "swingin'," began, the Eisenhower era of calm, quiet, middle-of-the-road suburban lifestyles was just then coming to an end. Welcome, then, to the all-too-brief Kennedy Years: A handsome youthful president and his gorgeous wife set the pace for a return to old fashioned glamour and a new sort of sexiness. Though the James Bond books had been available during the 1950s, no one filmed them. Word that JFK was a huge Ian Fleming addict led to Albert "Cubby" Broccoli initiating a series that brought the novels' unique, and for many unsettling, combination of sex and violence to vivid life onscreen. Seeing is believing; audiences watched and, while primarily being enter-

1

tained, learned something, for better or worse. Movies, even those that are designed as diversions, change us, if in ways we aren't always aware of.

The old MPAA code, around since 1933, had restricted what could or could not be shown in a studio release. This value system was immediately challenged. By decade's end, it would be discarded in favor of a Ratings System that more or less allowed for anything, from family fare to outright porn. That shift occurred between 1967-1969. At the end of the Sixties and beginning of the Seventies, an X-rating meant mild Nudies cranked out by crude Russ Meyer (*Vixen*, 1968; *Blacksnake,* 1973), or classy Radley Metzger (*Camille 2000*, 1969; *The Lickerish Quartet*, 1970). Also, with the occasional ambitious drama containing strong sexual content (John Schlesinger's Oscar-winning *Midnight Cowboy*, 1969); shortly such fare had to be re-considered and re-rated as 'R.'

The reason: penetration, once included only in the most vulgar stag films, went virile. As a result, the X-designation would then be applied only to those films deemed 'hard' (explicit as to the sex act). Gerard Damiano's *Deep Throat* (1972) ushered in a(n) (in)famous era heralded as Porno Chic. Shortly, *Behind the Green Door* (1972) by the Mitchell Broth-

THE BIRTH OF BOND CINEMA: In *Goldfinger*, third of the popular series, Shirley Eaton portrayed Jill Masterson, aka "The Gilded Girl."

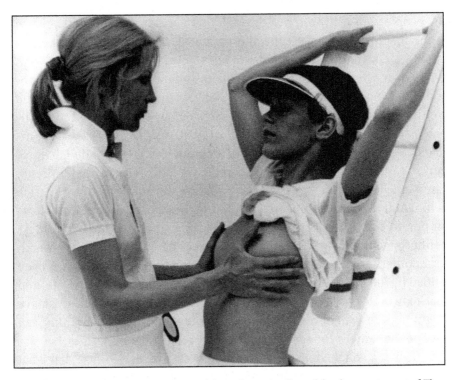

THE ERA OF EXPERIMENTATION: If the early 1960s allowed for the opening act of *The Sexual Revolution*, the late Sixties and early Seventies opened up the free love of Hippies to the vast mainstream; onscreen, Emmanuelle (Sylvia Kristel) gradually realizes that girl-girl action can be highly satisfying.

ers established that an X-rated film could be made with considerable artistry. The seamy sensibility of *Throat's* Linda Lovelace gave way to stunner Marilyn Chambers, who later navigated a shift into B-budget, R-rated Drive-In fare. There, she joined the femme fatales in those mainstream junk movies that, for the most part, this book enshrines. Do note, though, that A-films, including the aforementioned 007 series, are not excluded from these pages.

If the decade of the 1960s might be diagrammed as an ever rising line that charts the acceptance of graphic sex and violence into the mainstream, reaching an apex somewhere around 1969-1971, the 1970s can be seen as a similar line, contrarily moving in the opposite direction, ever in decline. If every movement, as Karl Marx once argued, produces its precise opposite, then once the pendulum has swung completely over to the far side, it automatically moves back toward where it came from. To consider one example that caught the 'journey' of Seventies cinema (and the people who really did live through that period), we need only glance at the first and last in the official *Emmanuelle* series. In the initial entry (1974), a conventional married woman (Sylvia Kristel), set in her ways if less than satisfied by her routine life, tossed away the old values to become a swinger with her husband as well as other men and women. She continued such passionate adventures in a far superior sequel. But the final installment, *Goodbye Emmannuelle* (1978), its title symbolic, has Emmanuelle, following the better part of a decade wallowing in divine decadence, come to realize that she misses the way things were. By film's end, Emmanuelle abandons La Dolce Vita (how significant that the Federico Fellini film of that title appeared in 1960, at the very tip of the Sexual Revolution iceberg) to pursue precisely what she had turned her back on. As her husband introduced her on to The Sweet Life, she drops him to search for another, more traditional, mate. Yet something significant has been gained by the process. You can't go home again, Thomas Wolfe wrote, and that may be for the best. No matter how retro her subsequent existence might appear—small house, white picket fence out front—nothing can ever be the same... for Emmanuelle or her real-life counterparts.

If such a couple does remain mutually exclusive, we sense that what happens behind closed doors, when the lights are turned off each night and they enter the bedroom, will never—*can* never—be conventional again. The joys of sex, back in the 1950s largely repressed, then emergent in the 1960s, exploding during the 1970s, will continue into the 1980s and beyond; reconfigured as an acceptable part of many re-imagined 'normal' American couples. The old Victorian adage that sex was, in and of itself, wicked, even among spouses, went out with the proverbial wash-water. By 1980, home video emerged as an important element in our popular entertainment. From then on, seemingly conventional husbands and wives might put on a Disney classic for the kids during the family hour. Still, an incredible number watched X-rated sex films after the little ones were fast asleep. Soon home video cameras inspired a few of those secret swingers to chronicle their own erotic experiences. Once the Internet existed, some couples went so far as to share their sex-capades with anyone and everyone, while still maintaining lifestyles that, on the surface, may have seemed like revivals of the Eisenhower era.

Meaning, of course, that the experience of the Sixties and Seventies, which seemed to soften during the Eighties, actually increased, at least behind the scenes. As to the Main Events? George Lucas (*American Graffiti, Star Wars*) and Stephen Spielberg (*Jaws, E.T.*) created nostalgia based retro-entertainment, relatively sexless films that proved popular with older, middle-aged, and young audiences alike. This may have been the result of a sexual overdose during the past two decades. First, an epidemic of Herpes created a cautionary attitude toward unprotected sex. Then the AIDS virus, which brought not only discomfort but death, drastically changed the sex habits of most people. Since popular culture consistently reflects the society that produces it, the movies which the public chose to see mirrored and motivated such attitudes. Not that sex entirely disappeared from the screen; only that the public had apparently lost interest in explicit depictions. The arrival of *Tattoo* (1981) in theatres was preceded by an advertising campaign featuring the image of a naked female (Maude Adams) in bondage, having become (to borrow from Ray Bradbury) The Illustrated Woman owing to her captor's mad obsession with tattooing every inch of her torso. Instead of creating a controversy, the film played to empty houses. Perhaps if the sexy space opera *Barbarella* (1969) had arrived onscreen in 1978 it might have been met with yawns. Likewise, had *Star Wars* premiered in 1969 it could have been a box-office bomb. Timing is everything, in life and in the film industry; movies must, to succeed, synch with the national psyche.

In due time, sex did return to the big screen. In the third Lucas-Spielberg collaboration, *Indiana Jones and the Last Crusade* (1989), the hero (Harrison Ford) and his father (Sean Connery), both (while fighting the

COULD LUCAS AND SPIELBERG HAVE BEEN INSPIRED BY THIS?: By the late 1980s, a wholesome 'family film' could contain a Nazi dominatrix; back in the mid-1970s, only Forbidden Cinema such as *Ilsa, She Wolf of the S.S.* with Dyanne Thorne, dared to include such a controversial character.

Nazis) become enamored of a beautiful bad girl, Elsa Schneider (Allison Doody). She tantalizes them with her blonde beauty, then ties them up and leaves a bomb to explode before she runs off. For those who only attend respectable films, this might have seemed an unprecedented innovation. For those who had regularly visited what might be tagged Forbidden Cinema, a sense of déjà vu set in. At third rate moviehouses, the aficionados of junk movies had seen it all before. In *Too Hot to Handle* (1977), bad girl Cheri Caffaro set precisely the same sort of bondage-and-bomb trap for one of her lovers. In *Ilsa, She Wolf of the S.S.* (1975), a notably similar sensuous but cruel Nazi blonde, incarnated by Dianne Thorne, dominated her male victims. Eventually, the pendulum swung once again, evidenced by Quentin Tarantino's *Pulp Fiction* (1994) and *Grindhouse* (2007), which openly brought B-movie sex-and-violence clichés back, now with an A-movie budget, his work playing at middlebrow Mall theatres.

Such a pushing of the limits was not confined to Tarantino's films. In the James Bond opus *GoldenEye* (1995), bad-girl Famke Janssen disposes of her lovers by strangling them with her long lovely legs even as the men reach orgasm. Everything old (and marginal, at least way back when) is new again, now salvaged from what was known as Forbidden Cinema, included in a re-imagined form of popular entertainment. A wicked Lolita, played by Patty Chandler, set the pace for that 007 sequence in a lowbrow junk flick *The Million Eyes of Su-Maru* (1967). Sex, particularly as embodied by the irresistible bad girl, had made her belated arrival. In truth, deadly beauty had been a staple of commercial movies from their birth during the early 1900s. The first true superstar of the silver screen was Theda Bara (1885-1955). Supposedly an arrival from the far east, her name meant 'Exotic Love That Leads to Death.' Actually, that phrase was made up by a press agent. The 'exotic enchantress' had been born Theodosia Goodman, daughter to a kindly tailor from Cincinnati. But the public bought into the fantasy; after all, all of us get enough grim reality in our daily lives. When most people buy a movie ticket, they do so to escape their actual existences. It's like visiting an exotic foreign country, only better, because the real deal can disappoint, whereas its dream-like fantastical reincarnation by Hollywood has been designed to satisfy, to make the impossible dream a tangible reality if only for two hours. But *what a wonderful* two hours. And how their images burn into one's memory buds, powerfully returning as we all walk along through ordinary existence, pretending to fully be a part of the world, sustaining ourselves with spellbinding fantasies drawn from The Movies.

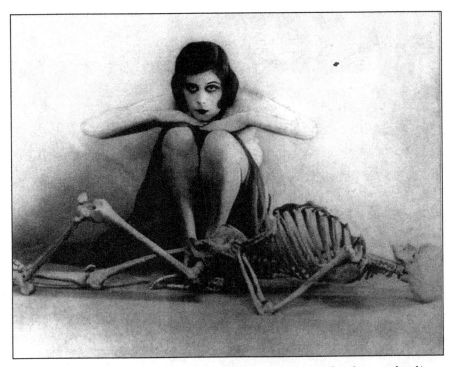

WHAT A WAY TO GO!: Theda Bara embodied the Victorian era fear that casual and/or pleasurable sex could only lead to death for the man involved with such a wicked woman.

As for Bara, her most famous film, *A Fool There Was* (1915), cast her as a Vamp (a realistic vampire, sans fangs or the ability to transform into a bat) who wins a hapless middle-aged businessman away from his wife and children, with a cautionary-fable caveat ending: The experience brings him 'up' briefly, then downward, long and hard, leading to his demise. At the time, Bara and fellow vamps—Nazimova, Pola Negri, Vilma Banky, etc.—boasted hair and make- up as midnight-black as their wicked souls. Conversely, natural blondes—Mary Pickford, Lillian Gish, Mae Marsh—represented The Good Girls (i.e. virgins utterly without sexual experience) during the days of a lingering Victorian moral sensibility. This came crashing down circa 1920, when the boys marched home from the First World War. Many had enjoyed the company of European women; nice enough, yet (surprisingly to such post-Victorian Americans) comfortable with their sexuality. Meanwhile, women had joined the workforce while the yanks were overseas. Many lived a swingin' lifestyle as the Roaring Twenties commenced. Yet if they were 'easy,' that didn't any longer imply that they were evil. Peroxide hit the market big-time, allowing blondes

A LIST VAMPS: In the 1930s, those near-twin mystery ladies from Europe, Greta Garbo and Marlene Dietrich, embodied the femme fatale image of the scornful temptress who seductively draws men to their all-too-willing destruction.

(Jean Harlow, Thelma Todd) to appear as trashy as brunettes had often been portrayed. The coming of sound to motion pictures caused all on-screen characters to appear more complex than the stick-figures of the Silent Era. This extended to Vamps, be they blonde or brunette: Greta Garbo and Marlene Dietrich might still seduce and abandon men, yet all their characters had likeable traits and won an audience's sympathy.

During World War II, the bad guys more often than not were German spies or agents of Japan, wickedly wanton in their exoticism. No sooner had the war ended, the promise of the best years of our lives dashed by economic problems, the nuclear stand-off with Russia, and a growing fear of fellow Americans owing to McCarthyism and worries that one's neighbors might be part of the Red Scare, than film noir was created to reflect that current malaise via the crime genre. Femme fatales, blonde or brunette, were deliciously duplicitous dames who drove a man mad with lust only to betray him at the end. Veronica Lake, Lana Turner, and Lauren Bacall all switched over from their early 1940s good-girls to late 1940s man-eaters. During the 1950s, such characters were softened somewhat. In movies like *Clash by Night*, *Niagara*, and *River of No Return*, Marilyn Monroe portrayed femme fatales who, despite their often wicked behavior, were nonetheless sympathetic to male and female viewers. Then came the Sixties. The birth control pill was immediately released onto the legal marketplace. A Sexual Revolution rapidly took form, and popular culture, particularly films, reflected this.

Though graphic sexuality (or violence, or some combination of the two) would not be possible onscreen (at least in Hollywood) owing to the lingering if ever more challenged Breen/Hays Office Code, movies swiftly grew ever more suggestive. These included the 007 films, unimaginable even ten years earlier; all the rage with the mass audience. Many of the Bond girls, as well as other international beauties, posed for *Playboy* pictorials; it could only be a matter of time before movies allowed female nudity. Sex was suddenly everywhere, the volume pumping up as the decade wore on. Here was when the femme fatale made her comeback, if contemporized for the current audience. Vampire girls, bad Bond babes, hit ladies, sword-and-sandals evil-queens, wild biker chicks, out of control hippies, gun molls, succubi from outer space, and prehistoric beauties were among the scantily clad females who swept across the screen. Apparently, they all enjoyed indulging in evil. Such situations grew ever more intense when female nudity, and then sex itself, were displayed throughout the 1970s. Nice girls got naked too, in life and onscreen. As always, though, it was the bad girl who caught the imagination of men.

BLONDES HAVE MORE FUN – FINALLY!: Veronica Lake in the 1940s and Marilyn Monroe in the 1950s debunked the old idea that all blondes were wholesome virgins.

Why? Alfred Hitchcock had a phrase for it: "the desire for the fall." This theme ran through *Vertigo* and most of the master's suspense classics. No one film depicts the syndrome as vividly as the little known *The Paradine Case* (1947). In it, a happily married attorney (Gregory Peck) defends a beautiful woman (Ann Todd) accused of murder. He becomes dedicated to his task, not only professionally, of ensuring that she is found innocent. Unconsciously, he becomes obsessed with her, though not simply as a result of her stunning looks. On some primitive level, he may possibly sense what everyone else does—in the courtroom, in the theatre, as audiences watch with growing fear and pity, as in a Greek tragedy—that she is indeed guilty. Perhaps only his loyal wife, with her sharp female instinct for the truth, truly understands what he wants: To set the guilty woman free, make love to her, and gleefully become her next victim. More than four decades later, this would be the premise of *Basic Instinct* with Sharon Stone; some three decades prior; it had been the essence of *A Fool There Was* with Theda Bara. The more things change (in terms of moviemaking styles), the more they stay the same substance-wise.

Importantly, the tradition of the femme fatale reaches way back before the birth of movies, and has been a part of our culture, ranging from the literary artistic elite to sordid pulp fiction, since Day One in the story

SHE'S BACK: Throughout the 1960s and early 1970s, Barbara Steele reinvented the hard-hearted vamp from the days of silent cinema, such a character now endowed with a contemporary 'edge.'

of mankind. Lilith for the Hebrews, Lamia for the Libyans; every ancient nation had its own Femme Fatale. During the Renaissance, a 1424 poem by Frenchman Alain Chartier warned of "La Belle Dame Sans Merci," the man-eater who swallows lovers whole during the act of sex. During the Romantic era of the early 1800s, Englishman John Keats wrote his own poem with a similar title and an identical theme. Good boys can't resist Bad girls: Of course, it works both ways. Why do nice girls always seem to fall for bad boys? That's a question for another writer, presumably female, to address in yet another book. Here, though, a heterosexual male scribe addresses the issue as it involves his gender, then and now.

Perhaps the greatest single moment in pulp-cinema history regarding the male desire for the femme fatale occurs in *Invasion of the Bee Girls* (1973). In Nicholas Meyer's smart script, a group of ordinary guys sit around in a sports bar, discussing the recent invasion of deadly but beautiful girls from outer space. One of their best friends was a recent victim; the scene of the crime revealed that he had been killed by this femme fatale while making love to her. "Just imagine," one of the guys sighs, "coming and going at the same time." That pretty much sums it all up for the appeal of the women found in this volume.

But to end where we began… those two film buffs, enjoying a meal in L.A., discussing their all-time favorite bad girls from their most warmly remembered era in moviemaking. They decided to create a list of the best of the best in descending order. Barbara Steele, Ingrid Pitt, Caroline

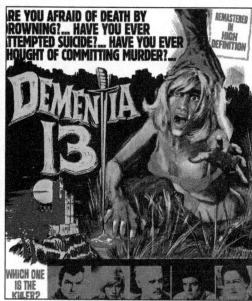

THOSE GREAT MOVIE POSTERS: The appeal of Italian-made Peplum and home-grown thrillers (the latter directed by a young Francis Coppola, no less!) draw in the audience with femme fatales receiving their just desserts; unfortunately, neither Anne Heywood or Luana Anders followed up on their momentary bad-girl status, which is why neither is included in this volume.

Munro, and Victoria Vetri were contenders for the top spot. That's when the two fellows became aware that their waitress, hovering nearby, was listening in with great fascination and concern. *What's up?*, the two guys wondered. Then, she smiled and stopped by the table to say hello. That's when they realized who this was: Victoria Vetri, aka Angela Dorian. Once *Playboy's* Playmate of the Year, then star of sci-fi horror (*Invasion of the Bee Girls*) and ancient world epic (*When Dinosaurs Ruled the Earth*). She thanked them for rating her so high on the list, assuring them she would soon make a comeback. This waitress job was only a temporary gig to pay the bills while saving as much as possible for a film she was determined to produce and star in. They wished her well and over-tipped. Each knew that her once potent beauty had faded. Likely, the film would never be made. In fact, it wasn't.

That was sad, though what followed for this former cult queen would be tragic. That story is told in her chapter. The point here is, such beauty, immortalized on celluloid, seems as if it will never fade. Also, there is a tendency among the general public, film buffs included, that anyone who has ever received star billing in a motion picture, and the adulation of many, is set for life. They must live in some magical zone where the necessity to make money, and do so on a regular basis, does not exist. As the quotes with which this introduction begins state, that's not the case. A few B-movies don't pay a tidal wave of incoming bills several years later. Many of the starlets showcased here ended up as minor league variations of Gloria Swanson as Norma Desmond in *Sunset Boulevard* (1950), desperate to believe they were still beautiful, always certain the next major role was right around the corner. Denial, in such cases, can be necessary for survival. Others continued their careers over a long period of time, in some cases seizing control of their projects. For every girl that gave in to alcohol and drugs, leading to an early death, there was another who left the industry, married, and raised a family; or set out on a new career, more often than not in the lucrative California real estate business. A few became superstars, though that was rare. Another few ended up in prison as a femme fatale in real life, as was the case with the aforementioned Victoria Vetri.

Here, then, is a book that brings them all together for the first time. This is a salute to those cinematic cult queen, international dream girls, B-movie babes (as well as several A-listers) who incarnated every guy's (and some girls' as well) darkest dreams of desire laced with... doom. There are the stars of Forbidden cinema from an era that remains vital in the memories of those who partook of the grindhouse and the Drive-In, as well as more respectable moviegoing venues. Thanks to home entertainment, such long-time fans can relieve those days (and nights) whenever they wish, while younger aficionados of edgy films can employ this volume as a handy guide to the best of the best—which the non-cogniscenti likely perceives as the worst of the worst. No matter: As always, there are those who 'get it' and those who do not. The Sixties and Seventies were a true golden age for the femme fatale. Those days are preserved here, as if under glass, for reconsideration by mature fans and an introduction for novitiates.

TO END WHERE WE BEGAN: Victoria Vetri, aka Angela Dorian, at the peak of her career as blonde queen of the brunette cave-girls, with Imogen Hassall (left) and Magda Konopka (right).

THE BRITISH LOLITA: Beginning in the early 1970s, Jenny Agutter offered an engaging variation on the popular Nymphet cliché, portraying females who existed halfway between over-developed girls and emergent young women.

Jenny Agutter

Birthdate: December 20, 1952; Taunton, Somerset, UK
Height: 5' 8"
Measurements: N/A

EARLY ON IN HER CAREER, Jenny Agutter became a major 'child star' in England owing to her appearances on the BBC TV series *The Railway Children* during the mid-1960s. A slender beauty even in her pre-teen years, with intense eyes, a charisma that reached everyone who watched the memorable family show (adults and kids alike), and a soft, sensitive manner of delivering her lines, the young, vibrant, yet reserved actress left people wondering if she might be one of the rare few child stars who went on to enjoy a long career. Initially, she seemed to have set her sights on a 'serious' stage career, circa 1970, playing the ingénue roles in Shakespeare's comedies and dramas. Then, Agutter surprised everyone by moving to Hollywood to pursue a film career there. More surprising still, the ultra-classy young woman accepted roles that other aspiring actresses had turned down owing to the necessity of performing in the nude. Shortly, Jenny established herself as one of the rare A-list actresses who had no hesitation at all about stripping down in front of the camera, and not only in high-tone films.

The first such project was an American-financed art film shot by English director Nicholas Roeg in Australia. *Walkabout* remains today one of the most memorable and remarkable cinematic projects from the early 1970s, even though it was not particularly successful at the box-office in its time. Barely sixteen and looking considerably younger (Jenny could pass for a swiftly-maturing twelve-year-old), she portrays a school girl who, with her young brother, is stranded in the outback after their businessman father goes mad. For most of the running time, this appears to be a G-rated movie about kids trying to survive in a hostile environ-

BRAVE NEW WORLD: Looking lovely (with co-star Michael York) in her futuristic costume for *Logan's Run*, Jenny also stripped down for a brief, entirely gratuitous nude scene.

ment. Then, about twenty minutes before the conclusion, Jenny's character (who has been aging as the film progresses) slips into the water for an outdoor bath. Not only is she nude: During the sequence, the camera lingers over her body, visually exploring every nuance of her flesh and blood make-up. Viewers are, step by step, ever more stunned by how far the film dares to go, creating one of the decade's first great debates (there would be many more, as chronicled in this book!) as to where art leaves off and pornography begins.

Agutter also appeared nude (briefly, and in terms of the narrative, unnecessarily) in the chintzy sci-fi film *Logan's Run*, as well as in Sidney Lumet's ultra-serious, ultra-ambitious film of the award-winning stage play *Equus* (Agutter is nude for the final half hour here). But for B-movie buffs, the most memorable such project has to be *China 9, Liberty 37*. On the surface, it is one more violent/sexual spaghetti Western. For those who look closer, here is filmmaker Monte Hellman's fascinating (despite the low budget) depiction of a singular woman's search for true love and also sexual satisfaction, which she learns along the way may not be a possibility with any one man, necessitating for her multiple relationships that, taken together, add up a to a sense of wholeness. All the genre trappings are present, redeemed here by an in-depth study of the female psyche. Agutter is glimpsed nude on regular occasions throughout the film, many of them involving her habit of bathing (perhaps a conscious allusion to *Walkabout*) in an isolated spring.

"NO NUDITY, PLEASE – WE'RE BRITISH??": Jenny Agutter belied that old cliché beginning with her still notorious nude swimming sequence in the arthouse film *Walkabout*.

No explanation has ever been given as to why Jenny's character in *An American Werewolf in London* features an obvious body double for her nude scene, as certainly audiences by then had come to know and appreciate her distinct lines and curves owing to much visual exposure over the years. When she passed the age of 30 and movie roles were no longer hers for the asking, Jenny returned to her roots: High-quality Brit TV and Shakespeare, as well as other classics, on the stage. Fantasy film buffs get a brief, shady glimpse of her, but can hear that distinctive voice, during her brief appearance at the end of *The Avengers* as the female member of the council. Agutter has been married to Swedish hotelier Johan Tham since 1990; they lived quietly with their son in London.

SELECTED FILMOGRAPHY:

A Man Could Get Killed (Linda Frazier, 1966); *Star!* (Pamela, 1968); *The Railway Children Movie* (Roberta "Bobbie" Waterbury, 1970); *Walkabout* (The Girl, 1971); *Logan's Run* (Jessica, 1976); *The Eagle Has Landed* (Molly Prior, 1976); *Equus* (Jill Mason, 1977); *China 9, Liberty 37* (Catherine, 1978); *Sweet William* (Ann Walton, 1980); *Othello* (Desdemona, 1981); *An American Werewolf in London* (Nurse Alex Price, 1981); *Dark Tower* (Carolyn, 1987); *The Avengers* (Councilwoman Hawley, 2012).

Anouk Aimee

Birthdate: April 27, 1932; Paris, France
Birth Name: Françoise Sorya Dreyfus
Height: 5' 8"
Measurements: N/A

ONCE UPON A TIME, a young girl was walking along the Rue Coli-
sée in Paris with her mother when a man stopped them and asked if the
daughter would like to be in a film he was then casting. The two women
thought this was a joke or perhaps something more menacing. As things
turned out, film director Henry Calef had been unable to cast the part of
Anouk, a fifteen-year-old girl. With *The House By the Sea* finished, this
budding actress took the name as her own, for several years billed simply
as that to create an aura of mystery around herself. One early success was
Lola, a Hitchcock-inspired film by Jacques Demy in which, like Kim Novak in *Vertigo*, Anouk played a dual role; years later, she and the director
teamed for a California-shot sequel, *The Model Shop*. Likewise, Anouk
enjoyed acclaim in Claude Lelouch's *A Man and a Woman*, a mid-1960s
romance which *Look* noted "allowed us to feel sophisticated about our
sentimentality." The eventual sequel, like *The Model Shop*, conveyed none
of the original's appeal.

Anouk's inclusion here is based on a single role: the queen of Sodom
in *(The Last Days of) Sodom and Gomorrah*, a spectacle loosely derived
from the Old Testament tale of Lot. Critics of the time sarcastically dismissed this as an over-long erotic cartoon. Co-directed by Robert Aldrich
and Sergio Leone, it rates as fascinating curio, breaking all sorts of taboos
about what could and could not be depicted onscreen at the time, with
hints of lesbianism (the Queen's relationship with a young African servant) and incest (she and her brother, Stanley Baker, engage in a bizarre
sado-masochistic relationship) helping to chip away at the Production

MIDNIGHT DREAMER: Even as a young girl, Anouk Aimee suggested the aura of class and mystery that would forever surround her in life and on film.

Code still held over from the 1930s. Here is the first Biblical epic to be played as surreal fantasy, ranking alongside daring works by Bunuel and Fellini.

Regarding the latter genius, Anouk won strong roles in two of the master's classics, *La Dolce Vita* and *8 ½*. As to her personality, Anouk's *A Man and a Woman* co-star Jean-Louis Trintignant found her as offputtingly aloof as most of the characters Anouk played. The critical and commercial failure of *Justine*, an opulent adaptation of Lawrence Durrell's legendary novel, ended any hopes for a mainstream career. Aimee continued to play odd roles in offbeat films for decades, always coming across as classy, sophisticated, mysterious, and very, very deep. Too bad Albert "Cubby" Broccoli did not see fit to cast her in the part this actress was born for: the enigmatic female lead in *Octopussy*, unique among Bond girls as this title figure is neither villainess nor heroine but a combination of the two. At age 75, she played a Holocaust survivor in *The Little Meadow of Birch Trees* (2002), a role that allowed her to come to terms with her own Jewish identity via an onscreen performance.

"WELCOME TO SODOM!" In a big scale Peplum co-directed by Robert Aldrich and Sergio Leone, Anouk played the queen of the wickedest city in the Bible.

DECADENT DISHABILLE: A recurring role for Anouk was as a high-price girl of the night, often going by the name of Lola.

SELECTED FILMOGRAPHY:

A House By the Sea (Anouk, 1947); *The Lovers of Verona* (Giorgia/Juliet); *Golden Salamander* (Anna, 1950); *The Paris Express* (Jeanne, 1952); *Nina* (Nina, 1956); *Lovers of Paris* (Marie Pichon, 1957); *Anyone Can Kill Me* (Isabelle, 1957); *La Dolce Vita* (Maddalena, 1960); *Lola* (Lola/Cécile, 1961); *(The Last Days of) Sodom and Gomorrah* (The Queen, 1962); *8 ½* (Luisa, 1963); *A Man and a Woman* (Anne Gauthier, 1966); *The Model Shop* (Lola, 1969); *The Appointment* (Carla, 1969); *Justine* (Justine, 1969); *A Man and a Woman: 20 Years Later* (Anne Gauthier, 1986).

Chelo Alonso

Birthdate: April 10, 1933; Central Lugareño, Camagüey, Cuba
Birth name: Isabella Garcia
Height: 6' 1"
Measurements: 35 1/4 – 21 – 36

FANS OF OUT-OF-THE-MAINSTREAM CINEMA had something of a shock in store when in 1968 they flocked to theatres to catch Sergio Leone's spaghetti Western *The Good, The Bad, and the Ugly.* Some twenty-two minutes into the movie, Lee Van Cleef, portraying the middle-billed character, arrives at a remote farm. This professional assassin has been paid to murder the humble man living there. Unaware of the stranger's reason for stepping inside, she silently serves him a meal. When her husband appears, Van Cleef shoots him down, also killing this woman's teenage son. Her entire life ended, the woman gasps in horror as 'The Bad' calmly steps by her and out of her life forever. "Hey," more than one fan of the era's great femme fatale stars whispered. "Wasn't that Chelo Alonso?" Indeed, it was. The woman who headlined opposite Steve Reeves in two of his (best) muscleman movies had, in a few years, slipped from superstar of Euro-lensed action movies to a bit player.

"The Princess of Peplum," one critic called Chelo. That term, often used to describe sand/sword/sandals films, refers to the short skirt-like costumes worn by the mighty men of valor. Alonso's father had been Cuban, her mother Mexican; at an early age she developed a dangerously sultry look recalling the Vamp stars from the Silent Era: Theda Bara, Nazimova, and Pola Negri. Drawn to dance of an eroticized nature, Chelo wildly performed in Havana clubs, her highly developed body allowing the girl to convince the owners she was seventeen long before she reached that age. Her unbridled sensuality caused the local press to dub this girl-woman "The Cuban H-Bomb," allowing her to rise above the seedier side of dark,

THE FIRST COUPLE OF PEPLUM: In *Goliath and the Barbarians,* sword and sandal princess Chelo Alonso co-starred with former Hercules Steve Reeves.

lurid entertainment, becoming a star at Cuba's National Theatre. Hailed as a latter-day Josephine Baker, she combined Afro and Cuban rhythms with key elements of middle-Eastern belly-dancing. Alonso headlined a tour of Puerto Rico, Haiti and, in America, Miami and New Orleans. Eventually she landed a steady job in Paris' Folies Bergère. Supposedly, "Che" Guevara tried, in 1963, to talk her into returning to Cuba and joining the revolu-

MEN ARE FROM MARS, WOMEN ARE FROM VENUS: This classic poster effectively displays the two sides of Peplum, with Chelo Alonso incarnating sensuality while Steve Reeves embodies violence.

tion. Chelo declined. Film historian Gary Brumburgh noted that she all but "slithered" on the screen, truly a mythic snake-goddess come to life, "with her volcanic temperament, highly distinctive cheekbones, and wild mane of dark hair." In pre-Sexual liberation days, before the R (much less X)-rating, few images were more dazzling than Chelo tearing into one of her abandoned dance routines in which she seemed ready to seduce and panther-like kill any of the men gazing at her, *Goliath and the Barbarians* offering her greatest onscreen Terpsichore.

Married to production manager Aldo Pomilia, Chelo Alonso abandoned not only films but, at 35+, live dance performance as well. Following her husband's passing in 1986, she is reported to have moved to Tuscany. Brumburgh reports that, last seen, Chelo was "breeding cats and operating a hotel (and adjacent) restaurant."

SELECTED FILMOGRAPHY:

Sign of the Gladiator aka *Sheba and the Gladiator* (Erica, 1958); *Top Secret* (Sherazad/ Soraya, 1959); *Goliath and the Barbarians* (Princess Landa, 1959); *The Pirate and the Slave Girl* (Princess Miriam, 1959); *At-*

AN INTERNATIONAL DREAM GIRL: Like so many female stars of the 1960s, Chelo Alonso introduced American audiences to the joys of mixed-race beauty.

tack of the Moors (Suleima, 1959); *Terror of the Red Mask* (Karima, 1960); *The Huns* (Queen Tanya, 1960); *Morgan the Pirate* (Consuela, 1960); *Son of Samson* (Queen Smedes, 1960); *Atlas Against the Cyclops* (Capys, 1961); *Girl Under the Sheet* (Maria, 1961); *The Good, the Bad and the Ugly* (Steven's wife, uncredited, 1966).

Ursula Andress

Birthdate: March 19, 1936; Ostermundigen, Bern, Switzerland
Height: 5' 5"
Measurements: 38 – 25 - 35

FOR FANS OF SPY CINEMA, Ursula's iconic moment comes about
halfway through the first official James Bond film, *Dr. No*. Sean Connery's
007 finds himself stranded on a Caribbean beach. To his surprise, there
comes a siren song from not far away. As the intrigued spy steps around
a dune, there is Honey Ryder: tall, natural, in a white bikini quite unlike anything that had been seen up until that moment in an American-
financed mainstream movie. She appears to be Venus, goddess of love—if
not quite standing on a half-shell then carrying just such an object in her
hands. She literally takes Bond's breath away, and that of the audience as
well. Here was the first great sex symbol for the Swingin' Sixties, a European (Andress was half Swiss, half German) beauty completely comfortable with her own sexuality.

Movies, and in fact life itself, would never be the same. If Brigitte
Bardot had introduced the bikini bathing suit in art films in the mid-
1950s, Ursula's acceptance by middle-of-the-road moviegoers near the
dawn of this new decade set the pace for even girl-next-door types like
Sandra Dee and Annette to wear them in beach films less than a year later.
In truth, Honey was not a femme fatale per se, but a good girl who could
hold her own alongside Bond in a fight with any of the title character's
minions. True Deadlier Than the Male status would come shortly. In *The
Tenth Victim*, a science-fiction film about a dystopian future society in
which people can elect to play a game in which they target and assassi-
nate one another, Ursula's character kills her prey by, in a face mask and
matching bikini, stripteasing for them, then shooting the enamored vic-

VENUS ON THE HALF SHELL: From the moment that Ursula emerged from the sea in *Dr. No,* viewers sensed that this girl was the new cinematic goddess.

tim dead via two shots from guns hidden in her bra. In her second James Bond outing, the non-official-series film *Casino Royale,* her secret agent appears to be in love with the dolt played by Peter Sellers. Toward the film's end, she kills the bad guys surrounding him with an automatic rifle, then decides not to spare him after all. "Never trust a spy," she laughs over his dead body. In Hammer's lavish remake of *She,* Ursula embodied H. Rider Haggard's queen of a lost tribe who has achieved immortal beauty via a pact with pagan gods.

There are those who claim that Ursula may have actually been something of a femme fatale in real life, if unknowingly. On the morning of September 30, 1955, James Dean asked Ursula to take a drive with him in his Spider Porsche. Apparently, she finally told Dean that she was going to marry actor-photographer Derek. Dean took off alone and died in a fiery car crash several hours later. Could his mind have been on other matters (i.e. Ursula) and not on the road? **Trivia:** In Ursula's eye-popping opening moment in *Dr. No*, the voice singing Calypso melodies (and summing up memories of the goddess of that name in The Odyssey) is actually Diana Coupland, while Honey's voice throughout the movie is dubbed over by Nikki van der Zyl. Ursula's own voice, and in fact her acting abilities, were, to be kind, sorely limited. Still, she radiated star quality, enough so that when a woman was needed who could convey Aphrodite, a variation on the Venus image that Ursula had incarnated early on, for the Ray Harryhausen F/X extravaganza *Clash of the Titans*, no one else was considered. When asked why she was so comfortable doffing her clothes for *Playboy* photos, Ursula smiled and shrugged and said: "Because I'm the most beautiful woman in the world." Highly recommended little-known B-film: *Slave of the Cannibal God*.

WHAT A LOVELY WAY TO DIE!: In *The Tenth Victim*, Ursula plays a futuristic huntress who kills her prey with bullets from guns embedded in her bra, then cuts and lifts the man's tie as a symbol of phallic castration.

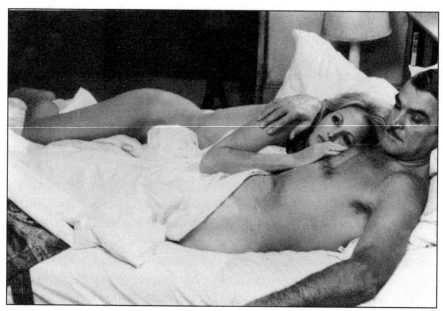

TO BED OR NOT TO BED: As the 1960s gave way to the 1970s, the new freedom of the screen allowed for ever more explicit sexual situations to be graphically displayed; here Ursula Andress shares 'cuddling time' with Stanley Baker in *Perfect Friday*.

SELECTED FILMOGRAPHY:

An American in Rome (Astrid, 1954); *Sins of Casanova* (Blonde, 1955); *Dr. No* (Honey Ryder, 1962); *Fun in Acapulco* (Marguerita Dauphin, 1963); *4 for Texas* (Maxine Richter, 1963); *Nightmare in the Sun* (Marsha Wilson, 1965); *She* (Ayesha, 1965); *What's New Pussycat* (Rita, 1965); *Up to His Ears* (Alexandrine, 1965); *The 10th Victim* (Caroline Meredith, 1965); *The Blue Max* (Countess Kaeti von Klugermann, 1966); *Once Before I Die* (Alex, 1966); *Casino Royale* (Vesper Lynd, 1967); *Anyone Can Play* (Norma, 1968); *The Southern Star* (Erica Kramer, 1969); *Perfect Friday* (Lady Britt Dorset, 1970); *Red Sun* (Cristina, 1971); *The Sensuous Nurse* (Anna, 1975); *Scaramouche* (Joséphine De Beauharnais, 1976); *Double Murder* (Princess Dell'Orso, 1977); *Mountain of the Cannibal God*, aka *Slave of the Cannibal God* (Susan, 1978); *Tigers in Lipstick* (The Widow, 1979); *The Fifth Musketeer* (Louise de la Vallière, 1979); *Clash of the Titans* (Aphrodite, 1981); *Cremaster 5* (Queen of Chain, 1997); *The Bird Preachers* (Madonna, 2005).

ONCE A GODDESS, ALWAYS A GODDESS: Unlike many sex symbols, Ursula Andress aged gracefully, playing beautiful women for many decades.

"BANG! YOU'RE DEAD!": In *Viva Las Vegas*, the red-headed femme fatale takes aim
at no less than Elvis Presley himself.

Ann-Margret

Birthdate: April 28, 1941; Valsjöbyn, Jämtlands län, Sweden
Birth name: Ann-Margret Olsson
Height: 5' 3 1/2"
Measurements: 36 (D) – 24 ½ - 35

ARRIVING IN AMERICA AT AGE SIX, Ann-Margret headed for Northwestern University after graduating high school. Following a short stay, the future superstar left to try and forge a show business career. One of the teenager's first mentors was George Burns, who secured her a record-deal with RCA. The event that put her over the top was a no-holds-barred "Hello, Swingin' 1960s; Goodbye, the Eisenhower Era" rendering of the theme song from Bob Hope's comedy *Bachelor in Paradise* (in which she did not appear) at the Oscars. No one had seen anything like it, at least from a woman (Elvis had introduced such stuff in 1956). Soon Ann-Margret's bad-girl (or good-girl gone bad) image seemed a far cry from the innocent she'd played in her first film, as Bette Davis' daughter in *Pocketful of Miracles*. When Ann-Margret assumed the role of the ingénue in the *Bye Bye Birdie* movie, her full-throttle frugging altered America's idea of who and what the girl next door had become.

Quickly, Ann-Margret found herself typecast as the baddest of bad-girls. One notable role in a tawdry B-noir cast her as a dangerous nymphet who lures middle-aged John Forsythe toward destruction in *Kitten with a Whip*. The danger—and she was smart enough to sense this—was typecasting of a sort that had in the previous decade limited Mamie Van Doren, also of Swedish origin. Ann-Margret would transcend any such stereotyping as a sleazy female despite major career mistakes, such as

35

"LOVE ME TONIGHT!!" In *Kitten With a Whip*, Ann-Margret played a bad girl pretending to be a good girl; in *The Swinger*, a good girl passing herself off as a bad girl.

turning down roles that went to Jane Fonda in *Cat Ballou* (1965) and Faye Dunaway in *Bonnie and Clyde* (1967) while agreeing to appear in B-movies including *C.C. & Company*, a biker-flick starring football great Joe Namath. Essentially, Ann-Margret (for the time being, at least) opted to appear in lucrative if non-ambitious projects. When major player Mike Nichols, sensing that here was a talent that had ripened, cast her in *Carnal Knowledge* (for which Ann-Margret received an Oscar nomination)

THANK HEAVEN (OR, IN THIS CASE, HELL!) FOR LITTLE GIRLS: In *Kitten With a Whip*, Ann-Margret employs the Lolita effect on naïve older man John Forsythe.

QUEEN OF THE HOLLYWOOD HIPPIES: In *The Swinger*, Ann-Margret displayed two sides of the sex symbol, first as a throwback to the elegant girls of the 1940s, then as the first hippie princess to engage in body-painting during a communal orgy.

UPDATING A TINSELTOWN DREAM: The most beautiful redhead since Rita Hayworth brought that 1940s' sex symbol's sulky allure to 1960s pop-culture.

she became a sought after star for serious projects, in time offering up a smart, nuanced performance of Blanche DuBois in a first-rate TV staging of Tennessee Williams' *A Streetcar Named Desire* (1984). Such a shame that the maturing actress didn't also play Maggie in Williams' *Cat on a Hot Tin Roof!*

Still, those early bad-girl roles are irresistible. *Bus Riley's Back in Town* has her cat-like scratching the drapes as the young nympho wife of a wealthy older man. A similar part came her way opposite Steve Mc-Queen in *The Cincinatti Kid*, seducing the title hero away from good-girl Tuesday Weld (as a character called Christian, no less!). She opted for the then-current craze of spy cinema with *Murderer's Row*, a Dean Martin/Matt Helm opus. Here she portrayed what at mid-decade had become her specialty: a hot-looking teenage chick who remains a virgin by choice. Though Suzie is too "clean-cut" to slip into bed with the middle-aged hero she flirts with, that doesn't preclude freaking out every time she steps onto a dancefloor, or taking a less than healthy pleasure in helping Helm kill bad guys (her face lights up with bizarre pleasure while strangling a young boat pilot).

Her most telling role came via the junk movie *The Swinger*, in which Ann-Margret plays a girl with her own actual last name. She's the virgin queen of a Hippie Commune (her means of travel is a 500cc Triumph Motorcycle) who goes in for the most rad sort of body-painting orgy but draws the line at sex with yet another middle-aged lech (this time, Tony

Fanciosca) who hungers after the nubile hippie. Essentially, the character is a remarkable new creation of the 1960s Sexual Revolution at its mid-point: the world's first virgin-nympho. Ann-Margret will not reveal the nature of her relationship with Elvis. She remains married to former actor Roger Smith despite his long, difficult decades of life-threatening illness.

SELECTED FILMOGRAPHY:

Pocketful of Miracles (Louise, 1961); *State Fair* (Emily Porter, 1962), *Bye Bye Birdie* (Kim McAfee, 1963); *Viva Las Vegas* (Rusty Martin, 1964); *Kitten With a Whip* (Jody Dvorak, 1964); *The Pleasure Seekers* (Fran Hobson, 1964); *Bus Riley's Back in Town* (Laurel, 1965); *The Cincinnati Kid* (Melba, 1965); *Made in Paris* (Maggie Scott, 1966); *Stagecoach* (Dallas, 1966); *The Swinger* (Kelly Olsson, 1966); *Murderer's Row* (Suzie, 1966); *The Tiger and the Pussycat* (Carolina, 1967); *C.C. & Company* (Ann, 1970); *Carnal Knowledge* (Bobbie, 1971); *The Train Robbers* (Mrs. Lowe, 1973); *Tommy* (Nora Walker, 1975); *Joseph Andrews* (Lady Booby, 1977); *The Cheap Detective* (Jezebel Dezire, 1978); *Magic* (Peggy Ann Snow, 1978); *The Villain* (Charming Jones, 1979); *52 Pick-Up* (Barbara, 1986); *Grumpy Old Men* (Ariel Truax, 1993).

SEDUCED AND ABANDONED: In many of her films, Laura Antonelli played trusting
virgins who are misused by men and then set out to seek revenge.

Laura Antonelli

Birthdate: November 28, 1941; Pola, Italy; Pula, Croatia
Birth name: Laura Antonaz
Date of passing: June 22, 2015; Ladispoli, Rome, Italy
Height: 5' 7"
Measurements: 36 (D) – 23 - 37

AT LAURA'S BIRTH, the city in which her family lived served as the capital of Italy's Istria province. They would move while Laura remained a girl first to Genoa, then on to Venice, and finally settling in Naples. Unlike so many other women in this book, who were perceived as great beauties beginning in their childhood and picked for stardom while still teenagers, Antonelli later recalled that "My parents... felt I was ugly, clumsy, insignificant." Owing to this perception, they insisted that their daughter constantly exercise in gymnasiums in hopes of becoming at least a little bit more appealing. Swiftly, she mastered the art of Rhythmic Gymnastics, which as she explained combined athletics and dance into a unique form. Breaking with her family at last, Antonelli moved to Rome where she became a teacher in a secondary school, explaining the delay in trying to make it in movies. In this more sophisticated setting, her great if offbeat beauty allowed her to win modeling jobs, then film roles. One of the earliest was in the Italian-lensed follow-up to A.I.P.'s *Dr. Goldfoot and the Bikini Machine*, with Vincent Price again playing a mad megalomaniac not unlike villains in the James Bond films.

One of the oddest things about Laura's movie career is that she did not become an important international sex symbol until the mid-1970s. This, despite the fact that she had been born at around the same time as Elke Sommer, Romy Schneider, Rosanna Schiaffino, Senta Berger, and so many other European beauties that began to dominate the screen (and in many cases decorate the pages of *Playboy*) beginning in the early 1960s.

41

HUSBAND AND WIFE: In one of the most bizarre erotic sequences ever, Giancarlo Giannini seduces his wife (Laura Antonelli) though aware she has recently become pregnant by another man.

For one thing, Antonelli got something of a late start, her first film appearances occurring in the mid- rather than early- Sixties. For another, her beauty was more subtle and nuanced than those aforementioned women, causing her to more resemble Edwige Feniche, Corinne Clery, and Silvia Kristel, who all achieved fame during that decade when the Sexual Revolution that had been fought and won throughout the Sixties exploded into mainstream culture during the following ten years. Understandably, her appeal was not that of a nubile young beauty but a mature woman. As such, her stardom might be thought of as a reflection of the Women's Movement taking place simultaneously with her greatest screen appearances. For here, certainly, was a woman, not another good-looking girl. The point was, even as those temptresses from the 1960s began to fall out of favor, Laura gained a following.

While appearing opposite Jean-Paul Belmondo in a light-hearted swashbuckler, the two became deeply involved and would remain a couple throughout the decade of the 1960s. As the 1960s segued into the 1970s, and censorship restrictions lightened up even in a country as Catholic as Italy, producers began to turn out inexpensive sex farces of a leering nature, cartoonish in style, vulgar in intent. These were junk movies, pure and simple. Had nothing more intriguing followed, likely Laura would be completely forgotten today. Then came an offer to star in what would turn out to be the final film from an acclaimed master, Luchino Visconti. For most of its running time, *The Innocent* is a griping if off-putting tale of a difficult (to say the least) marriage. Sumptuously produced, no one would confuse this film with superficial porn. At the midpoint, however, there appeared one of the most intense sex scenes of the decade. In it, Laura's unpleasant husband (Giancarlo Giannini), knowing that she has become pregnant by another man, seduces her in what might be considered a non-violent intra-marital rape. The scene is not only erotic in nature but exhilarating in terms of character development, particularly the uneasy relationship between the wife and husband.

Her other best known movie from that era is *Wifemistress*, similar to a degree in theme if not in style. Here, Antonelli plays a frustrated wife whose husband is unable to satisfy her. Setting aside all the old conventions that a generation earlier would have caused a self-respecting Italian woman to grin and bear it, she becomes a sex monster: crazily seducing one man after another, these encounters filmed in vivid close-ups that leave little to the imagination without ever spilling over into the hardcore that would have netted an X-rating.

DO WITH ME WHAT YOU WILL: In another of Laura Antonelli's bizarre sexual situations, she finds herself lying alongside a mannequin designed precisely on her own proportions.

Trivia: After Antonelli retired, a 1991 police raid led to cocaine being discovered in her home. The legal system convicted her though she was confined to a house arrest rather than prison. Laura spent the following ten years fighting to have the conviction over-turned and, in due time, it was.

SELECTED FILMOGRAPHY:

16 Year Olds (The Girl-Woman, 1965); *Dr. Goldfoot and the Girl Bombs* (Rosanna, 1966); *The Sexual Revolution* (Liliana, 1967); *Venus in Furs* (Wanda, 1969); *Bali* (Daria, 1970); *A Man Called Sledge* (Ria, 1970); *Without Apparent Motive* (Juliette, 1971); *How Funny Can Sex Be?* (Assorted roles, 1973); *Malicious* (Angela, 1974); *Lovers and Other Relatives* (Laura, 1974); *Till Marriage Do Us Part* (Eugenia, 1974); *The Divine Nymph* (Manoela, 1975); *The Innocent* (Giuliana Hermil, 1976); *Wifemistress* (Antonia De Angelis, 1977); *Tigers in Lipstick* (Businesswoman, 1979); *Passion of Love* (Clara, 1981); *The Venetian Woman* (Angela, 1986); *The Trap* (Marie, 1986); *Malizia 2000* (Angela, 1991).

Claudine Auger

Birthdate: April 26, 1941; Paris, France
Birth name: Claudine Oger
Height: 5' 8"
Measurements: 36 (D) – 23 - 37

ALL FEMME FATALES OF THE 1960S AND 1970S were beautiful; few could also be described as classy. One who fit that bill was Claudine, winner of the Miss France competition at age fifteen. Shortly, she came in second in 1958's Miss World competition. A graduate of the St. Joan of Arc College and the Paris Drama Conservatory, Claudine made an auspicious debut in Gallic genius Jean Cocteau's sequel to his phantasmagoria *Orphee* (1951). In the follow-up, Auger played a lovely ballerina, establishing art-house credentials that were, sadly, never fulfilled. Roles in minor movies led nowhere. While on vacation in Nassau, Claudine was noticed by members of the crew who were preparing to film *Thunderball*. Up until then, Domino (mistress of the title character played by Adolfo Celli), betraying her rich benefactor after bedding Sean Connery's James Bond, was to be played as an Italian girl, most likely by Luciana Paluzzi. So impressed were the higher-ups that they not only hired Claudine but rewrote the script to make the character French, so that there would be no need to fake an accent.

Her first marriage, to writer-director Pierre Gaspard-Huit (her senior by 23 years) eventually folded, though she later had a successful union with businessman Peter Brent, remaining with him until his passing in 2008. They had one child. A follow-up to *Thunderball* was another spy saga, this one with a World War II setting: *Triple Cross* starred Christopher Plummer as real-life agent Eddie Chapman, with Yul Brynner as

A RECURRING WEAPON: In a surprising number of 1960s films, strong and seductive women employ spear guns to dispatch menacing men; Claudiner Auger in *Thunderball* may have been the first.

a Nazi officer. Auger joined several other Bond girls for medium-budget productions, co-starring with Barbara Bach and Barbara Bouchet in *Black Belly of the Tarantula*, a memorable Giallo (Italian thriller inspired by the word 'yellow') and Ursula Andress in *Anyone Can Play*. Her natural acting abilities allowed her to play mature character roles for years thereafter.

SELECTED FILMOGRAPHY:

The Testament of Orpheus (Minerve, 1960); *The Seven Deadly Sins* (A Servant, 1962); *The Iron Mask* (Isabelle, 1962); *In the French Style* (Clio, 1963); *Kali Yug – Vendetta* (Amrita, 1963); *Games of Desire* (The Girl, 1964); *Thunderball* (Domino, 1965); *Triple Cross* (Paulette, 1966); *The Devil in Love* (Maddalena de Medici, 1966); *The Killing Game* (Jacqueline,

THREE OF A KIND: A trio of Bond babes on the beach (from left to right) Martine Beswick, Claudine Auger, and Lucianna Paluzzi in *Thunderball*.

MENACED BEAUTY: Another frequently recurring image of 1960s cinema has a gorgeous girl (in this case, Claudine Auger) threatened, while in bed, by an unknown male.

1967); *Anyone Can Play* (Esmerelda, 1968); *The Bastard* (Barbara, 1968); *Black Belly of the Tarantula* (Laura, 1971); *Summertime Killer* (Michèle, 1972); *The Bermuda Triangle* (Sybil, 1978).

Ewa Aulin

Birthdate: February 13, 1950; Landskrona, Sweden
Birth name: Ewa Brigitta Aulin
Height: N/A
Measurements: 36 ½ (B) – 24 - 35

ANYONE SEARCHING FOR PROOF during December, 1968, that the cultural Zeitgeist in America had altered (in fact, virtually reversed itself) during the Sixties needed to look no further than billboards along every roadside advertising the big holiday film. Less than fifteen years earlier,

CANDY IS DANDY: The gorgeous Scandinavian teenager perfectly embodied in the 1960s that Lolita-like Nymphet from Terry Southern's earlier novel, which in the 1950s no one believed could ever be made as a major film.

middle-Americans would have seen sentimental images of Bing Crosby, Rosemary Clooney, and Danny Kaye singing carols in *White Christmas* (1954). Now, people peered out their car windows at a take-your-breath-away image of an underage blonde bombshell, nearly nude, her arms extended upward and outward spread eagle fashion, she seemingly bound and waiting for some older man to approach... In fact, her hands were not actually tied, though more than one passer-by imagined invisible cuffs. Here was an image that outdid such previous paradigm-shifting icons as Carol Baker rolling around in bed in *Baby Doll* (1956) and Sue Lyon sunbathing in a bikini in *Lolita* (1962). Incredibly, this image appeared at what many living in the U.S. still considered the holiest time of the year!

Aged eighteen at the time, the pretty Scandinavian was not, like the girl she played, underage. Yet her wide eyes and blank stare suggested a combination of idiocy and innocence, precisely right for the heroine of Terry Southern's once controversial and often banned book about a nymphet whose erotic adventures follow a similar arc to those in Voltaire's classic *Candide*. What had been considered the ultimate in Underground reading in the late 1950s was, in our reconfigured world, the new mainstream. For this was not some daring arthouse item but a studio film; the men who alternately succeeded or failed at scoring with Ewa were played by, among others, Marlon Brando, Richard Burton, Walter Matthau, and James Coburn.

At the time, the general impression was that Ewa Aulin had never before appeared in a film. Actually, she was a veteran of several low-budget Italian-lensed exploitation flicks, filmed after discovery in her homeland by Gunnar Fischer. Searching for a model for a short film he was completing, Fischer realized that his neighbor's daughter was perfect. At age fifteen, she was crowned Miss Sweden, then went on to win the title of Miss Teen International. After *Candy*, Aulin only found one worthy film project, a fine if forgotten comedy, *Start the Revolution Without Me*. Directed by Budd Yokin, this period-piece set during the French Revolution starred Donald Sutherland and Gene Wilder in early leading roles. Ewa, in a decorative part, shows off the stuff in period costumes. After that, her best part came in Monty Python's Flying Circus' *Full Frontal Nudity* (1969).

There were two marriages, the first to Roberto Loyola (1968-1972), which led to divorce following one child, the next to Cesare Paladino, beginning in 1974. Ewa's given reason for dropping out of The Biz was that she lost interest in acting, though possibly the industry lost interest in her

BATHING BEAUTY: During the 1960s, an obligatory image of any premiering star featured her in as skimpy a suit as possible, half in and half out of the water.

once she was no longer youthfully charismatic. One of her sex-charged thrillers is worth searching for: *The Legend of Blood Castle*, one of many movies shot during the 1970s based on the female Dracula, Countess Ersbeth Nadasdy Bathory. Warning: Watch the uncut version!

SELECTED FILMOGRAPHY:

Don Juan in Sicily (Wanda, 1967); *I Am What I Am* (Jane, 1967); *Death Laid an Egg* (Gabrielle, 1968); *Candy* (Candy Christian, 1968); *Start the Revolution Without Me* (Princess Christina, 1970); *Miscroscopic Liquid Subway to Oblivion* (Elizabeth, 1970); *The Double* (Lucia, 1971); *Quest for Love* (Isina, 1972); *Rosina Fumo* (Rosina, 1972); *Death Smiles on a Murderer* (Greta, 1973); *The Legend of Blood Castle* (Marina, 1973); *When Love Is Lust* (Beautiful Blonde, 1973); *Long Lasting Days* (Anna, 1973).

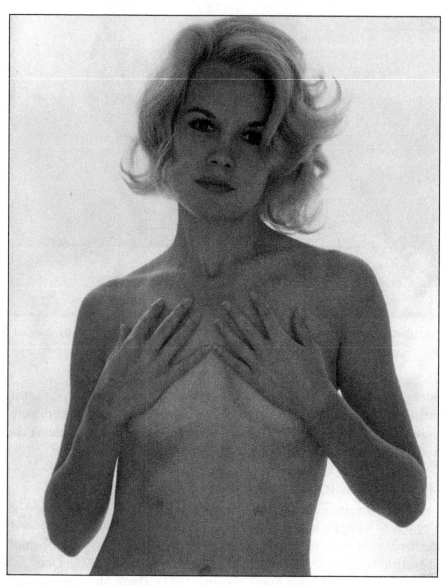

NOW YOU SEE ME, NOW YOU DON'T: In the early 1960s, Hollywood flirted with nudity though actual exposure wouldn't be possible until the decade's final years; here, Carroll Baker brings exposure about as far as the then in-effect Production Code allowed.

Carroll Baker

Birthdate: May 28, 1931; Johnstown, Pennsylvania
Birth name: Karolina Piekarski
Height: 5' 5"
Measurements: 35 (B) – 24 - 35

IF, **BACK IN 1956,** someone had suggested rising young star Carroll Baker would eventually appear in lurid low-budgeters, that person would have been considered as crazy as anyone who suggested that in a decade and a half Grace Kelly would headline *Ilsa, She Wolf of the S.S.* Yet in the case of Carroll Baker, the call would have been correct. The Actor's Studio alum did not appear in a single film between 1956-1958 owing to her refusal to allow Warner Bros. to exploit her ripe image from their hit *Baby Doll*, in which she created that postwar sex symbol, The Nymphet. The high-profile project was written by Tennessee Williams and directed by Elia Kazan. Accepting the offer to star but fearful of typecasting, she refused to show up on the set to film *God's Little Acre*. Shortly, she appeared in such towering blockbusters as *The Big Country* (with Gregory Peck and Charlton Heston) and *How the West Was Won* (opposite James Stewart). These, Baker alternated with smaller, well-received black-and-white indie films like *Bridge to the Sun* (playing an American married to a Japanese man during World War II) and *Something Wild* (one of the first films to deal honestly with rape, directed by her then-husband Jack Garfein).

In her autobiography *Baby Doll*, Baker insists everything went downhill when she allowed producer Joseph E. Levine to cast her in a series of extravagantly glossy, incredibly shallow melodramas such as *Harlow*, *The Carpetbaggers* (in which she played a Jean Harlow type), and the dreadful retro-noir *Sylvia*. Following her ever more ripe histrionics in such proj-

FROM HOLLYWOOD TO ROME, WITH LUST: If Carroll Baker's earliest top-drawer sex films were shot by gifted American directors like Elia Kazan, her later Giallos were exploitation flicks filmed cheaply in Italy.

ects, few in Hollywood would cast Baker in serious pictures. So off it was to Italy. Baker found work in the slick/sordid sexploitation films then being churned out assembly-line style. She recalls that the entire period was something of a blur, Baker often not certain which film she was currently starring in, as so many had near-identical plots and interchangeable names. Three of the most memorable, at least for genre fans and Baker addicts, were *The Sweet Body of Deborah*, *Paranoia*, and *A Quiet Place to Kill*, which showed off Baker's super-skinny body, often in bondage shots. She eventually became a Queen of Camp, appearing for that master of cinematic oddity, Andy Warhol, in *Bad*; in it, Baker mocked Norma Desmond (Gloria Swanson) from Billy Wilder's classic Hollywood send-up *Sunset Boulevard* (1950). In time Baker redeemed her reputation via strong roles in such serious-minded films as *Ironweed* in which she played a supporting role to Jack Nicholson and Meryl Streep.

Trivia: She was Nicholas Ray's first choice for Judy (Natalie Wood) in *Rebel Without a Cause* though Baker turned down that classic to spend time with then-husband Garfein.

PEROXIDE BLONDE: Baker played 'Rina Marlowe,' a Jean Harlow type, in *The Carpetbaggers*, then went on to enact the real deal in *Harlow*.

SELECTED FILMOGRAPHY:

Easy to Love (Clarice, 1953); *Giant* (Luz Benedict II, 1956); *Baby Doll* (Baby Doll Meighan, 1956); *The Big Country* (Patricia Terrill, 1958); *But Not for Me* (Ellie Borden, 1959); *The Miracle* (Teresa, 1959); *Bridge to the Sun* (Gwen Terasaki, 1961); *Something Wild* (Mary Ann Robinson, 1961); *How the West Was Won* (Eve Prescott, 1962); *Station Six-Sahara* (Catherine, 1963); *The Carpetbaggers* (Rina Marlow Cord, 1964); *Cheyenne Autumn* (Miss Deborah, 1964); *Sylvia* (Sylvia West, 1965); *The Greatest Story Ever Told* (Veronica, 1965); *Mister Moses* (Julie, 1965); *Harlow* (Jean Harlow, 1965); *Her Harem* (Margherita, 1967); *Jack of Diamonds* (Herself, 1967); *The Sweet Body of Deborah* (Deborah, 1968); *Paranoia* (Kathryn West, 1969); *So Sweet... So Perverse* (Nicole, 1969); *A Quiet Place to Kill* (Helen, 1970); *Deathwork* (Maude, 1971); *The Devil Has Seven Faces* (Julie/Mary, 1971); *Knife of Ice* (Martha, 1972); *Baba Yaga* (The Witch, 1973); *The Flower With the Deadly Sting* (Evelyn, 1973); *The Body* (Madeliene, 1974); *Private Lessons* (Laura, 1975); *Bait* (Carol, 1976); *Bad* (Hazel Aikin, 1977); *The World is Full of Married Men* (Linda, 1979); *Bloodbath* (Treasure, 1979); *The Watcher in the Woods* (Helen Curtis, 1980); *Star 80* (Dorothy Stratten's Mother, 1983); *The Secret Diary of Sigmund Freud* (Mama Freud, 1984); *Native Son* (Mrs. Dalton, 1986); *Ironweed* (Annie Phalen, 1987); *Kindergarten Cop* (Eleanor, 1990); *Blonde Fist* (Lovelle, 1991); *Cyber Eden* (Madame, 1992); *In the Flesh* (Elaine, 1995); *The Game* (Ilsa, 1997).

Brigitte Bardot

Birthdate: September 28, 1934; Paris, France
Nickname: Bebe
Height: 5' 7"
Measurements: 36B – 19 ½ - 36

SHORTLY AFTER A BEVY OF BEAUTIFUL ITALIAN GIRLS, Gina
Lollabrigida and Sophia Loren most memorable among them, took America by storm, Brigitte Bardot established the French connection. While
her career does not include the kind of classics those world-class beauties
occasionally appeared in, Brigitte had the greatest impact on popular culture, in America and elsewhere; then and now. Bebe's legend has less to
do with the quality of individual movies than their content, particularly a
through-line that connects the dots of disparate projects. Bardot changed
the way men look at women and, more importantly, the way women look
at themselves, and each other. A child of the upper-middle classes, Bardot
in the early 1950s (before she swept the U.S. by storm with the release
of... *And God Created Woman* in 1957), had redefined what a girl could
do, in public and on the screen, as to what had previously been considered 'naughty' behavior. She was the first actress to dare wear the then-
new and highly controversial bikini bathing suit, in real life and on the
screen; this at a time when professional models (oooh-la-la French girls,
at that) were so frightened of the prospect of appearing in one that the
original display of the bikini at swimsuit shows had to be turned over to
exotic dancers. Bardot personally embraced and openly flaunted the suit,
which became inseparable from her image: A girl-woman claiming absolute right to her sexual identity, her daring and charm swiftly destroy-

"...BUT THE DEVIL CREATED BARDOT!": That was the follow-up line to the title of Roger Vadim's mega-hit,... *And God Created Woman*, launching the career of one of the world's famous love goddesses.

ing old attitudes and moralistic clichés. The very titles of Bardot's earliest films—*School for Love, The Girl in the Bikini, Naughty Girl*—made clear that this singular person would change everything in terms of the New Woman of the postwar era claiming, as men had always done, the right to enjoy sexuality without this necessarily being an act of true love and total commitment. Good girls; bad girls? After Bardot, that dichotomy finally began to disappear, at least in terms of women's sexual decisions concerning their own bodies and acceptance of the pleasure principle as a non-evil choice for both genders. To recall Nietzsche, Bebe existed beyond good and evil. The New Morality, following Bardot, had to fully extend to women any female's worth, defined by her intellect, emotions, and spirituality rather than whether she was or was not a virgin. Equal rights for women had to begin somewhere. Not surprisingly, feminism—like everything that matters most in society—began in the bedroom.

Her aforementioned breakthrough film for then-husband Roger Vadim proved the point: Even as Bebe's character gleefully cheats on her husband, played by Jean-Louis Trintignant, so did this seeming Trilby cheat, and with that very leading man, on her supposed Svengali. Cheating, though, is the wrong word. Bardot brazenly announced her right to enjoy any man (and, in a later Vadim film in which she plays a female Don Juan, any woman too), refusing to be pigeonholed as superficially promiscuous. Bardot made clear that human sexuality in general, a woman's in particular, was something profound. Her daring act of bodily display via the bikini made itself felt in Hollywood, even as the most wholesome

OF BIKINIS, BLACK LEATHER, AND MOTORCYCLES: Though hailing from the upper-classes, 'Bebe' dared to wear the then-controversial bikini bathing, switching to black leather for a ride on her cycle; in so doing, she legitimized the entrance of White Trash Culture into a swiftly altering nouveau-mainstream.

COME DANCE WITH ME: Brigitte Bardot sways to an emergent international language that, throughout the 1960s, would combine elements of jazz, rock 'n' roll, and the Caribbean beat into an ever less modest form of self-expression.

California girls (Annette Funicello, Sandra Dee) came to accept near-nudity as 'the way' of the 1960s, Bebe of course the true pioneer razing the dark forest of Puritanical beliefs about the body's wickedness. Bardot then further challenged the status quo via a series of photographs displaying her in black leather jacket and dominatrix boots, striding a motorcycle. Her latest icon was influenced by Marlon Brando in *The Wild One* (1952); in the Sixties, Bebe announced in images rather than in words, women (like herself) of social status and "good breeding" could playfully adapt aspects of White Trash Culture into their individual styles. Even suburbanites, by mid-decade, took on the characteristics of outlaws as Harley Davidsons became symbols of success every bit as much as the Porsche. The comic book character Barbarella was based on Brigitte, though by the time a film was finally made (by Vadim) the more mature Bebe might have been been cast as The Grand Tyrant, a role that went to Anita Pallenberg. Likewise Bardot was too mature to play the lead in a film version of *The Motorcycle*, written as a tribute to Bebe's ability to balance an upscale everyday life with sudden walks (or rides) on the wild side (Marianne Faithfull played that part).

BEBE IN BONDAGE: The bad girl gets her just desserts at the hands of a multitude of men she has casually mistreated.

A decade later, this one-time revolutionary suddenly came to appear to many as a reactionary. Bardot dismissed 1970s porn stars, many of whom idolized her, as trashy. In retrospect, there is but a minimum of nudity in Bebe's movies. What she symbolized was the power of suggestion, the joys of sex not when clinically revealed but as a glimpse of stocking (or naked thigh), which works wonders on the human mind. Bardot might have claimed, as actor Charlton Heston did when asked about a transition from liberal in the 1950s to conservative in the 1970s: "I didn't change. The world shifted around me."

SELECTED FILMOGRAPHY:

Crazy for Love (Javotte Lemoine, 1952); *The Girl in the Bikini* (Manina, 1952); *Act of Love* (Mimi, 1953); *School for Love* (Sophie, 1955); *Doctor at Sea* (Hélène Colbert, 1955); *Helen of Troy* (Andraste, 1956); *Naughty Girl* (Brigitte, 1956); *Nero's Mistress* (Poppea, 1956); *Her Bridal Night* (Chouchou, 1956);... *And God Created Woman* (Juliete Hardy, 1956); *La Parisienne* (Brigitte, 1957); *Love Is My Profession* (Yvette, 1958); *The Female* (Eva Marchand, 1959); *Babette Goes to War* (Babette, 1959); *Come Dance with Me!* (Virginie Dandieu, 1959); *Testament of Orpheus* (Ella-même, 1960); *The Truth* (Dominique, 1960); *A Very Private Affair* (Jill, 1962); *Love on a Pillow* (Geneviève, 1962); *Contempt* (Camille Javal, 1963); *Agent 38-24-36* (Penelope Lightfeather, 1964); *Viva Maria* (Maria I, 1965); *Two Weeks in September* (Cecile, 1967); *Spirits of the Dead* (Giuseppina, 1968); *Shalako* (Irina, 1968); *Les Femmes* (Clara, 1969); *Les Novices* (Agnès, 1970); *Pistoleros,* aka *The Legend of Frenchie King* (Louise, 1971); *If Don Juan Were a Woman* (Jeanne, 1973).

Alexandra Bastedo

Birthdate: March 9, 1946; Hove, East Sussex, UK
Date of passing: January 12, 2014; West Sussex, England, UK
Height: 5' 6"
Measurements: N/A

ABOUT A THIRD OF THE WAY THROUGH *Casino Royale*, elderly
Sir James Bond (David Niven) drives his elegant touring car across the
lush British countryside. Suddenly, a beautiful blonde appears in a sports
car. Her assignment: Eliminate Bond by using electronic controls to ease a
bomb-on-wheels up behind the semi-retired spy's car. Meg may be a bright
young thing, but under-estimating Bond proves fatal. Sir James makes a
sharp turn; moments later the moving bomb appears on the lethal lady's
tail. Unforgiving, Bond uses his controls to enter into a gated area, making
sure the iron entranceway closes tightly behind him. This leaves the dis-
traught girl forced to stop there and, for several horrifying seconds, glance
back to watch as the wheeled bomb inexorably closes in, perpetrator now
ironically turned victim. One more Bond bad-girl bites the dust. In those
brief moments, Alexandra Bastedo made a strong impression.

Shortly, B-films and TV did happily provide a strong venue for
such elegant beauties. Soon Bastedo followed in Goldengirl Shirley Eaton's footsteps, playing a beautiful bad-girl on *The Saint*, opposite future
Bond Roger Moore, in an episode titled "The Counterfeit Countess." This
Brit-lensed series was followed by another in which Alexandra played
the female lead: an odd, short-lived, but memorable series, *The Champions* (1968-1969). Produced by Lew Grade for ITV, here was a 30-epi-
sode 1968-1969 series combining elements of the popular spy cycle with
science-fiction, also allowing a hint of Sir Arthur Conan Doyle's Sherlock

COME SPY WITH ME: Alexandra Bastedo incarnated the deadly-dangerous spy girl in TV's *The Champions*.

Holmes mystery stories into the mix. Otherworldly super-heroes (mentored by an aged Tibetan seer in a Shangri-La-like Himalayan hideaway) included Craig Stirling (Stuart Damon), Richard Barrett (William Grant), and Bastedo as a cool-as-ice agent, Sharron Macready. Bolstered by supernatural abilities, the three fought a SPECTRE-like force of evil called Nemesis. Many Bond-like gimmicks were employed within the budget limitations. Never as popular as *The Avengers* or *The Prisoner*, the show created enough interest that it was picked up as an NBC summer-replacement item.

Even as the spy cycle diminished in the late 1960s, Bastedo moved on to the increasingly popular horror films. A craze for Karmilla Carnstein movies (from the Sheridan Le Fanu 1870s novella) led to her being cast as the Baroness of Blood in a contemporary version, *The Blood Spattered Bride*. This was among those early 1970s female-oriented vampire films to create a sensation with lesbian-inclined succubi. As to the star's life journey: Appearing every bit the Mod Brit babe so popular during the Carnaby Street era, Bastedo had made her screen debut in a bizarre film from schlockmeister William Castle called *13 Frightened Girls*, about nubile nymphets helping a spy catch enemy agents. Like most 1960s celebrities, Bastedo dated such jet-set darlings as actor Omar Sharif and interviewer David Frost (she said 'no' to Steve McQueen) before settling into a long-term marriage with Patrick Garland, which lasted from 1980 until his passing in 2013. She became close friends with Prince Charles, ran an animal-rights sanctuary, and lived as a vegetarian. In later years, she appeared in Brit TV series like *Boon*, *Absolutely Fabulous*, and *EastEnders*

KISS THE BLOOD OFF MY HANDS: In *The Blood Spattered Bride*, Alexandra Bastedo took her turn at playing Sheridan Le Fanu's legendary fictional vampire Carmilla Karnstein.

SECRET AGENTS WITH SUPER-POWERS: In a prime example of cult Brit TV,
Alexandra Bastedo joined Stuart Damon and William Grant for a classic
combination of spy adventure and science-fiction.

(as Cynthia), and remained striking enough in appearance to portray a
British society dame in Christopher Nolan's *Batman Begins*. Bastedo suc-
cumbed to cancer in 2014.

SELECTED FILMOGRAPHY:
13 Frightened Girls (Alex, 1963); *The Liquidator* (Radio Girl, 1966);
That Riviera Touch (Roulette Table Girl, 1966); *The Haunted Man* (Blonde
Victim, 1966); *Casino Royale* (Meg, 1967); *My Lover, My Son* (Cicely
Clarkson, 1970); *The Sicilian Affair* (Spy Girl, 1970); *The Blood Spattered
Bride* (Mircalla Karstein, 1972); *The Ghoul* (Angela, 1975); *Stigma* (Anna,
1980); *Draw!* (Bess, 1984); *Batman Begins* (Society Dame, 2005).

Brigid Bazlen

Birthdate: June 9, 1944; Fond du Lac, Wisconsin
Birth name: Brigid Mary Bazlen
Date of passing: May 25, 1989; Seattle, Washington
Height: N/A
Measurements: N/A

YOUNG BRIGID, AGE SEVEN, was waiting at her school bus stop when an NBC exec drove by, spotted the beautiful child, and exclaimed: "That's the next Elizabeth Taylor." Shortly, she was being prepped to join Hollywood's aristocracy. First there was the small screen. Despite her youth, Bazlen earned several distinctions during the Golden Age of Live-TV. As little Nellie Corrie, she was a part of what many cite as TV's first soap-opera (at the time referred to as "A Mid-Day Novel"), *Hawkins Falls* in 1955. Brigid next had the lead in one of the first live TV shows produced for children, also broadcast in color, *The Blue Fairy*, developed at Chicago's

MORE BY WAY OF OSCAR WILDE THAN THE BIBLE: The conception of young Salome (Brigid Bazlen) in Nicholas Ray's *King of Kings* is more based on an influential nineteenth century play than anyting to be found in the Gospels.

"COME AND SEE THE CREATURE IN MY CAVE": A teenage river pirate
(Brigid Bazlen) tempts a mountain man (James Stewart) who really ought
to know better in *How the West Was Won*.

WGN. As one TV historian noted, "Appearing in a blue gown, diamond
tiara, and clasping a silver wand, Bazlen, suspended by wires, would fly
across the small television stage, lip sync(h) 'I'm the Blue Fairy, I'll grant
you a wish, to make all your dreams come true...'" Bazlen was the first
actress to play a teenage girl (Pam Blake) as the lead on a TV series on the
brief-lived *Too You to Go Steady*. Critics marveled at her ultra-natural acting, moreso her striking resemblance to the young Elizabeth. Then came
several bad decisions, as when Brigid's mother turned down offers for her
daughter to co-star with Mary Martin in *The Sound of Music* on Broadway
and a young Jewish girl relocated in post-war Palestine in *Exodus*. Shortly,
Brigid played the debutante lead in *The Honeymoon Machine*, a romantic
comedy opposite young Steve McQueen. By this time, Bardot was all the
rage, incarnating a new kind of rebellious youth, and seductive P.R. spin
doctors posited Brigid as the logical American version. She won showy
roles in two big movies: as the legendary temptress (or so Oscar Wilde,
more than The Bible, had informed the world) Salome, dancing for Herod
in exchange for John the Baptist's head; and Dora, the dangerously seduc-

tive daughter of river pirate Walter Brennan who lures mountain man James Stewart to his near-demise in *How the West Was Won*.

Even before that CinemaScope Western hit the screen, Brigid's career was dead in the water. It's difficult to explain in retrospect why the press turned on her, in an unnecessarily vicious manner. *King of Kings* was picked out as the Biblical-epic genre's whipping boy, labeled "I Was a Teenage Jesus" owing to star Jeff Hunter's good looks and blue eyes. Perhaps the wrath directed at Bazlen had to do with a "we made you, now we'll break you" attitude. Entertainment reporters ridiculed her performance of Salome as a teen-temptress, performing a dance, scantily clad, not unlike the one Bardot offered up in ... *And God Created Woman* (1956). In fact, this film, released a year and a half before *Lolita*, introduced the underage femme fatale as a movie staple for the 1960s. Bazlen is radiant, she and the film long-since reclaimed as a classic. Bazlen later reflected: "Some people are surprised that I used no veils in my dance, but it is a false assumption that Salome did a strip tease. I had to form my seductive charming of Herod with a pure Oriental-African dance movement of the

WHEN THINGS WERE ROTTEN: Pontius Pilate (Hurd Hatfield), Herod (Frank Thring), and Salome (Brigid Bazlen) weigh the consequences of executing John the Baptist in *King of Kings*.

period." Audiences enjoyed her immensely yet MGM dropped Brigid's contract at once.

In desperation, she returned to TV soap-operas: *Days of Our Lives* in 1965, *Bright Promise* in 1969, before retreating from The Biz altogether. A 1966 marriage to Jean-Paul Vignon led to one child, then dissolved. A second, to a Nashville musician, also did not last. Bazlen lived quietly with her mother, who was not well. Soon Brigid became sick, too, likely as a result of her huge dependency on tobacco. She died in obscurity of cancer at age 44.

FILMOGRAPHY:

The Honeymoon Machine (Julie Fitch, 1961); *King of Kings* (Salome, 1961); *How the West Was Won* (Dora Hawkins, 1962).

Jeanne Bell

aka: JEAN BELL
Birthdate: November 23, 1943 (some sources say 1944);
   St. Louis, Missouri
Birth name: Annie Lee Morgan
Height: 5' 4"
Measurements: 34 – 23 - 36

HALFWAY THROUGH *TNT JACKSON,* the heroine, a courageous African-American crime fighter named Diane, finds herself surrounded by Hong Kong hoodlums. As they close in on the diminutive girl, she swirls about in a remarkably choreographed karate-style move, then flips up into the air. There's a quick cut to another part of the room as this agent, nicknamed TNT, lands on her feet with the deftness and agility of a cat. As she does, the audience realizes something that doesn't appear to have made an impression on the bad guys: Our strong, smart, sexy girl is now wearing a totally different costume. No, this is not a Diana Prince/Wonder Woman transformation but something more mundane: One of the worst continuity gaffs in film history, even in such a B-budget item. Instead of booing, urban audiences roared with laughter, even applauded. Here was the heart and soul of such pictures that, in our own time, Quentin Tarantino has established as a self-conscious aesthetic for mainstream movies.

Not satisfied with the limited choices awaiting Jean in her hometown, St. Louis, the ambitious youngster set out to achieve fame and fortune via the only means open to her: Exploit the many possibilities of her beauty. The first step was to become *Playboy's* second African-American centerfold (October, 1969). In addition to sex symbol, Jean became a media pioneer for civil rights in all areas of life and popular culture, American

STREET SMARTS: Pam Grier in her most famous role as 'Coffy' had considerable competition from another star of urban-action, Jeanne Bell in *TNT Jackson*.

style. If the then still new feminist movement put Jean down for appearing nude in a male-oriented publication, most of the nation (women as well as men) took pleasure in Jean's tastefully done layout.

Most of Jean's screen appearances were in movies designed as black-exploitation items. An exception: Early in Martin Scorsese's trail-blazing indie *Mean Streets*, Harvey Keitel's character exits the sanctuary of a Roman Catholic Church and steps down into a Little Italy cellar club. There, alcohol, music, and strippers dominate. One gorgeous African-American dancer flirts with him. Her next two films, though shot on A-movie budgets, were disasters. She worked with Richard Burton and Lee Marvin in *The Klansman* (not a remake of D.W. Griffith's *Birth of a Nation*, originally released under that title in 1915); this expose was so terrible that many theatres wouldn't play it. Likewise, co-starring in the much heralded film version of bestselling former policeman Joseph Wambaugh's *The Choirboys*, particularly under the direction of action-expert Robert Altman (*The Dirty Dozen*), must have seemed like a dream come true. But it too fizzled—taking down with it Jean's dreams of mainstream stardom.

The first great love of Jean's life was actor Richard Burton, during one of his frequent splits from Elizabeth Taylor. Joining the alcoholic star in Céligny, Switzerland, she was instrumental in helping him put aside the bottle. According to some sources, Jean encouraged her lover to patch things up with Queen Liz. Charmed by her clean, clear new environment, Jean settled in nearby Geneva. For eight years, she dated a wealthy businessman, Gary Judis. Following their marriage vows they shared one son. In 1979, after several years of retirement and virtual anonymity, Jean returned to the publication where it began for her, doffing her clothes once more (and still looking gorgeous) in a "Playmates Forever" nostalgia pictorial.

SELECTED FILMOGRAPHY:
Melinda (Jean,1972); *Trouble Man* (Leona, 1972); *Black Gunn* (Lisa, 1972); *Cleopatra Jones* (Terry, 1972); *Mean Streets* (Diane, 1973); *Policewoman* (Pam, 1974); *TNT Jackson* (Diana Jackson, 1974); *Three the Hard Way* (Polly, 1974); *(The) Klansman* (Mary Anne, 1974); *The Muthers* (Kelly, 1976); *Disco 9000* (Karen, 1976); *Some Like it Cool* (Fatme, 1977); *The Choirboys* (Fanny Forbes, 1977).

QUEEN OF THE DAMNED: In *Prehistoric Women*, which the star once called "one of the silliest movies ever made," Martine Beswick strikingly captures the very essence of a femme fatale.

Martine Beswick

aka: MARTINE BESWICKE
Birthdate: September 26, 1941; Port Antonio, Jamaica
Birth name: Mary Beswick
Height: 5' 6"
Measurements: 37 – 22 ½ - 35

WHEN PHOTOGRAPHED, Martine's perfect facial features, often described as sweet by people who met her in real life, were reconfigured by the photographic process in such a manner that her image projected pure, absolute evil. While this ensured a long line of deadly-dame roles it also interfered with the sort of serious career she would have liked to pursue. Almost always cast as a Scream Queen, Martine discovered early on that the mood on an escapist movie set was not likely to be of the professional nature that she sought: "I always go into my films with absolute commitment, and there was (none) from the other people involved. And so I put my all into it, and it's a little frustrating because what comes out is not what I put in." Born in Jamaica as Mary Beswick, she traveled to England as a teenager to attend school, afterwards heading home. Mary found work as a secretary and also entered the Miss Jamaica pageant, though she was not chosen as a finalist, much less the winner. Then it was back to England where she pursued a film career. Now calling herself Martine to suggest an exotic aura, she tested for the role in *Dr. No* that eventually went to Ursula Andress. Any disappointment was tempered by her being cast as the exotic dancer in that film's famed opening credits. Meanwhile, a cover shot of her on London's *Daily Mail* had the populace asking: "Who *is* that *girl?*" Terence Young recalled her vividly, casting the in-embryo femme fatale as one of two gypsy girls who engage in what may well be

OF SEX AND VOLENCE: Beswick's Barbarian Queen in *Prehistoric Women* entices unwary men into her animalistic boudoir, then fights for domination over one of her blonde slave girls.

the screen's greatest cat-fight in *From Russia With Love*. Clearly, though, her Bond Girl potential had not yet been fulfilled. In *Thunderball*, she played what had already become known as The First Girl: The one who becomes involved with 007 early on but is killed by the evil empire, spurring James to seek revenge. Surprisingly, her character was 'good,' an aid to the hero after he reaches Jamaica, instead of the villainess.

The house of Hammer recognized her potential. Martine next engaged in another classic cat-fight, this one with Raquel Welch, in *One Million Years B.C.*, the film that made that other girl a major star. With Raquel's hair colored a light brown/near-blonde, Martine was free to play the crazed beauty threatened by cave man John Richardson's attraction to the recent arrival in their camp. (Martine, not Raquel, shortly married the male star.) Martine dies screaming in pain and horror (something she was remarkably adept at) when an earthquake eventually claims her. The potential on view in a supporting role there led to her lead as an evil empress on the order of Barbarella's Great Tyrant in *Prehistoric Women*. Martine enacted the leader of a tribe of raven-haired Wiccans who en-

"TAKE THAT, YOU...!": Martine Beswick at her baddest, as the second-billed title character in *Dr. Jekyll and Sister Hyde*, a thriller from Hammer.

slave (and essentially cannibalize) the more demure nation of blondes. All the girls wear animal-skin bikinis; Martine's full-throttle performance as the sadistic/ nymphomaniacal worshipper of the White Rhinoceros rates as one of the great Camp performances in film history. "It was probably the silliest movie ever made," Martine reflected.

Perhaps. Still, *Prehistoric Women* rates as a cult classic, in part owing to the semi-surreal quality of its minimalist sets and a time-warp theme that recalls some of the most intriguing *Star Trek* episodes from the same era. Other notable villainesses included a mystery woman who arrives at the title place in *The Penthouse*, where she tortures a young couple who only wanted to sneak away for some free sex. Hammer offered Martine the female side of the title team in *Dr. Jekyll and Sister Hyde* when their first choice, Caroline Munro, refused to appear nude. In this version (extremely effective despite the off-putting title) the doctor transforms into a deadlier-than-the-male seductress. A stunning resemblance between Beswick and the male star, Ralph Bates, helped make the concept click. Moving to Hollywood, she played leads in silly R-rated items like *The Happy Hooker Goes Hollywood*, in which she portrayed famed madam Xaviera Hollander, as well as finding an occasional character role in a top movie like *Melvin and Howard*. After serving in the Tinseltown trenches for years, Beswick retired and returned to London where she founded a removal business. She did, however, return to 'Bondage' as one of twelve former 007 girls who appeared together on an April 2013 BBC reunion show.

Trivia: She was mistakenly billed as 'Martin' in From *Russia With Love,* and chose to be billed as 'Beswicke' in several of her final films.

SELECTED FILMOGRAPHY:

Dr. No (Dancing Girl in Credit Sequence, 1962); *From Russia With Love* (Zora, 1963); *Saturday Night Out* (Barmaid, 1964); *Thunderball* (Paula, 1965); *A Bullet for the General* (Adelita, 1966); *One Million Years B.C.* (Nupondi, 1966); *The Penthouse* (Harry, 1967); *Prehistoric Women* (Kari, 1967); *Dr. Jekyll and Sister Hyde* (Sister Hyde, 1971); *(The) Kiss of Death* (Nara Kotosky, 1974); *Seizure* (The Queen, 1974); *The Last Italian Tango* (The Girl, 1975); *The Happy Hooker Goes Hollywood* (Xaviera Hollander, 1980); *Melvin and Howard* (Reality Agent, 1980); *Evil Spirits* (Vanya, 1990); *Trancers II* (Nurse Trotter, 1991); *Critters 4* (Angela, voice only, 1992); *Wide Sargasso Sea* (Aunt Cora, 1993); *(The) Night of the Scarecrow* (Barbara, 1995).

"HELLO, MR. BOND...": Martine Beswick was one of the rare girls to appear in three installments of the 007 franchise: *Dr. No*, *From Russia With Love*, and *Thunderball*.

A SWEET PACKAGE FROM ITALY: Though Daniela Bianchi played a Soviet spy in *From Russia With Love*, the dazzling beauty came to the Bond franchise by way of Rome.

Daniela Bianchi

Birthdate: January 31, 1942; Rome, Italy
Height: 5' 7"
Measurements: N/A

LIKE MANY OTHER BOND GIRLS, Daniela Bianchi was picked for her role after being spotted at a beauty contest. Daniela won the Miss Rome title in 1960, then was named runner-up for Miss World later that year. Being voted Miss Photogenic by the press in attendance at the event helped launch a movie career. She had appeared in several films prior to becoming the second 007 "final girl" in *From Russia With Love*, including one Peplum about El Cid that ought not to be confused with the major-league production starring Charlton Heston and Sophia Loren. The role of Tatiana, a simple Soviet shipping clerk persuaded to enter "the dirty game" of spying, can be taken metaphorically, as can the film's title. During the early 1960s, many hoped that, despite such events as the Cuban Missile Crisis, the Cold War might finally thaw. The idea of a British agent and a Russian spy sleeping together—though not, as each had originally planned, killing one another—implied that such a state of *detante* might yet be achieved, rogue terrorists here targeted as the true enemy of each super-power. Likewise, casual sex in a mainstream movie (Bond and Tatiana enjoying one another without hesitance on first sight, she wearing nothing but a sheet and black choker) further popularized the 1960s Sexual Revolution.

If Bianchi projected presence and charisma, no one ever accused her of acting. When cast, she spoke nearly no English and, as numerous members of the crew have attested, had to whisper each of her lines phonetically. An excellent Brit stage actress, Barbara Jefford, provided

A TASTE FOR DANGER: Daniela Bianchi and Sean Connery overcome their Cold War enmity to fight super-villains in *From Russia With Love*.

the vocal accompaniment. After, Daniela appeared in several Euro-spy B-junk movies that scored on the international box-office, though most were never released in the continental U.S. The exception was *Operation Kid Brother*, aka *Double 007*, aka *Secret Agent 00*. Neil Connery, Sean's younger brother, at the time an out-of-work carpenter suffering from appendicitis, essentially played himself: sibling to the world's greatest spy star. Rounding out the 007 element were Lois Maxwell and Bernard Lee, cast as spin-offs of Miss Moneypenny and M. When asked why they would take the risk of angering Albert 'Cubby' Broccoli, both admitted that they couldn't resist the paychecks, higher than any they had received for any of the official films. Broccoli was too savvy a businessman to fire the pair, more or less taking the grin and bear it approach. And of course Bianchi (having already played a lead Final Girl) had nothing to worry about as she was not likely to be asked back. Here her character is the villainess during the film's first half but, after bedding young Connery, turns into a heroine.

Adolfo Celli, who had played *Thunderball*'s title villain, has a similar role. Anthony Dawson, a secondary villain in *Dr. No* as well as the voice of Blofeld in *From Russia With Love* and *Thunderball*, is up to no good again. Ennio Morricone created music that sounded almost identical to what appeared in Broccoli's films. Toward decade's end, Bianchi retired from such nominal stardom. In time, she married a wealthy shipping magnate from Genoa. They have one son and continue to maintain a successful relationship.

SELECTE'D FILMOGRAPHY:

Love Is My Profession (Girl, uncredited, 1958); *Demons at Midnight* (Blonde, 1961); *Always on Sunday* (Donatella, 1962); *Attack of the Cid* (Elvira, 1962); *From Russia With Love* (Tatiana, 1963); *Code Name: Tiger* (Mehlica Baskine, 1964), *Slalom* (Nadia, 1965); *Weekend, Italian Style* (Isabella, 1965); *Balearic Caper* (Mercedes, 1966); *Special Mission* (Lady Arabella Chaplin, 1966); *Requiem for a Secret Agent* (Evelyn, 1966); *Dirty Heroes* (Kristina, 1967); *Operation Kid Brother* (Maya Rafis, 1967).

QUEEN OF CARNABY STREET: During the era of The Beatles and the Rolling Stones, few young women made as huge a splash as mini-skirted Jane Birkin.

Jane Birkin

Birthdate: December 14, 1946; Marylebone, London
Birth name: Jane Mallory Birkin
Height: 5' 8 3/4"
Measurements: 32 – 24 - 37

"I WAS VERY CONVENTIONAL," Birkin once said, reflecting on her Swingin' Sixties' status. "At eighteen, I was the oldest virgin in Chelsea." Swiftly, the gorgeous model turned actress (and eventual balladeer) shed any inhibitions. Jane emerged as, alongside Twiggy, the most visible symbol of The New Female who dared wear mini-skirts and sleep around with rock stars. In her first (brief) screen appearance, in *The Knack...* (directed by Richard Lester, avatar of Beatles films) Jane was seen cruising around Mod London on the back seat of a motorcycle driven by one of the era's notorious Teddy Boys. Soon thereafter she played one of two underage teen-girl would-be models (she's the blonde) who seduce trendy photographer David Bailey (David Hemmings) into trading sex for future studio sessions in Michelangelo Antonioni's *Blow-Up*. That was a cinematic masterpiece which happened to include several risqué sex scenes. Birkin, who now felt as free about sex as her predecessor from France (whom she resembled), Brigitte Bardot, starred in slight, shallow films which existed solely to titillate an audience. If there was any message to *Catherine & Company*, it was that all inhibitions ought to be shed in favor of free love. Speaking of Bardot, the two beauties shared a bedroom sequence in *If Don Juan Was a Woman*, directed by Roger Vadim, Bardot's onetime husband.

Daughter of a stage actress, Jane found herself in the right place at the right time for her life to segue into the Brave New Beatles' Era World. Yet she maneuvered the difficult journey, soft-porn aside, of being taken

THE MANY LOVES OF A 'HIPPIE-CHICK': In *Blow-Up*, the young Jane Birkin warily enters into a love affair with David Hemmings; in *If Don Juan Were a Woman*, she wholeheartedly embraces Brigitte Bardot (in the title role).

seriously both as an actress and songstress. Her two best femme fatale roles in mainstream movies occurred in a pair of Agatha Christie-based detective thrillers, *Death on the Nile* and *Evil Under the Sun*, starring Oscar winner Peter Ustinov as Belgian detective Hercule Poirot. In 1985 Jane deservedly won the Best Actress award at the Venice Film Festival for her performance in *Dust*. Like her contemporary Marianne Faithfull, she survived the Sixties and moved on to true stardom in recording and concert performances. Initially, such success derived from her teaming with pop artist Serge Gainsbourg who, simultaneous with Jacques Brel, developed a breezy but earnest Gallic form of contemporary music including elements of rock and folk, though not limited by any narrowing sense of genre. The most famous disc (as the French liked to call records) by Birkin and Gainsbourg, "Je t'aime... moi non plus," contained such sexually explicit language that it was banned from radio play in many countries. Gainsbourg had earlier begun to compose this song for a lover, Bardot; after their split rewriting it for Jane. Eventually, Birkin found the confidence to strike out on her own, writing the lyrics and composing the music for her own albums. A leftish activist, she has championed the cause of democracy in Burma, along with embracing and being a spokesperson for other progressive causes.

NICE GIRLS DON'T SUCK THEIR THUMBS!: Jane Birkin strikes an innocent pose.

Trivia: A haute fashion staple, the Hermès Birkin bag, was designed by Jean-Louis Dumas to capture Jane's free-spirited image and share it internationally with women who refuse to let their unavoidable aging interfere with an ongoing open embrace of sensuality. Jane received the Order of the British Empire in 2001 from the Queen of England.

SELECTED FILMOGRAPHY:

The Knack... and How to Get It (Blonde on a Motorcycle, 1965); *Kaleidoscope* (Exquisite Thing, 1966); *Blow-Up* (Blonde Teenager, 1966); *Poor Cherry* (Judy, 1967); *Wonderwall* (Penny Lane, 1968); *La Piscine* (Pénélope, 1969); *Slogan* (Evelyne, 1969); *The Pleasure Pit* (Jane, 1969); *Sex-Power* (Jane, 1970); *Romance of a Horsethief* (Milja, 1971); *Dark Places* (Alta, 1973); *If Don Juan Were a Woman* (Clara, 1973); *Seven Dead in the Cat's Eye* (Corringa, 1973); *Private Screening* (Kate, 1973); *Serious as Pleasure* (Ariane Berg, 1975); *Catherine & Co.* (Catherine, 1975); *The Devil in the Heart* (Linda, 1976); *Death on the Nile* (Louise Bourget, 1978); *Melancoly Baby* (Olga, 1979); *Evil Under the Sun* (Christine, 1982); *La Pirate* (Alma, 1984); *Love on the Ground* (Emily, 1984); *Dust* (Magda, 1985); *The Woman of My Life* (Laura, 1986); *Comédie!* (Elle, 1987); *Daddy Nostalgia* (Caroline, 1990); *One Hundred and One Nights* (Celle, 1995); *This is My Body* (Louise, 2001); *Around a Small Mountain* (Kate, 2009).

Honor Blackman

Birthdate: August 22, 1925; Plaistow, Newham, East London
Height: 5' 11"
Measurements: 37 C – 23 - 36 ¼

PICTURE THIS, IF YOU CAN: PUSSY GALORE, the onetime lesbian transformed into a male-loving nymphomaniac after being raped (watch that barn sequence again!) by Bond... working as a dispatch rider during World War II. While the naughtily named fictional character (that's pronounced 'Poooo-sie,' of course) may be impossible to imagine in such a situation, that's how Honor Blackman served her country during England's darkest hours. Previously, this denizen of London's East End (her dad was a civil service statistician) had studied for a career in the arts at the Guildhall School of Music and Drama. Originally interested in live theatre, she appeared in several West End productions until offered a movie role opposite Sir Michael Redgrave in her film debut, *Fame Is the Spur*.

For several years during the mid-1950s, Blackman dropped out of sight. Few knew that she had suffered a nervous breakdown and had to be hospitalized. Now divorced from first husband Bill Sankey, Honor gradually found the strength to return to the screen. If not a generic Peplum, *Jason and the Argonauts* allowed her to play the goddess Hera in a world-class retelling of the Greek myth, bolstered by state-of-the-art special effects by Ray Harryhausen. Earlier, she landed the lead role of "Mrs. Cathy Gale," a swingin' spy (clad mostly in black leather) in a TV predecessor to the upcoming James Bond films. She and Patrick Macnee, as the dapper John Steed, took on super-villains, the edgy "heroes" licensed to kill at will (Honor seemed to enjoy dispatching the pug-uglies far beyond any sense of duty). The show was so cheaply produced and recorded that when

THE VERY PICTURE OF ELEGANCE: The ever-stylish Honor Blackman as one of the most legendary Bond babes, Pussy Galore.

England's American cousins decided to broadcast *The Avengers* once the Bond phenomenon had begun, it was necessary to shoot new episodes that were produced with employment of high-quality film stock. Surprisingly, Honor passed on the offer to continue in her role, Diana Rigg replacing her as "Mrs. Emma Steed." This freed Honor to play a somewhat similar role in *Goldfinger*, Pussy Galore providing an "origination story" for *The Avengers'* female lead. Blackman beating up the bad boys for the Brit series, judo skills included, served as her audition for *Goldfinger*.

Fans of the film in general, Honor Blackman in particular, recall the introduction of her character at the mid-point. She approaches Bond on an airplane as he comes to consciousness, introducing herself. "I must be dreaming," Bond says upon hearing her name while considering her beauty. The line won a laugh, though not nearly as big a one as might have been the case had what originally appeared in the script been used. "I'm Pussy Galore," Honor was to have said. "I can see that," Bond was to have replied. "What's your name?" However mild that may seem today, it was a bit much for the censors in 1964. Such success did not lead to strong film offers. So Blackman returned to the stage, often working with second husband Maurice Kaufmann, though they too in time divorced.

Trivia: Honor is a long-time political liberal and member of the Labour Party. Her only topless sequence appears in the uncut original version of *The Last Roman*. She hates to be called "a Bond girl" since the term refers to bimbos, while Pussy Galore was always her own woman.

SELECTED FILMOGRAPHY:
Fame Is the Spur (Debutante, 1946); *Daughter of Darkness* (Julie Tallent, 1948); *Quartet* (Paula, 1948); *Conspirator* (Joyce, 1949); *So Long at the*

DIANA WHO?: Long before Ms. Rigg joined *The Avengers*, it was Honor Blackman who solved crimes alongside John Steed (Patrick Macnee).

A MEMORABLE ROLE IN THE HAY: Pussy Galore (Honor Blackman) appears to have enjoyed her mid-movie encounter with James Bond in *Goldfinger*.

Fair (Rhoda, 1950); *Come Die, My Love* (Eva, 1951); *Green Grow the Rushes* (Meg, 1951); *The Glass Cage* (Jenny, 1955); *A Night to Remember* (Liz Lucas, 1958); *Jason and the Argonauts* (Hera, 1963); *Goldfinger* (Pussy Galore, 1964); *The Secret of My Success* (Baroness Lily, 1965); *Moment to Moment* (Daphne, 1965); *Shalako* (Lady Daggett, 1968); *The Last Roman* (Amalaswintha, 1968); *The Virgin and the Gypsy* (Mrs. Fawcett, 1970); *Night Legs* (Helen, 1971); *To the Devil a Daughter* (Anna Fountain, 1976); *The Cat and the Canary* (Susan Sillsby, 1978); *Tale of the Mummy* (Chief Inspector Shea, 1998); *Bridget Jones' Diary* (Penny Husbands-Bosworth, 2001).

Barbara Bouchet

Birthdate: August 15, 1943; Reicehnberg, Bohemia
Birth name: Barbara Gutscher
Height: 5' 5 ¼"
Measurements: 36 ½ – 23 - 34 ½

FOR MOST GLAMOROUS ACTRESSES of the 1960s and 1970s, there could be no greater glory than being chosen as either the 'good (and final) girl' or 'bad (doomed to die) girl' in a James Bond film. Consider, then, the curious case of Barbara Bouchet. Though she never appeared in any of Broccoli's official 007 opuses, Bouchet did play roles resembling both sides of Bond's female dichotomy. Bouchet's first memorable part was in a 1964 episode of TV's Bond imitation *The Man from U.N.C.L.E.*, Barbara cast as 'Narcissus Darling.' Her next spy-girl role also had TV connections. *Agent for H.A.R.M.* was filmed as the pilot for another TV series. Bouchet played Ava Vestok, a seemingly innocent beach-bunny who frugs and twists on the seashore in ultra-skimpy bikinis, practices her archery skills, and seduces the film's nominal hero (Peter Mark Richman). Eventually it's revealed that she's a cold-blooded assassin. Bouchet's ability to transform from wide-eyed innocence to deadly cruelty in a split-second suggests what a fine candidate she might have been for one of the more upscale entries in Cubby's official series.

The following year, Bouchet did indeed play a Bond-ed good-girl in the decade's only 007 film *not* a part of the ongoing franchise. Charles K. Feldman, who owned *Casino Royale*, decided to cash in on 007's heady success. He settled on the 'romp' style that had succeeded two years earlier in *What's New Pussycat?* thanks to Woody Allen's clever script. *Casino Royale* (boasting many of *Pussycat*'s cast members—Allen included,

THOSE LIPS, THOSE EYES, THAT HAIR: When Barbara Bouchet failed to make it in Hollywood, she shifted her sights to Europe and became a leading figure in exploitation flicks.

though he did not write this disappointing failure) sunk like lead owing to its lack of good gags. Bouchet does shine through, as Miss Moneypenny, rescued from secondary status, now the 007 leading lady.

At the time, Bouchet was a mere 23. Having survived the Nazi occupation of Czechoslovakia, the Gutscher family moved to Munich when she was ten. Young Barbara studied ballet, then moved, again with family, to San Francisco. A talent search for a "new Gidget" led to a screen-test, modeling gigs, and such pageant titles as "Miss China Beach" and "Miss Firecracker." Though the old studio system was fast-failing, Bouchet did go the starlet route with window-dressing roles in such big films as *A Global Affair*, *What a Way to Go!*, *Good Neighbor Sam*, and *Sex and the Single Girl*, all 1964. A seven-year-contract with major-league producer-

"SHE WAS AFRAID TO COME OUT OF THE WATER...": Despite Brian Hyland's legendary rock 'n' roll song about bikinis, Barbara Bouchet shows no fear at all as she emerges from the sea as yet another legendary goddess come to life in 1960s cinema.

director Otto Preminger allowed her to play Kirk Douglas's adulterous wife in *In Harm's Way*. Sensing that Preminger all but owned her, Bouchet asked for a release, causing her career to slip into B-budget filmmaking. However, what may be her best onscreen performance occurs in yet another low-budget Bond type film (this, though, a great one): *Danger Route*. She went the Playboy route, appearing in two pictorials, one in 1965, the other in 1967.

When the American B-movie industry bottomed out, Bouchet moved to Europe. Bouchet starred in several sexy/silly comedies, always willing to do mild nudity. More importantly, she became the queen of the Giallo, these shot in gaudy color and with large/graphic doses of sex and violence. Though few were imported to America, The Blonde (as many now referred to Bouchet) ruled. Married to Luigi Borghese from 1974 to 2006, she opened a prominent health club in Rome, then created her own production company to film videos instructing women of the world how to, like Barbara, remain youthfully beautiful. Today, Barbara remains best

LIVE FAST, DIE YOUNG: As Kirk Douglas's adulterous wife, Barbara dies early on in the film *In Harm's Way*; despite this publicity picture, she expires not while on the beach (with Hugh O'Brian) but shortly thereafter in a car crash.

known for her *Star Trek* appearance as the seductive Kelinda opposite William Shatner in "By Any Other Name" (2/23/1968).

SELECTED FILMOGRAPHY:

In Harm's Way (Liz, 1965); *Agent for H.A.R.M.* (Ava Vestok, 1966); *Casino Royale* (Moneypenny, 1967); *Danger Route* (Marita, 1967); *Sweet Charity* (Ursula, 1969); *Intimacy* (Signora Marchio, 1970); *Nights and Loves of Don Juan* (Esmeralda, 1971); *Black Belly of the Tarantula* (Maria Zani, 1971); *The French Sex Murders* (Francine, 1972); *The Lady in Red Kills Seven Times* (Kitty, 1972); *Don't Torture a Duckling* (1972); *Sex With a Smile* (1976); *Death Rage* (Anny, 1976); *Gangs of New York* (Mrs. Shermerhorn, 2002).

PORTRAIT OF A DOOMED BEAUTY: Elisabeth Brooks, appearing stunning before the application of make-up in The Howling.

Elisabeth Brooks

Birthdate: July 2, 1951; Toronto, Canada
Birth name: Elisabeth Brooks Luyties
Date of passing: September 7, 1997; Palm Springs, CA
Height: N/A
Measurements: N/A

DURING THE MID-1970S, two competing film companies set out to "reinvent" the old werewolf film by bringing the genre more in line with contemporary graphic sex and violence well as featuring the swiftly advancing world of F/X. John Landis's *An American Werewolf in London* stole all the steam, partly because a major distributor's backing allowed the movie vast publicity. Less noticed but far superior, despite a smaller budget, was *The Howling*, which spawned a series of ever-less-impressive sequels. The first was not only a modern version of the ancient tale but one of the first post-modernist films to come out of a still-emergent New Hollywood. Joe Dante continuously deconstructed the drama to keep his audience aware that what they were watching was not only a werewolf movie but a movie *about* werewolf movies. Horror/sci-fi veterans ranging from John Carradine to Kevin McCarthy put in appearances; a smart script by indie filmmaker John Sayles constantly undercut the horror with humor. A then young Rob Bottin did what he could with a tight budget to construct striking special effects. Still, audiences were most eager to talk about Elisabeth Brooks as the seductive succubus.

During the movie's remarkable mid-point sequence, she literally rips an eager victim's skin from his body while they experience hot and nasty sex in the woods. Fans of such femme fatales compared her to past favorites including Barbara Steele, Caroline Munro, and Martine Beswick.

Here was the moment Brooks had been eagerly awaiting since she started acting at age five in any production she could talk her way into. During the 1970s, she appeared in the high-status TV mini-series *Rich Man, Poor Man* and had a regular role on a daytime serial, *The Days of Our Lives*. There was plenty of episodic TV work, including an appearance in one cult show, *Kolchak: The Night Stalker*. A single mother, she took jobs outside the industry (including waitressing) to make ends meet and support herself and her son. A long term friendship developed with actress Kristy McNichol. Gifted beyond performance abilities, Brooks wrote and directed a play, *Orphan Dreams*, which was performed in several venues.

DEMON OF THE NIGHT: Despite her one great role as a femme fatale, everyone who knew Elisabeth insists she was a sweet and 'righteous' woman.

The Howling's success begged for a sequel and executives were keenly interested in retaining only one holdover from the original: Elisabeth. Those putting together the follow-up were devastated upon meeting with her: Brooks had gained weight; her once radiant face had become flaccid, wrinkled, and drawn almost overnight. This may well have been the result of a necessary hysterectomy shortly after filming of the first *Howling* had been completed. Some sources insist she was indeed offered the role but backed out. Sybil Danning received the part and Brooks, diagnosed with brain cancer, survived for another three years in her trailer park home. As to her most famous sequence, she always damned the inclusion of full-frontal nudity, as well as the images from it published in *Playboy*, insisting she had been promised the sequence would be suggestive, not explicit; her personal combination of Christian values and feminist leanings conflicted with such a portrayal. One final tribute appeared: the producers and designers of the video game *Return to Castle Wolfenstein* (2001) included a "special thanks" to Elisabeth.

SELECTED FILMOGRAPHY:
Family Plot (Girl in Café, 1976); *The Howling* (Marsha Quist, 1981); *Deep Space* (Mrs. Ridley, 1988); *The Forgotten One* (Carla, 1989); *Jaded* (Rita, 1989).

BAD ASS ATTITUDE/GREAT ASS PHYSICALLY: In films that she co-produced and designed for herself, Cherri Caffaro set the pace of many of today's onscreen action babes.

Cheri Caffaro

Birthdate: April 29, 1945; Miami, FL
Height: N/A
Measurements: 36 (B) – 24 - 36

WHILE A TEENAGER IN PASADENA, and a student at the city's
famed Playhouse, Cheri Caffaro won a Brigitte Bardot lookalike contest.
Rather than opt for offers to do Cormanesque B-films, she seized control
of her career and collaborated in creating a character all her own. Not
only did Caffaro play the lead in three Ginger films; she involved herself in writing, production, even costume design for her ultra-low-budget
items. Initially, her ultra-violent, ultra-sexy opuses were rated X; with a
little trimming, they were re-rated R for the emergent home video market, where Caffaro emerged as a cult queen. Here was a succubus sans
fangs, Ginger all but physically devouring the men who, as a top secret
government agent assigned to take out the trash, she met during her lurid adventures. Watching her elicited a Death Wish reaction on the part
of men who became obsessed with her blonde beauty and cold-blooded,
calculated approach to the males that she met onscreen: Oh, what a thrill
to be her next victim… *what a way to go!*

Perhaps her most famous erotic-kill occurs in the initial *Ginger* film.
A spoiled rich boy (J. Calvin Culver, aka Casey Donovan) has been selling
drugs to the kids in a small town. Ginger's job is to shut down the operation.
She flirts with the youth; he is cocksure that he's on the edge of bedding her
though Ginger always remains elusive. Finally, it comes time to put up or
shut up. When they arrive at a motel, she knocks him out, ties him tight to
the bed, and wraps a wire around his private parts. Upon coming out of his
stupor, Ginger calmly explains to her victim that if he doesn't tell her ev-

erything about the drug deals she'll yank the wire, castrating him. While he desperately spills the beans, she first performs a striptease, then slips onto the bed, tantalizingly kissing her prey. When he's told everything he knows, and he foolishly addresses her via the 'b word,' Ginger smiles cruelly and yanks the wire anyway. In the original theatrical cut, the onscreen image was shocking beyond belief; for video versions, several seconds were cut. To this day, fans of the original still search for the missing footage.

In her last auteurist effort, *Too Hot to Handle*, Caffaro left the female Bond image behind to play one of the earliest incarnations of what would

MEAN AS THEY COME: Following her three Ginger mini-epics, Cheri portrayed a Hit Woman who enjoys lovemaking with men marked as her intended prey.

SOFT SIDE OF A HARD GIRL: In each of her Ginger films, Cheri Caffaro has at least one moment in which she goes "girly-girl" – though soon it's back to kicking and killing.

soon become an ongoing icon: the gorgeous female assassin. In the first killing, she joins an unawares male victim in a hot tub, having slipped him a knock out drop. As he freezes, unable to move but aware of all that's going on, she enjoys watching as he slowly sinks under the water and drowns. She then goes on to murder male and female victims, all the while enjoying a sexual affair with the handsome male agent assigned to stop her. Particularly appealing was that, at the end, she slips away scott free, rather than, like other female assassins in *The Next Man* and TV's *Hit Lady*, having to pay the ultimate price for her transgression.

Caffaro scored roles in a few mainstream TV shows like *Baretta* and *Delvecchio*, both in 1977. She also wrote the story and screenplay for *H.O.T.S.* (1979), one of the many raunchy youth films turned out in the wake of *Animal House*'s popularity. Thereafter, she disappeared from the Biz, having split with her collaborator-husband Don Schain. Caffaro apparently still lives in the Los Angeles area, where she raises honeybees in hopes of replacing their dwindling number in order to preserve the ecosystem. If gone and mostly forgotten, rest assured that such characters as Uma Thurman's role in Tarantino's *Kill Bill* films pay homage to Cherri Caffaro.

SELECTED FILMOGRAPHY:

Ginger (Ginger McAllister, 1971); *The Abductors* (Ginger McAllister, 1972); *A Place Called Today* (Cindy Cartwright, 1972); *Girls Are for Loving* (Ginger McAllister, 1973); *Savage Sisters* (Jo Turner, 1974); *Too Hot to Handle* (Samantha Fox, 1977).

Audrey Campbell

Birthdate: August 5, 1929; Cincinnati, OH
Date of passing: June 8, 2006; New York, NY
Height: 5' 7 ½"
Measurements: N/A

"I MADE A CAREER OUT OF PLAYING LESBIANS," Audrey Campbell once reflected on her other-than-mainstream moviemaking during the early 1960s, when the sordid grindhouse that had been located out on the far end of town gave way to rural Drive-In passion pits. There, what previously ranked as Forbidden Cinema was discovered by the first wave of American teenagers, all at once affluent and able to afford cars. None of Audrey's characters had the same impact on audiences (or pop culture to come) as incredible Olga. "To this day," Campbell recalled in her later years, "people recognize me on the street. I'm not quite sure what the appeal of the films is, exactly, since so many different kinds of people enjoy them." Her point is well taken, particularly when we glance back at Audrey as Olga from our post-Tarantino perspective. Now, pretty much everyone admits to seeing films with titles such as *Pulp Fiction* and *Grindhouse*, Quentin's salutes to the sordid cinema of yore. The longstanding myth: back in the good/bad old days, only people living on The Fringe level of society would venture out to the decrepit theatres where such stuff played. In fact, even then there was a large, if largely secretive, audience for films that dared to take a walk on the wild side and bring their viewers—as Audrey said, *all sorts of people*—along for the trek. The difference is that in our own time, the Underground has come up and out. A mass audience can watch such raunchy stuff at a 'respectable' mall theatre.

Incredibly, the woman who would embody Olga had originally planned to be either a singer (she once performed in a legitimate stage production of a Gilbert and Sullivan operetta) or a high-style fashion model. In Cincinnati, Audrey worked with the prestigious Playhouse in the Park theatre group

BAD GIRLS GO TO HELL: But only after getting lots of nice gifts like jewelry, the case for Audrey Campbell in all of her Olga mini-epics.

LAST DAYS OF THE GRINDHOUSE: In the early 1960s, the first of the Olga movies opened at dreary downtown theatres; at mid-decade, the final installment showed up at Drive-Ins, the new home of such sordid projects.

and, in the late 1940s, was one of TV's earliest stars via a show called *The Girl in the Window*. Hoping to break into the Met or appear on Broadway, Campbell moved to Manhattan, where schlockmeister Joe Sarno offered the young beauty a role in his exploitation flick *Lash of Lust*. There could be no turning back. Some observers believe that Campbell's finest performance is in *Sin in the Suburbs*, a bizarre combination of sharp social commentary and cheapjack softcore porn. Check out the 1964 pictorial spoof in *Playboy* featuring Peter Sellers in a variety of classic roles; you'll spot Audrey as the female beside him. In time, she gave up junk movies and rejoined the mainstream with regular roles on such soap operas as *The Guiding Light*, *Ryan's Hope*, *As the World Turns*, and the vampire soaper *Dark Shadows*.

During the early 1960s, the Olga films drew from the popular if Underground bondage pictures of Bettie Page either tying up other women or being tied up herself. As played by Audrey, Olga works for a crime syndicate, as the overseer of gangland's prostitution ring, also dealing drugs on the side. A sadist who despises heterosexual lovelies, Olga keeps her girls chained, down in a basement. There, ancient devices for torture are employed on any pretty-pretty who makes the mistake of displeasing their Boss. Campbell was a pioneer of sorts; without her, there could never have been Dyanne Thorne as *Ilsa, She Wolf of the S.S.*, or the other wicked wardens in women's prisons as played by cruel, coldhearted "bi-sexual bitches" like Barbara Steele and Sybil Danning. The Olga films, unlike their later progeny, were locked into a retro-1950s frame of mind, designed as "documentaries," sharing the horror with ordinary citizens in the guise of a cautionary fable and "educational" film experience. Doubtless, such movies inspired Russ Meyer to abandon his nature-girl nudies, moving on to *Faster, Pussycat! Kill! Kill!* As to Audrey, her last theatrical appearance was in a family film, Carl Reiner's *The One and Only*, featuring Henry Winkler as a Gorgeous George-type wrestler.

SELECTED FILMOGRAPHY:

The Woman at Bernardo's (Patron, 1961); *K.I.L. 1* (Attractive Lady, 1962); *Lash of Lust* (Poetrix, 1962); *She Should Have Stayed in Bed* (Woman, 1963); *1,000 Shapes of a Female* (Margot, 1963); *Olga's House of Shame* (Olga, 1964); *Sin in the Suburbs* (Geraldine Lewis, 1964); *White Slaves of Chinatown* (Olga, 1964); *Olga's Girls* (Olga Saglo, 1964); One Naked Night (Barbara, 1965); *The Sexperts* (Stripper, 1965); *A Woman in Love* (Bea, 1968); *The One and Only* (Woman, 1978).

Gianna Maria Canale

Birthdate: September 12, 1927; Reggio di Calabria, Italy
Date of passing: February 13, 2009; Florence, Italy
Height: N/A
Measurements: N/A

'REGAL' IS THE TERM to best describe this woman's beauty, so it comes as no surprise that she was almost always cast as a queen, good or bad in the Peplums that all but defined her. A generation older than most of the femme fatales included here, Gianna had been active in sword-and-sandals mini-epics preceding the 1960s franchises, appearing in *Hercules*, the first such items to be imported into the U.S. for the Drive-In circuit by distributor Joseph E. Levine. One of Canale's earlier successes on the continent had her playing historical Theodora, a benign ruler, though decked out in revealing costumes. In *Hercules*, Steve Reeves and his fellow Argonauts are temporarily seduced by the Amazon queen (Gianna) and her fetching warrior-women. That middle-section of the movie, in which Gianna Maria Canale's large eyes burningly size up the hero, proves as memorable today as it did for 1950s teenage audiences way back when.

Like Sophia, Gina, and a horde of others, Canale had hoped to break into Hollywood, aka The Big Time. Most every Italian leading lady received at least one studio-movie role; hers was in *Go for Broke*, an intriguing MGM item starring Van Johnson as the Texas-born leader of Japanese-Americans who volunteer to fight the Nazis. Gianna plays one of those Italian girls who, during the German occupation, had to somehow survive, hopefully with a sense of integrity. Canale played the role well, perhaps because she had lived it in real life. Nothing much happened afterwards, so she returned to the Peplums and, in time, the emergent sex-

THE SENSUOUS SWASHBUCKLER: In a pair of Italian-lensed pirate films, Gianna Maria Canale portrayed an Anne Bonny-like lady buccaneer.

vampire films as well; a mystery lady in several international espionage films that predated the Bond cycle perhaps inspiring them. *The All Movie Guide* praised her "enigmatic" quality while playing dangerously powerful women. Her must-see Peplum is *Colossus and the Amazon Queen*, which plays less as a genre piece than a Mel Brooks-type spoof of the entire syndrome. Also recommended: Gianna's pair of Pirate Queen movies, in which she embodies the She-Wolf of the Seven Seas. She married filmmaker Riccardo Freda, the two remaining a couple until his passing in 1999. The couple made it a point to work together whenever possible so as not to suffer the vagaries of geography and time that destroy so many movieland marriages. She retired in 1964, dedicating herself to her family.

SELECTED FILMOGRAPHY:

Return of the Black Eagle (Tatiana, 1946); *The Mysterious Rider* (La Contessa, 1948); *Dead Woman's Kiss* (Nora O'Kira, 1949); *The Iron Swordsman* (Emilia, 1949); *Daughter of d'Artagnan* (Linda, 1950); *Go for Broke!* (Rosina, 1951); *Revenge of the Black Eagle* (Tatiana, 1951); *Sins of Rome* (Sabina, 1953); *The Man from Cairo* (Lorraine, 1953); *Theodora,*

THE POSTER SAYS IT ALL: In one of her most memorable films, Canale played the historical empress of Rome in all her glory, able to whip up a good time as a dominatrix but also able to surrender to the man of her dreams.

EVIL TYRANT OF THE ANCIENT WORLD: Though many actresses played such roles, few proved as memorable as Canale, seen here in *Colossus and the Amazon Queen.*

Slave Empress (Teodora, 1954); *The Sword and the Cross* (Julia, 1956); *Lust of the Vampire* (Giselle, 1957); *Hercules* (Antea, 1958); *The Warrior and the Slave Girl* (Amira, 1958); *Pirate of the Half Moon* (Infanta Caterina, 1959); *The Devil's Cavaliers* (Baroness Elaine of Faldone, 1959); *The Night They Killed Rasputin* (Czarina Alexandra, 1960); *The Queen of the Pirates* (Sandra, 1960); *Colossus and the Amazon Queen* (La Regina, 1960); *Goliath and the Vampires* (Astra, 1961); *The Centurion* (Artemide, 1961); *The Slave* (Claudia, 1962); *Clash of Steel* (Princess Fausta Borgia, 1962); *Tiger of the Seven Seas* (Consuelo, 1962); *The Adventures of Scaramouche* (Suzanne, 1963); *The Avenger of Venice* (Imperia, 1964).

Ahna Capri

Birthdate: July 6, 1944; Budapest, Hungary
Birth name: Anna Marie Nanasi
Date of passing: August 19, 2010; California
Height: N/A
Measurements: 36 (C) – 23 - 35

"BUXOM" IS THE TERM SEVERAL CRITICS have used to describe Ahna Capri, born in Europe, raised in America since her early childhood. As a glowing teen, Anna appeared on family-oriented late-1950s TV series including *The Danny Thomas Show*, *Father Knows Best*, and *Room for One More*, on which she had a recurring role. At thirteen, the drop-dead gorgeous blonde appeared in movies, including a role in United Artists' B-budget *Outlaw's Son*, billed as Anna, later altering her name, apparently at her agent's suggestion, for something more provocative. Much of Ahna's cult-fandom results from a singular (if in truth supporting) role: Tania, the glamorous secretary to (and, by implication, mistress of) villainous Han (John Saxon) in the martial arts classic *Enter the Dragon*. Most well-remembered of Bruce Lee's films and to this day the most popular on DVD and cable-TV, *Enter the Dragon* collapsed the visceral excitement of Hong Kong-lensed "chop-socky" films with conventions drawn from the Bond movies. The bad guy summons world-class competitors to his remote island, which he rules over with a statuesque blonde by his side. Lee, playing an Asian Bond in this one, not only wins the bouts but destroys Han's plans for world domination. One key difference between *Enter the Dragon* and a 007 opus is that the trope of the bad-girl betraying her 'master' for the handsome hero is not present. Ahna's Tania dies along with most other members of Han's evil army during the final battle.

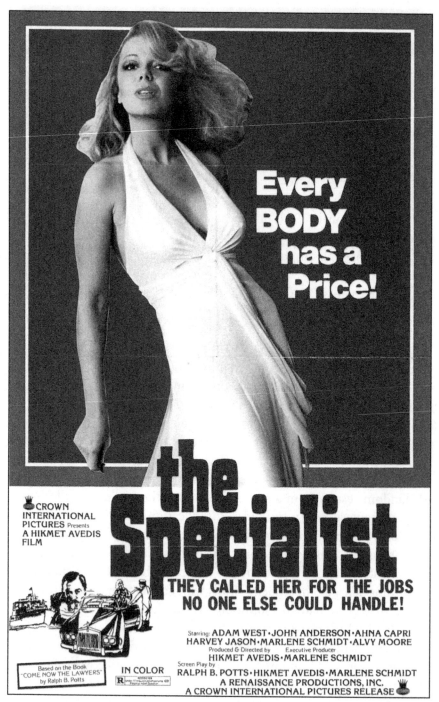

GINGER 2?: In a blatant (and not all that good) rip-off of the Cherri Caffaro films, Ahna Capri plays a secret investigator who enjoys inflicting violence almost as much as she does sex.

Ahna also died in one of her other most memorable roles, if here she did 'embrace' the hero before her hasty departure. In the all-but-forgotten *Darker than Amber*, the pilot-film for a Travis McGee movie or TV series that never emerged, she's the companion of evil muscleman William Smith but falls for hero Rod Taylor. Capri appeared Amazonian in a barely-there bathing suit. Sadly, the film was little-seen. Still, there was plenty of episodic TV, including the cult UFO series *The Invaders* and, earlier, such spy-cinema small-screen efforts as *The Wild, Wild West*, *I Spy*, and *The Man from U.N.C.L.E.* A few horror items—*The Brotherhood of Satan* and *Piranha, Piranha*—did assure lasting if minor-league cultdom. The offbeat indie item *Payday*, a serious drama in which Ahna was cast opposite the esteemed Rip Torn, revealed her acting chops. She did win one lead role in the low-budget actioner *The Specialist*. Ahna played an early example of the many hit-women who would soon grace the silver screen, seducing and then murdering her prey. Adam West, TV's *Batman*, was the male lead.

Capri left film and TV even as the 1980s dawned. She never married, spending most of her time from then on with her sister/best-friend Rose. At age 66, on August 9, 2010, while driving from her San Fernando Valley

"ARE YOU SURE YOU AREN'T BRUCE WAYNE?": Ahana Capri co-starred with Adam West in her only lead role, *The Specialist*.

home to North Hollywood, Ahna's car smashed into a 5-ton truck. After 11 days on life-support during which she remained in a coma, Capri quietly passed away.

SELECTED FILMOGRAPHY:

Outlaw's Son (Amy, 1957); *The Girls on the Beach* (Arlene, 1965); *One of Our Spies Is Missing* (Do Do, 1966); *Darker Than Amber* (Del, 1970); *Company of Killers* (Maryjane, 1971); *Brotherhood of Satan* (Nicky, 1971); *Piranha, Piranha!* (Terry, 1972); *Payday* (Mayleen Travis, 1973); *Enter the Dragon* (Tania, 1973); *The Specialist* (Londa Wyeth, 1975).

Marie-Pierre Castel

aka: MARIE-PIERRE, aka PONY TRICOT
Birthdate: February 5, 1946 (alternative date 1950); Villejuif,
   Val-de-Marne, France
Height: N/A
Measurements: N/A

SEVERAL ACTRESSES CONTAINED in this volume appeared in movies by Jesse (Jesus) Franco (1930-2013), whose erotic vampire thrillers
were so graphic that for decades they remained unseen by mainstream
viewers. Difficult as it may be to believe, there was at the same time (mid-
1970s) a director whose work contained so many controversial images of
violence and sexuality in tandem with one another that his films made
Franco's appear conventional in comparison. Jean (Michel) Rollin (Roth
Le Gentil) (1938-2010) created in France a succession of works that, not
unlike Franco's in Spain, broke all previous existing barriers between what
was considered pornography and what might be thought of as art. Many
fundamentals present appear to be exploitive in their graphicness. Always,
though, such elements are balanced with a serious, even intellectual desire
to penetrate beyond the surface of such threatening material. For many,
this—as well as his unique 'signature' style—qualify Rollin as an artist, his
cinematic renderings of bondage and torture recalling the literary oeuvre
of the Marquis de Sade. Whereas a handful of beauties vie for the position
of Franco's greatest onscreen inamorata, in Rollin's case, one girl comes
immediately to mind: the eerily enchanting Marie-Pierre Castel.

   For most of Castel's adoring fans, *Requiem for a Vampire* stands
as Marie-Pierre's (and Rollin's as well) piece-de-resistance. Two pretty
teenage girls (who may in fact be violent madwomen) slip into an aban-

TWO ORPHAN VAMPIRES: Castel (left) and a companion find themselves menaced in a spooky castle – even as they previously menaced older men.

doned castle to hide out. There they discover that they are surrounded by monsters. The film's considerable impact is based on our awareness that, pretty as these two Lolitas may be and how ugly their enemies are, the child-like beauties are in truth more evil than those attacking them. Yet we root for them to win, and for one reason only: they are beautiful females. This fascination with the philosophic nature of beauty, coupled with an appearance and reality theme, underlines all Rollin's work, but seems specifically strong in his films with Castel. In fact, her part here was originally intended for Marie-Pierre's twin sister, Catherine. A series of personal issues that developed between Catherine and Rollin shut down their working relationship, at least for the time being. This offered Marie-Pierre the opportunity to step in and assume center stage, first in *Shiver of the Vampires*, shortly followed by *Requiem*.

Unlike Franco, who draws on both the British Hammer horror tradition and the Italian Giallo thriller to create an onscreen sensibility marked by vivid, sometimes florid color, Rollin prefers a pastel-inspired lyricism that recalls the sweet visual sensibility of the French impression-ists. He then ironically sets his bloodthirsty succubus tales against such an initially alluring backdrop. Other infamous Rollin-Castel collaborations include *The Nude Vampire* and *Lips of Blood*, both starring Marie-Pierre and her sister Catherine. Their joint appearance played into a Hitchcock homage that honored the two Kim Novak characters in *Vertigo*, though here there actually were two strikingly similar girls onscreen. Initially, these films were mostly shown at private screenings, ranging from adult

SELL IT WITH SEX!: Jean Rollin's vampire cinema went to such extremes that he actually made Jess Franco seem almost mainstream by comparison.

porn clubs to campus film societies. This explains why they remained un-known at the time even to fans of Jess Franco, whose movies did make it into theatres, if not necessarily the most respectable ones. The current term para-cinema developed from the 1970s situation in which such threatening films were seen by small pockets of highbrows and lowbrows, totally bypassing the mass audience and creating a bizarre parallel be-tween those who sought out daring art and others who were interested only in the cheap thrill of graphic sex and violence.

In time, Rollin entered the hardcore market in order to try and sat-isfy a public that had become jaded after seeing so many of the R-rated sex films that had flooded the market during the early 1970s, when pretty much all the old restrictions were suddenly gone. Even VHS's move into the mainstream failed to bring most Rollin-Castel collaborations to a wider, broader public, this occurring only with the advent of DVD. Fi-nally, apparently lost films are now readily available. Torn as to whether or not she should appear in X-rated work, Castel initially appeared to acquiesce, though shortly after starring in several, she abandoned her still lucrative career in 1977. Ever since, she has attempted to maintain as low a profile as possible.

SELECTED FILMOGRAPHY:

The Nude Vampire (Blonde Servant, 1970) *Requiem for a Vampire* (Marie, 1971); *The Shiver of the Vampires* (Pretty Maid, 1971); *Erotic Diary* (Pony, 1974); *Fly Me the French Way* (A Blonde, 1974); *Once Upon a Virgin* (Pretty Blonde, 1975); *Lips of Blood* (Young Vampire, 1975); *Depravities* (Girl, 1975); *My Vampire* (Jurmelle, 1976).

Marilyn Chambers

Birthdate: April 22, 1952; Providence, Rhode Island
Birth name: Marilyn Ann Briggs
Date of passing: April 12, 2009; Santa Clarita, California
Height: 5' 7"
Measurements: 35C – 23 - 35

"I'M GOING TO BE THE FIRST PORN STAR to cross over and be accepted as a mainstream actress." How many times have you heard *that* since the creation of the X-rated film industry in the late 1960s? No question, though, that Marilyn Chambers was the first blonde beauty to make such a statement. Her initial film work was in big, reputable Hollywood productions (though her parts were small) including *The Owl and the Pussycat* starring Barbara Streisand and George Segal. She played the silent girlfriend of Robert Klein. Marilyn less resembled a typical porn star on the order of Linda Lovelace than she looked like Farrah Fawcett, Cheryl Ladd, and Heather Locklear, those zippy blondes who achieved TV stardom during the early 1970s. She spotted an ad for a casting call and showed up at the office of Chuck Traynor, searching for a wholesome girl of the Tuesday Weld/Sandra type to play the lead in *Behind the Green Door*, an upcoming hardcore item. This was at a time when hardcore was filmed rather than videotaped, allowing for a certain patina of style. Mood-drenched, *Behind the Green Door* relates the story of an abducted socialite, forced to perform sex acts for a paying audience. The neat trick is that, as Chambers' character passes through all sorts of humiliations, the look on her face and ripples of her body language suggest she may be learning to love such sado-masochistic treatment. If virtually everyone believed at that time that *Deep Throat* had provided the ultimate in porno chic, here was the film that rebooted hardcore: Feminists mostly damned

THE GOLDEN GIRL OF PORN: Though Linda Lovelace preceded her as the first superstar of contemporary hardcore, Marilyn Chambers was the most beautiful such girl of the 1970s.

the movie as an extreme example of what would come to be called The Male Gaze, allowing/inciting men to watch a woman's humiliation. As Second/Third Wave feminist thinking gave way to post-feminism, members of the next generation of American women perceived the film differently, as an everday woman overcame her conventional inhibitions and found liberation of an unconventional order.

All of this caused a great amount of consternation over at Ivory Soap headquarters. They'd recently put model Marilyn on their box covers, embodying a demure young upper-middle-class mom holding an adorable child. To continue the ad campaign and sell lots and lots of soap or abandon it in the name of good taste and see sales plummet? Decisions, decisions! Marilyn dreamed of becoming the new Monroe. It almost happened, thanks to two notably different femme fatale roles. First came *Ra-*

"I USED TO BE (IVORY) SNOW WHITE, BUT I DRIFTED": A post-porn Marilyn mockingly holds the soap box that earlier had introduced this model to the public at large.

bid, directed by Canadian David Cronenberg, even then redefining horror. The first contemporary vampire film, *Rabid* featured Marilyn as a female biker who, after a near-fatal accident, undergoes surgery that transforms her into a blood-craving creature. Old gothic clichés were nowhere to be seen as this film offered a scientifically realistic approach to the genre. Also, Marilyn won the lead in *Angel from H.E.A.T.*, a mild spoof of the spy films from the previous decade, only with a female lead—as in the Cherri Caffaro *Ginger* films, albeit more mainstream. Still, these were B-movies. Marilyn would navigate back and forth between direct-to-video softcore exploitation flicks and hardcore items that paid considerably more. One, *Insatiable*, is often considered a classic of its kind. There was much talk about mainstream roles, including the possibility that legendary director Nicholas Ray (*Rebel Without a Cause*, *Johnny Guitar*, etc.) would helm the project, but funding fell through. Marilyn began to make personal

FROM HARDCORE TO HORROR: Canadian-born director David Cronenberg gave Marilyn Chambers a shot at mainstream stardom in his contemporary vampire thriller *Rabid*.

appearances based on her notoriety, drank too much, and passed away at an early age. She married three times, to Doug Chapin (1971-1974), her porn mentor Chuck Traynor (1974-1985), and William Taylor, Jr. (1991-1994).

SELECTED FILMOGRAPHY:

The Owl and the Pussycat (Blonde in Bed, 1970); *Together* (Pretty Blonde, 1971); *Behind the Green Door* (Gloria, 1972); *(The) Resurrection of Eve* (Eve, 1973); *Rabid* (Rose, 1977); *Insatiable* (Sandra Chase, 1980) *Up 'n' Coming* (Cassie Harland, 1983); *Angel of H.E.A.T.* (Angel Harmony, 1983); *Insatiable II* (Sandra Chase, 1984); *My Therapist* (Kelly, 1984); *The Marilyn Diaries* (Marilyn, 1990); *Breakfast in Bed* (Marilyn, 1990); *New York Nights* (Barbara Lowery, 1994); *Sextrospective* (Marilyn, 1999).

MOVE OVER, SANDRA DEE: Co-starring with Annette Funicello, Patty Chandler
initially seemed the most clean-cut blonde on the California beaches.

Patti Chandler

Born: December 8, 1943; Culver City, CA
Birth Name: Patricia Ann Lauderback
Height: N/A
Measurements: 36 – 22 - 35

TAKE YOUR PICK! Two stories have long circulated as to how Patty Chandler landed her first role in a *Beach Party* film. One has it that she participated in a radio contest on KRLA and, at age 21, won the small role of a twisting bikini-clad beauty. The other: Patti had moved to Hawaii, where she worked as Water Sports Counselor on Waikiki Beach. A photographer, marveling at her clean-cut sensuality, inquired as to whether she'd like to become a model. However it happened (perhaps some combination of the two?), Patti soon found herself at American International Pictures, where she swiftly moved up the ladder from one more nameless beach bunny to a top-liner of those giddy, campy items, even allowed to use her own name in a continuing role. *Look* magazine featured a spectacular layout which, to everyone's surprise, allowed Patti far more coverage (though she was mostly uncovered) than supposed queen of the beach, Annette Funicello. *Look* followed this up with a cover featuring Patty. The banner "Success Overtakes Patti Chandler" implied that she was on the verge of a big breakthrough.

Nothing of the sort occurred. Sheer Magic cosmetics did employ Patti for several print advertisements. Patti then negotiated a turn from wide-eyed innocent to femme fatale. She appeared with Vincent Price in each of the *Dr. Goldfoot* comedies (his character's name a rip-off of 007's Goldfinger). Price's mad doctor (played in Grand Guignol fashion) creates an army of bikini-clad female robot bombs. Sweetly smiling girls approach

WHEN GOOD GIRLS GO BAD: In *The Million Eyes of Su-Maru*, Patti Chandler employs those lovely legs to slowly suffocate a helpless male captive while fellow Slaygirls watch.

unwitting men who can't resist their charms though, upon a first kiss, both members of the temporary couple explode. But the best (or worst) was yet to come. Along with Beach buddy Frankie Avalon, Patti headed for Hong Kong to film *The Million Eyes of Su-Maru*. This time around, it's a beautiful evil female mad-genius (Shirley Eaton) who hopes to take over the world. No girl in Su-Maru's entourage is more lethal than Patti. In an early sequence, she wraps her long legs around a bound and gagged man, applying pressure to his corpulent neck with her knees, grinning with pleasure even as he cringes in fear of what's to come. Patti glances at the Slaygirls seated around her, Patti's eyes brightening with cruel pleasure as, one after another, each, including Eaton, turns a thumbs down. At last, Patti's eyes widen and we hear the sound of a sudden crack.

Later in the film, she drowns a fellow bikini-clad bad-girl suspected of being a traitor. This sequence played as so much giddy fun, as if we were watching a girlish seaside romp rather than a murder. Interviewed by *Photoplay* magazine as to whether this former good-girl had any problems playing a murderess who, at the finale, not only gets away with all her crimes but ends up in the arms of the hero (George Nader), Patty laughed, insisting this had been the opportunity of a lifetime: "I usually run around in bikinis... in *Su-Maru* for the first time in my life I play— a *killer!*" No one dared ask whether this meant that within Patti Chandler, and perhaps every good girl, there's a naughty one just clawing to get out. That was it for movies. On TV, she enacted an Indian maiden in a 1967 episode of *The Big Valley* opposite Lee Majors, with whom Patti became involved. Show Biz 'player' Burt Sugerman and serious actor Albert Finney also occupied her time. Other than brief appearances in made-for-TV movies like *The Feminist and the Fuzz* (1971) and several bits on the popular ABC comedy *Love, American Style*, the *Look* prediction failed to crystalize. As Tom Lisanti noted in *Drive-In Dream Girls*, Patti "dried herself off... after marrying a very successful businessman" and set out to live the good life.

SELECTED FILMOGRAPHY:
Bikini Beach (Beach Girl, 1964); *Pajama Party* (Pajama Girl, 1964); *Beach Blanket Bingo* (Patti, 1965); *Ski Party* (Janet, 1965); *How to Stuff a Wild Bikini* (Patti, 1965); *Sergeant Dead Head* (Patti, 1965); *Dr. Goldfoot and the Bikini Machine* (Robot Blonde, 1965); *The Ghost in the Invisible Bikini* (Patti, 1966); *Fireball 500* (Race-Track Fan, 1966); *The Million Eyes of Su-Muru* (Louise, 1967).

THERE'S SOMETHING ABOUT A FRENCHWOMAN: Corinne Clery as 'O' undergoes
bondage, torture, and humiliation in the process of becoming a worthy mistress.

Corinne Clery

Birthdate: March 23, 1950; Paris, France
Birth name: Corinna Piccolo
Height: 5' 7"
Measurements: N/A

WHERE DOES ART LEAVE OFF and eroticism begin, or is it impossible to answer that question about a film that makes some serious attempt to understand human sexuality? That issue was raised in 1954 by *Story of O*, a supposedly fact-based novel by Pauline Réage, nom-de-plume for Gallic author Anne Desclos. The Underground classic dealt with an unnamed Asian woman who, on her lover's request, agrees to journey to an island chateau in order to attend a course on sexual submission. She is humiliated by her masters/mentors in extreme sado-masochistic games; O is stripped, blindfolded, chained to a wall, and whipped, then forced to endure any sexual acts, however perverse, imposed on her. There is a final twist: O uses her supposed status as a powerless person to seize control and burn a little O on Sir Stephen's hand with her cigarette. That this book might have been filmed back then appeared impossible, even in France. In America, *The Story of O* (only the notorious Grove Press would agree to publish it) did not sell at mainstream bookstores, only at offbeat, edgy places frequented by Beats in Greenwich Village, New York, and Haight-Ashbury, California. Then came the sexual/cultural revolutions of the 1960s. Early in the next decade, director Just Jaeckin mounted a sumptuous film from a German-French co-production team.

In the U.S., *The Story of O* initially opened at arthouses, mostly in college towns, then 'went wide' as the mainstream, subscribing to a New Normal, turned this into a cult sensation. Indeed, in the age of such hardcore porn as the then-current *Deep Throat*, the once radical tale hardly

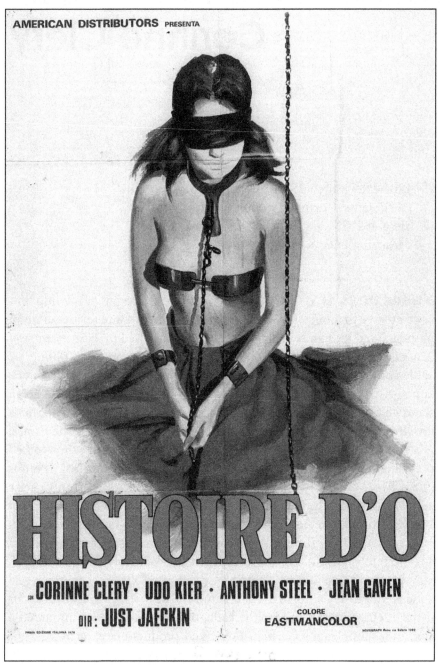

SEX SELLS: All advertising for *The Story of O*, released during the height of mid-1970s porno-chic, primarily emphasized the film's bondage theme.

raised eyebrows. Despite Jaeckin's off-putting aura of pretentiousness (here and in all his other films), viewers were fascinated by the gorgeous actress playing O, changed for the film to a Gallic girl. Her onscreen surrender to a frightful combination of pain and pleasure caused ticket-buyers to be convinced the filmmakers had found an embodiment of just such a woman. But five years later, while granting press interviews for

"TIE ME UP! TIE ME DOWN!": Like 'O' herself, actress Clery submits fully.

her appearance in a bad-girl role in the James Bond film *Moonraker*, the mere mention of *O* caused Clery, a shy, quiet woman, to visibly shudder. "For me," she coldly stated, "every morning, when I woke up, the question was: Do I kill myself today or do I go to the set?" The project's very concept had put her off; the notion of any woman, particularly herself, going through such an imprisonment a horrific thing to imagine. Simply, she had been young and few roles were being offered to her at the time; this just might be a star-making part. Her part in the 007 project, while casting her as a femme fatale, at least allowed her to play a sexy woman in a PG movie. That was true too of her Peplum, *Yor, the Hunter from the Future*, in which she donned the requisite fur bikini. Years later, Corinne was still perceived (and typecast) as a sexy siren: in a lavish TV version of *The Odyssey* (1991), she played the enchantress Circe. She did marry, then divorce Luca Valerio and Hubert Wayaffe but precise details have never been made public. She married Giuseppe Ercole in 2004 and maintained a relationship with him until his death in 2010.

SELECTED FILMOGRAPHY:

Les Poneyttes (Corinne, 1967); *The Story of O* ('O,' 1975); *Holiday Hookers* (Senine, 1976); *High Rollers* (Charlotte, 1976); *Stormtroopers* (La Donna, 1976); *Striptease* (Anne, 1976); *Plot of Fear* (Jeanne, 1976); *Three Tigers* (La Balia, 1977); *Hitch Hike* (Eve, 1977); *Covert Action* (Anne Florio, 1978); *The Humanoid* (Barbara, 1979); *Moonraker* (Corinne Dufour, 1979); *The Tunnel* (Pina, 1980); *I Hate Blondes* (Angelica, 1980); *The Last Harem* (Sara, 1981); *Yor, Hunter from the Future* (Ka-Laa, 1983); *The Gamble* (Jacqueline, 1988); *The King of Paris* (Betty, 1995); *God Willing* (Valeria, 1995).

Joan Collins

Birthdate: May 23, 1933; Paddington, London
Birth name: Joan Henrietta Collins
Height: 5' 5 1/2"
Measurements: 36 (D) – 24 - 34 ½

THE LEGENDARY WOMAN who would create some of the most no-table femme fatales the big and small screens have ever known originally prepared to be a classically trained actress. Joan dreamed of winning roles in stage productions following her studies at London's Royal Academy of Dramatic Arts. Even as her equally gorgeous younger sister Jackie Collins decided on a literary route, Joan won parts in movies. Britain's reigning Rank organization wanted to sign Joan but Hollywood won her away. Collins played in big films of the 1950s, mostly for 20th Century Fox. For Warner Bros. she did headline a big-budget Peplum, *Land of the Pharoahs*, a Howard Hawks film. Collins commanded the screen as a scheming femme fatale who destroys the life of a well-meaning pharaoh (Jack Hawkins), only to find herself undone when, during his burial, she is locked away with him in the pyramid for eternity. Her absolute ferocity convinced Fox execs that this was the right woman to play Cleopatra in a new retelling of that old tale. Disastrously, they instead signed Elizabeth Taylor. The legendary Liz and Dick antics on the set caused that film to go horrendously over budget. Always ultra-professional Joan would have caused no such problems.

During the 1960s, her greatest successes were on TV. "The City on the Edge of Forever," the second to last episode of *Star Trek*'s first season (# 28), written by Harlan Ellison, is rightly considered among that series' greatest triumphs. Collins played a sympathetic character: Edith Keeler,

PEPLUM, HOLLYWOOD STYLE: In 1955, Joan Collins played an evil sand-and-sandals temptress in *Land of the Pharoahs*, directed by Howard Hawks for Warner Bros.

who cares for the poor during the Depression while preaching pacifism, attracting time-traveler James Tiberius Kirk (William Shatner). Then it was back to her wicked ways, as lovely but deadly guest villainess The Siren in two episodes of *Batman*'s third season.

Joan's most visible film project was the disastrous *Can Hieronymous Merkin...*, written, directed by, and starring her then-husband Anthony

Newley, of "Stop the World, I Want to Get Off!" fame. The movie vilified his wife as a middle-aged monster attempting to keep him out of the arms of a beautiful blonde *Playboy* model, Connie Kreskie. Collins quietly completed the project, then divorced Newley.

The 1970s featured a comeback, if in B-movie monster junk, which at one point had her fending off army ants with preacher-turned-actor Mar-

"TAKE IT OFF! TAKE IT ALL OFF!" Collins demonstrates the art of striptease in the little-seen but engaging caper film, *Seven Thieves*.

joe Gortner. Best among this era's roles was Black Belle, a British highway-woman, in the R-rated (nudity, but no hardcore sex) version of *Tom Jones*. Accepting that villainy was now her stock in trade, Joan appeared in two contemporary films, *The Bitch* and *The Stud*, both written by her sister. *Dynasty* in 1981 created the great comeback. As Alexis, the bitch to end all bitches, Joan engaged in world-class cat fights with the blonde goodie-two-shoes Krystal (Linda Evans). Collins pulled in a hefty $120,000 an

THE BITCH: Even before *Dynasty*, Collins embraced the bad girl mystique in a film written specifically for her by sister Jackie Collins.

episode early-on, with so many raises once the show was a huge hit that the producers ceased using her in every episode out of financial necessity.

Her five marriages include Maxwell Reed (1952-1957), Newley (1963-1971), Ronald Kass (1972-1984), Peter Holm (1985-1987), and Percy Gibson, 32 years her junior (2002-present). Other men in Joan's life included Warren Beatty (to whom she was briefly engaged), Dennis Hopper, and Ryan O'Neal; she claims to have turned down 'offers' from Frank Sinatra, Dean Martin, and Robert Kennedy because they were married. In 1991, Joan finally had the opportunity to live out a long-held dream by starring in a 'serious' play (Noel Coward's *Private Lives*) on Broadway. She continues always to upapologetically indulge in The Sweet Life.

SELECTED FILMOGRAPHY:
Bikini Baby (Beauty Queen Contestant, 1951); *I Believe in You* (Norma Hart, 1952); *Decameron Nights* (Pampinea/Maria, 1953); *The Slasher* (Rene Collins, 1953); *The Good Die Young* (Mary Halsey, 1954); *Land of the Pharoahs* (Princess Nellifer, 1955); *The Virgin Queen* (Beth, 1955); *The Girl in the Red Velvet Swing* (Evelyn Nesbit Thaw, 1955); *The Opposite Sex* (Crystal, 1956); *Sea Wife* (The Nun, 1957); *The Wayward Bus* (Alice, 1957); *Island in the Sun* (Jocelyn, 1957); *The Bravados* (Josefa, 1958); *Rally 'Round the Flag, Boys!* (Angela, 1958); *Seven Thieves* (Melanie, 1960); *Esther and the King* (Esther, 1960); *The Road to Hong Kong* (Diane, 1962); *Can Hieronymus Merkin Ever Forget Mercy Humppe and Find True Happiness?* (Polyester Poontang, 1969); *The Executioner* (Sarah Booth, 1970); *Up in the Cellar* (Pat, 1970); *Tales That Witness Madness* (Bella, 1973); *The Bawdy Adventures of Tom Jones* (Black Bess, 1976); *Empire of the Ants* (Marilyn Fryser, 1977); *The Stud* (Fontaine, 1978); *The Bitch* (Fontaine, 1979); *Homework* (Diane, 1982); *Decadence* (Helen/Sybil, 1994); *The Flinstones in Viva Rock Vegas* (Pearl Slaghoople, 2000).

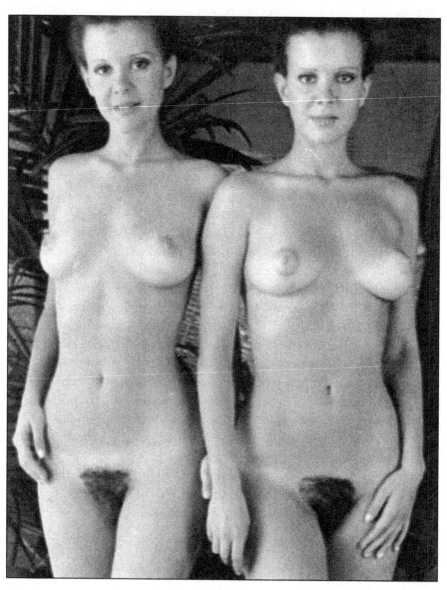

TWIN PLAYMATES AS VIRGIN VAMPIRES: The first identical siblings (that's Mary on the right) enjoyed brief-lived stardom for England's Hammer studio.

Mary Collinson

Birthdate: July 22, 1953; Isle of Malta
Height: 5' 6"
Measurements: 36 – 25 - 36

BEFORE THE BARBI TWINS there were the Collinson sisters, and while their fame did not make quite so enormous an impact or last nearly so long, these British-born twins enjoyed a kind of Warholian fifteen minutes of fame. Mary and Madeleine began appearing together in films while still teenagers and held the distinction of being *Playboy*'s first twin Playmates of the Month in October, 1970. Shortly after Mary and Madeleine arrived in England (at age sixteen each), they were spotted by photographer Harrison Marks who sensed something very special in their child-like beauty that hinted at a secret sensuality deep down below the demure surface. Publication of a photo of the two girls in the then popular *Continental Film Review* brought the Nymphettes, who looked to be underage but were old enough to legally model in the nude, further attention, both from Hugh Hefner in America and the Carreras family at London's Hammer productions. Their female vampire films, which had begun with *Vampire Lovers*, continued to prove financially successful. For the third and final such Le Fanu adaptation, the brass at England's house of horror decided to go the Lolita route, with twin girls, one good and one bad. (The original title was to have been 'Virgin Vampires'). In this prequel to the two previous lesbian vampire projects (that element toned down considerably here), Mary and Madeleine played Maria and Freida Gellhorn, a pair of naifs who arrive in an isolated village where Freida plays by the rules that her strict Puritanical uncle (Peter Cushing) sets in place.

DARK CHILD OF THE FULL MOON: While her sister remains pure, Mary sets out
to seduce and destroy men and women in her wake.

Mary's character, however, surrenders to the dark side, heading up
to that forbidden castle up on the hill for erotic and bloody adventures
with a handsome aristocrat. Shortly, she is deeply involved in his deadly
games, the problem for the villagers being that they can't tell which twin
is the good one, making it difficult to decide who should be burned at
the stake. The film is particularly interesting in its combination of both
vampiric and Wiccan traditions, suggesting that they are two sides of the
same evil coin. The film opened in America at the same time that their

Playboy appearance caused a huge if brief flurry of fascination. The girls granted many interviews and even appeared on *The Tonight Show* with Johnny Carson, who seemed taken with their giddy little girl behavior. Surprisingly, there were few if any follow-up offers for film or photographic model work, and the twins soon disappeared from sight. Today, Mary lives in Milan with a fellow identified only (by sister Madeleine) as "that Italian gentleman," with whom Mary has shared her life for well over twenty years. The couple have two daughters.

SELECTED FILMOGRAPHY:
Some Like It Sexy (Twin in White Dress, 1969); *Permissive* (Groupie, 1970); *I Am a Groupie* (Twin Groupie, 1970); *Passion Potion* (Janet, 1971); *The Love Machine* (Debbie, 1971); *Twins of Evil* (Maria Gellhorn, 1971).

GIRLS WILL BE GIRLS: Like all of Hammer's female vampire films, *Twins of Evil* emphasized the lesbian element of death's kiss.

DANGEROUS: If Yvonne Craig began her screen career as a beach bunny in *Gidget*, she soon moved on the roles that insisted this girl carry a gun.

Yvonne Craig

Birthdate: May 16, 1937; Taylorville, IL
Date of passing: August 17, 2015
Height: 5' 4"
Measurements: 37 (C) – 23 - 36

"**WHOM THE GODS WISH TO DESTROY**," Euripides wrote several thousand years ago, "they first make mad." TV writer Lee Ermey drew from that classic quote for a striking *Star Trek* episode (1/3/1969; Season 3, Episode 14), while borrowing from the Edgar Allen Poe short story "The Strange System of Dr. Tarr and Prof. Fether"; also, one of the first great horror-thriller films, *The Cabinet of Dr. Caligari* (1919-1920). Kirk and Spock, visiting an outer-space asylum for the criminally insane, wonder if the man in charge, Garth (Steve Ihnat), may be crazier than any of the inmates. The heroes become involved with Marta, one of those green dream-girls (an Orion female) who always spell some sort of trouble for our space cowboys. Yvonne (Joyce) Craig played the role, employing her considerable gifts as a dancer as well as an actress to create a series of jarring movements for Marta that keep *Enterprise* officers (and the home-viewing audience) guessing as to whether she's quite normal or absolutely mad.

From her earliest TV and film roles, the darkly beautiful Craig, raised in Dallas TX, almost always played something of a femme fatale. Yvonne had set out to become a professional dancer, discovered by George Ballanchine, training at Denham's Ballet Russe de Monte Carlo. Choosing to leave that company, she in 1959 played the female lead opposite Pat Wayne (in his first starring vehicle) as a lovely but impetuous Spanish beauty in *The Young Land* and a small role in *The Gene Krupa Story* with Sal Mineo. Acting more like a 1950s juvenile delinquent than a period-

FANTASY ON THE TUBE: When theatrical movies failed to provide her with suitable roles, Craig went the TV route as Batgirl on *Batman* and as one of the most memorable of all Green Girls on *Star Trek*.

piece girl from Krupa's era, Yvonne seizes the key to Gene's room and stuffs it into her bathing suit. To retrieve it, the aspiring drummer grabs the girl by her legs, turns her upside down, shaking her until the key falls out. During the process, the remarkable size and shape of Craig's breasts are as fully revealed as could be without any actual nudity.

Yvonne dated Elvis and appeared with him in two films. She became a spy-girl figure in the mid-1960s, appearing on *The Man from U.N.C.L.E.* and, in a cameo opposite James Coburn, in *Our Man Flint*. The latter part she won over other hopefuls because the film demanded a beautiful girl with dancing experience. TV audiences loved her as Barbara Gordon, aka Batgirl, in the third season of the Adam West ABC series. Though Craig played a good girl, viewers noticed how much pleasure the character (and the actress?) took in beating and kicking the villains. Craig was married to teen actor Jimmy Boyd (who had a hit record with "I Saw Mommy Kissing Santa Claus") for two years (1960-1962) and later to Kenneth Aldrich. Eventually Craig left Show Biz for the more dependable real estate industry and became a devoted world traveler. Her autobiography was appropriately titled "From Ballet to the Batcave and Beyond."

Trivia: Her espionage film *One Spy Too Many* was actually a compilation of two episodes from *The Man from U.N.C.L.E.* series. Fans are

AN ENCHANTRESS IN REPOSE: Yvonne Craig models the latest in bikini bathing suits.

encouraged to seek out her erotic dance sequence in *The Wild Wild West* episode "The Night of the Grand Emir," in which her villainess employs Salome-like skills to entice men she intends to murder. Yvonne may have been the first American girl ever to wear a bikini-style bathing suit in a Hollywood teen-oriented film as one of Sandra Dee's best friends in *Gidget*.

SELECTED FILMOGRAPHY:

Eighteen and Anxious (Gloria, 1957); *The Young Land* (Elena de la Madrid, 1959); *The Gene Krupa Story* (Gloria Corregio, 1959); *Gidget* (Nan, 1959); *High Time* (Randy 'Scoop' Pruitt, 1960); *Seven Women from Hell* (Janet Cook, 1961); *By Love Possessed* (Veronica, 1961); *It Happened at the World's Fair* (Dorothy, 1963); *Quick Before it Melts* (Sharon Sweigert, 1964); *Kissin' Cousins* (Azalea Tatum, 1964); *Advance to the Rear* (Ora, 1964); *Ski Party* (Barbara, 1965); *One Spy Too Many* (Maude Waverly, 1966); *One of Our Spies Is Missing* (Wanda, 1966); *Mars Needs Women* (Dr. Marjorie Bolen, 1967); *In Like Flint* (Natasha, 1967).

IF WOMEN HAD BALLS: During the second phase of her career, Sybil Danning established herself as the first significant action babe of junk cinema.

Sybil Danning

Birthdate: May 24, 1952; Wels, Upper Austria
Birth Name: Sybille Johanna Danninger
Height: 5' 7"
Measurements: 37 – 23 - 36

A YOUNG SPACE CADET (Richard Thomas), bearing more than a passing resemblance to Mark Hamill as Luke Skywalker, sets about recruiting a Magnificent Seven-like team to take down a ruthless galactic dictator (John Saxon). While gathering male warriors, he's approached by a futuristic Valkyrie (Sybil Danning) eager to join up. A typical male chauvinist, he scoffs at the thought that a girl could fight alongside Space Cowboy (George Peppard). But when the fighting commences, Saint Exmin fully lives out her philosophy of live fast, fight hard, die young. Without her, and the swift sword she wields, the mission could never succeed. The screen has witnessed its first contemporary macho woman. Lara Croft, Black Widow, and others would follow. The woman who would become known as the first great female action star of B-movies had played just such a role early on while still living and working in Europe. At the tender age of nineteen, Sybil embodied that remarkable figure of German myth, Kriemhild. An army brat (her adoptive father was an American major, her mother Austrian), she grew up on varied U.S. bases. When dad was transferred to California, Danning found herself within reaching distance of Hollywood. Yet stardom did not occur until she made the return journey home, eventually abandoning plans to become an oral surgeon or a beauty expert, realizing she was far more gorgeous than many of those models for whom she provided make-up. Seriously tackling the movie industry, Sybil originally seemed likely to become one more of the stunning

AT LONG LAST STARDOM: When Sybil co-starred in *Battle Beyond the Stars*, she was perceived as a minor figure in the drama; by the time that publicity was released for both the film and its soundtrack, she was photographed alone in her Valkyrie costume or placed front and center among the group.

dream girls who decorated the 1960s. At the time, Danning's career did not click. During the mid-1970s, her tough-girl image matched the audience's newfound interests. Sybil won roles in several high-profile films, including *Bluebeard* and *The Three Musketeers*. Everything changed when she won the Amazonian role in Roger Corman's spaced-out adventure, designed to cash in on the success of George Lucas's 1977 *Star Wars*.

With a larger budget than most quickies, also memorable F/X thanks to a then-young James Cameron, *Battle* amasssed a cult-following. Much of the film's appeal derived from the iconic image of Sybil in her epic-fantasy costume. Simply, she was the pioneer who set the way for *Xena, Warrior Princess* on television, a role Danning might well have played! Briefly, Albert Broccoli considered her for the lead in *Octopussy*. Unfortunately, the franchise's avatar chose a less charismatic woman and the film failed. Sybil's best Giallo was *The Woman in Red Kills Seven Times*. Her evil queen in the Lou Ferrigno version of *Hercules* (recalled for its unconvincing CG effects) bolstered an otherwise ordinary Peplum. Sybil then inherited the werewolf woman role from Elisabeth Brooks for *The Howling II*. No wonder that when John Landis wanted someone for the sort of role that Laurie Mitchell incarnated in 1958's *Queen of Outer Space,* he picked Danning for the lead celestial dream girl in *Amazon Women in the Moon*. Decades later, Sybil was Quentin Tarantino's first (some say only) choice for a caricature of Ilsa, She Wolf of the S.S. in *Grindhouse: "Werewolf Women of the S.S."*

Things did not always go easily. A pair of herniated discs sent Sybil to the hospital for nearly a year. Her *Playboy* pictorial became a collector's item. Attempting to explain herself, and her screen persona, Danning stated: "I love being a strong female onscreen. It suits me and I think

REMEMBER WHEN?: Early-on, Sybil Danning went the conventional dream girl route, though she didn't achieve notoriety until after the actress deserted such *Playboy*-type stuff in order to pursue a career as a kick-ass action babe; sometimes good, more often bad.

it's nice that young girls can see some of their own inner fantasies on film. Boys have Clint Eastwood. I hope that girls enjoy seeing me."

SELECTED FILMOGRAPHY:

Komm Nur (Lorelei, 1968); *Liebesmarkt in Dänemark* (Diane, 1971); *The Long Swift Sword of Siegfried* (Kriemhild, 1971); *Freedom for Love* (Sybille, 1971); *Resort Girls* (Ina, 1971); *Sex Olympics* (Phyllilia, 1972); *The Lady in Red Kills Seven Times* (Lulu Palm, 1972); *Bluebeard* (Prostitute, 1972); *Naughty Nymphs* (Elizabeth, 1972); *The Three Musketeers* (Eugenie, 1973); *The Four Musketeers* (Eugenie, 1974); *God's Gun* (Jenny, 1975); *The Twist* (Secretary, 1976); *The Prince and the Pauper* (Mother Canty, 1977); *The Cat in the Cage* (Susan, 1976); *The Concorde... Airport '79* (Amy, 1979); *Cuba Crossing* (Veronica, 1980); *The Man With Bogart's Face* (Cynthia, 1980); *How to Beat the High Co$t of Living* (Charlotte, 1980); *Cobra* (Brenda, 1980); *Nightkill* (Monika Childs, 1980); *The Salamander* (Lili, 1981); *S.A.S. à San Salvador* (Countess Alexandra Vogel, 1983); *Chained Heat* (Ericka, 1983); *Hercules* (Ariadne, 1983); *They're Playing with Fire* (Diane, 1984); *Jungle Warriors* (Angel, 1984); *Panther Squad* (Ilona, 1984); *Malibu Express* (Contessa Luciana, 1985); *Howling II:... Your Sister Is a Werewolf* (Stirba, 1985); *Young Lady Chatterley II* (Judith, 1985); *Private Passions* (Kathrine, 1985); *The Tomb* (Jade, 1986); *Reform School Girls* (Warden Sutter, 1986); *Warrior Queen* (Berenice, 1987); *Amazon Women on the Moon* (Queen Lara, 1987); *The Phantom Empire* (Alien Queen, 1988); *L.A. Bounty* (Huntress, 1989); *Grindhouse* (Gretchen Krupp, "Werewolf Women of the S.S." segment, 2007); *Halloween* (Nurse Wynn, 2007).

Susan Denberg

Birthdate: August 2, 1944; Pomerania, Germany; Polczyn-Zdrój, Poland
Birth name: Dietlinde Zechner
Height: 5' 7"
Measurements: 35 (C) – 25 - 34

BORN IN A SECTION OF GERMANY now belonging to Poland, Dietlinde Zechner moved to Austria and began performing as a chorus girl, continuing this career in London and then Vegas. At eighteen she was *Playboy*'s August 1966 Playmate of the Month. Susan seemed likely to be one more of those beautiful European blondes who captured, in their iconography, the essence of the New 1960s Youth. Clearly comfortable with display (including full nudity) of her awesome body, and with a nice-naughty face that combined elements of France's Brigitte Bardot and America's Kim Novak, she soon found herself in front of the cameras. Playing one of a trio of sensuous Space Cadets in *Star Trek*'s "Mudd's Women" (with Roger C. Carmel, 1966), Susan demonstrated little acting ability though a radiance did show through. Next came a small, showy role as the German femme fatale Ruta in a disastrous film version of Norman Mailer's novel *An American Dream*. Warner Bros. went so far as to sponsor a national contest. Adoring fans were asked to come up with the perfect Tinseltown name for the latest dream girl. Most entries were so... let us say... unmentionable that in the end all were rejected. Then came Susan's single starring role, *Frankenstein Created Woman*. Its title was intended as a humorous allusion to Brigitte Bardot's breakthrough film... *And God Created Woman* from a decade earlier. What might have been a potent gag in 1958 (when this film was conceived) no longer meant anything to the public at large by the time it surfaced in 1967. Directed by the esteemed Terence Fisher, here was a transition between the male-oriented monster movies Hammer had been turning out and the decidedly female

ONE MORE SCANDANAVIAN DREAM GIRL: Susan Denberg was introduced in *Playboy* and then briefly made a bid for movie stardom on the order of Elke Sommer and Britt Ekland.

thrillers they would focus on in the early 1970s. Though Peter Cushing was cast as the doctor, Denberg his gorgeous female creature (as prone to kill as her clumsy male predecessor), the film was burdened by a weak narrative and snail-slow pace. The public's anger, even outrage at the time had less to do with such faults than a dishonest advertising campaign.

The film was preceded into theatres by a P.R. attempt to sell it via a series of promotional images in which Cushing carries Denberg (as Christina) around the castle, she wearing a brief bikini. The photographs were taken as an afterthought; nothing of the sort occurs in the film. Viewers

"THE HORROR! THE HORROR!": For male viewers, the most horrifying thing about *Frankenstein Created Woman* was Hammer's failure to live up to its advance hype (seen here) and display the beautiful body of its young starlet.

WELCOME TO THE ENTERPRISE: Denberg (right) and other lovelies pay a visit to Kirk, Spock, and the crew as "Mudd's Women."

grew furious when the film concluded sans any sexiness. Nonetheless, offers poured in, mainly for more horror films, plus 'decorative' roles in bigger pictures. Susan turned them down, swept up by the drug-fueled late night party scene, sleeping most of the day, finally rising to begin her diet of drugs. It's uncertain whether Susan turned down the lead in *Girl on a Motorcycle/Naked Under Leather* or if the producers decided instead on Marianne Faithfull. Her money and Jet Set status gone, the deeply depressed blonde abruptly disappeared from The Scene. Rumors spread that she was dead of an overdose. In time, the story took on an aura of actuality. In fact, Susan, then (and now) had returned to her home in Klagenfurt. She lived with her mother, though there were reports of violence between them, also rumors that she had been temporarily institutionalized. Apparently they reconciled and now live in willful oblivion.

SELECTED FILMOGRAPHY:

An American Dream (Ruta, 1966); *See You in Hell, Darling* (1966); *Frankenstein Created Woman* (Christina/Creature, 1967).

Catherine Deneuve

Birthdate: October 22, 1943; Paris, France
Birth name: Catherine Fabienne Dorléac
Height: 5' 6"
Measurements: 34D – 25 ½ - 35

BORN TO HARD-WORKING ACTORS, Catherine (like her doomed redheaded sister, Francoise Dorléac) never considered any course in life other than that of movie star. The woman who would in time replace Brigitte Bardot as France's favorite daughter became the darling of international audiences thanks to Jacques Demy's scintillating musical-drama *The Umbrellas of Cherbourg*, Catherine playing an innocent provincial girl. Such a shock, then, to see her less than a year later in Roman Polanski's *Repulsion*, this her first great femme fatale role. Deneuve presents a variation on the hugely popular Lolita image, a gorgeous if mostly silent girl, living in swingin' London, who rarely makes contact with anyone, gradually goes stark raving mad, then ruthlessly murders a nice boy who tries to help. Shortly, there would be the erotic classic *Belle de Jour* for Luis Bunuel, a high-style work of cinematic art that also played to the audience's darkest desires to see S&M graphically revealed on the screen. As an upscale wife who secretly works by day in a lurid bordello, Catherine created a dual personality resembling Kim Novak in Alfred Hitchcock's *Vertigo*. What a shame Hitch did not seize upon Catherine as his star for the Sixties in *The Birds* and *Marnie*! Other (European) filmmakers reaped the rewards.

Surprisingly, attempts to turn Deneuve into a Hollywood star, opposite Jack Lemmon in a comedy, *The April Fools*, Burt Reynolds in a noir, *Hustle*, and Gene Hackman in a French foreign legion tale, *March or*

CLASSY LADIES LOVE BONDAGE, TOO!: In one of her most (in)famous roles, Deneuve plays an upscale housewife who spends her afternoons in a perverse bordello in *Belle de Jour*.

Die, failed to pay off. On the other hand, she played another dual role as good-girl/bad-girl in *Mississippi Mermaid*, Francois Truffaut's homage to Hitchcock. Never allowing herself to be typecast, Catherine played a wonderful woman in Truffaut's *The Last Metro* who hides her Jewish husband from the Nazis, though inevitably the pendulum swung back to femme fatale territory. In *The Hunger*, a bloodthirsty female vampire outing shot

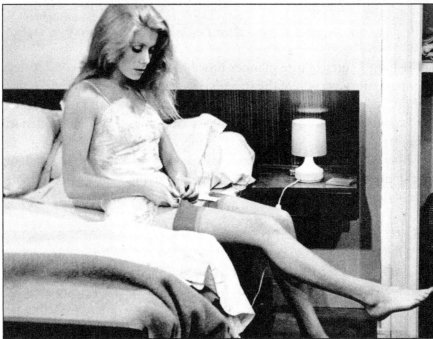

TO BED OR NOT TO BED?: Part of the appeal of watching a Catherine Deneuve film was getting to see the most beautiful woman in the world stripping down for action or already assuming 'the position.'

I, VAMPIRE!: Later in her career, Deneuve went the succubus route, portraying the most elegant of all mature screen bloodsuckers in *The Hunger*.

in the most haute couture manner possible, director Tony Scott created a contemporary version of the succubus as mature beauty, a modern day Bathory seducing and abandoning men (David Bowie) and women (Susan Sarandon) alike. To this day, Deneuve continues to act, most often in queenly roles, appropriate for this true queen of the cinema.

Trivia: Catherine's sister Francoise died in an automobile accident shortly after they completed their only co-starring venture, *The Young Girls of Rochefort*.

.SELECTED FILMOGRAPHY:

The Twilight Girls (The Beauty, 1957); *Tales of Paris* (Sophie, 1962); *And Satan Calls the Turns* (Manuelle, 1962); *Male Hunt* (Denise, 1964); *The Umbrellas of Cherbourg* (Geneviève, 1964); *Repulsion* (Carol, 1965); *Song of the World* (Clara, 1965); *The Young Girls of Rochefort* (Delphine, 1967); *Belle de Jour* (Séverine Serizy, 1967); *Benjamin,* or *Diary of an Innocent Boy* (Anne, 1968); *Mayerling* (Maria Vetsera, 1968); *Heartbeat* (Lucile, 1968); *The April Fools* (Catherine, 1969); *Mississippi Mermaid*

(Julie Roussel/Marion Vergano, 1969); *Tristana* (Tristana, 1970); *Donkey Skin* (The Princess, 1970); *Love to Eternity* (Liza, 1972); *Zig-Zag* (Marie, 1975); *The Savage* (Nelly, 1975); *Hustle* (Nicole Britton, 1975); *March or Die* (Simone Picard, 1977); *The Last Metro* (Marion Steiner, 1980); *The Hunger* (Miriam Blaylock, 1983); *Scene of the Crime* (Lili Ravenel, 1986); *Agent Trouble* (Amanda Weber, 1987); *Frequent Death* (Jeanne, 1988); *Indochine* (Eliane, 1992); *One Hundred and One Nights* (Fantasy Femme, 1995); *Thieves* (Marie, 1996); *Night Wind* (Hélène, 1998); *Dancer in the Dark* (Kathy, 2000); *The Musketeer* (The Queen, 2001); *8 Women* (Gaby, 2002); *Family Hero* (Alice, 2006); *Persepolis* (Mom, 2007); *A Christmas Tale* (Junon Vuillard, 2008) *The Girl on the Train* (Louise, 2009); *Hidden Diary* (Martine, 2009); *The Big Picture* (Anne, 2010); *Beloved* (Madeleine, 2011); *God Loves Caviar* (Empress Catherine II, 2012); *3 Hearts* (Madame Berger, 2014).

JAMES BOND'S GREAT GERMAN LOVE: Like Lucianna Paluzzi in *Thunderball*,
Karin Dor's villainess in *You Only Live Twice* proved to be one of those bad-to-the-bone
babes who cannot be won over to the side of righteousness – not even after bedding
down with 007.

Karin Dor

Birthdate: February 22, 1938; Wiesbaden, Hesse, Germany
Birth name: Kätherose Derr
Height: 5' 5"
Measurements: N/A

DESPITE ITS JAPANESE SETTING and the presence of two lovely Asian actresses as The First and Final Girl, the villainess of *You Only Live Twice* was played by Karin Dor. A German actress, she had an opportunity to create one of the most memorable of all the Bond bad-girls, in terms of her entrance as predecessor to the 1970s femme fatale 'Ilsa, She Wolf of the S.S.' (Dor, incidentally, might have been perfect for that role). Connery's Bond confronts the mysterious Mr. Osato of the chemicals industry he is investigating. Considered a security risk, Bond knows too much and must be eliminated. However, Osato's secretary, the cruel beauty Helga Brandt, must (as is the way with such bad Bond girls always) have her lurid pleasure first. Not unlike the villainess played by Lucianna Paluzzi in *Thunderball*, Helga takes time out from the killing game to hit the sheets with 007, pretending afterwards that she's been "won over." They will fly away together in her plane, or so it seems until she locks him in his seat while she parachutes to safety. Bond escapes the inevitable crash, of course. When he's recaptured (this time by Blofeld himself), Bond along with Helga must face a mock trial. Seemingly forgiving Helga, the master criminal allows her to step across a bridge to supposed safety. He then de-activates a device in the walkway, causing Helga to fall down into the water below, prey to the man-eating monster fish, the piranha. "Bon appetit," Bond glibly muses.

Though most of Dor's screen work must be considered minor, she did appear in a number of interesting exploitation items. One project was based on Dr. Mabuse, a super-villain who in the silent era had, when created by Fritz Lang, set the pace for all Bond bad guys to come. Several of her murder mysteries were based on tales by Edgar Wallace. Though his name may not be remembered today, Wallace's popularity in the early 20th

DRESSED TO KILL: Like most of the great Bond babes, Karin Dor wears outfits that are conducive to her line of work – murdering men.

century rivalled that of Stephen King in later years. There were also Teutonic Westerns based on the work of Karl May, a German writer whose Old Shatterhand and Winnetou were carbon copies of Hawkeye and Chingachgook from James Fenimore Cooper's Leatherstocking books.

Karin's relationships included failed marriages to Günther Schmucker and Harald Reinl. A successful one to George Robotham ended with his death in 2007. Most of her life has been spent in Los Angeles or Munich, where she won acclaim for various stage portrayals, including the lead in "Der Neurosenkavalier." Her only other notable film was *Topaz*, last of Alfred Hitchcock's spy thrillers. The best moment in this overlong production goes to Karin. As a relatively innocent woman involved in (overly) complicated espionage situations, she steps forward to embrace a man whom she considers to be her friend and lover. This brief encounter was filmed in the conventional medium shot. To her shock, he then murders her. Hitchcock deftly cuts to a bird's-eye-view shot in which the human element becomes purposefully lost: As Karin ever so slowly falls to the ground, we have the impression of looking down as a gorgeous rose crumbles in the kind of stop-action photography that allows such a lengthy real-life happening to occur onscreen in a matter of seconds.

SELECTED FILMOGRAPHY:
As Long as You Live (Pepita, 1955); *Little Man on Top* (Meike Brauns, 1957); *Sin Began with Eve* (Dinah, 1958); *False Shame* (Christa Reik, 1958); *The Blue Sea and You* (Helga, 1959); *The Terrible People* (Nora Sanders, 1960); *The White Horse Inn* (Brgitte, 1960); *The Green Archer* (Valerie, 1961); *The Forger of London* (Jane Clifton, 1961); *The Invisible Dr. Mabuse* (Liane Martin, 1962); *The Carpet of Horror* (Ann Learner, 1962); *Room 13* (Denise, 1964); *Winnetou: The Red Gentleman* (Ribanna, 1964); *The Last Tomahawk* (Cora Munroe, 1965); *The Face of Fu Manchu* (Maria Muller, 1965); *The Sinister Monk* (Gwendolin, 1965); *The Spy with Ten Faces* (Helen, 1966); *Killer's Carnival* (Denise, 1966); *Die Nibelungen* (Brunhilde, 1967), *You Only Live Twice* (Helga Brandt, 1967); *The Torture Chamber of Dr. Sadism* (Baroness Lilian van Brabant, 1967); *Topaz* (Juanita de Cordoba, 1969); *Assignment Terror* (Maleva, 1970); *Dark Echoes* (Lisa, 1977); *I Am the Other Woman* (Frau Winter, 2006).

BONNIE AND C.W. (MOSS, THAT IS): Faye Dunaway and Michael J. Pollard as part of the 1930s rural gang that terrorized the Midwest, eventually becoming legendary bandit figures.

Faye Dunaway

Birthdate: January 14, 1941; Bascom, Florida
Height: 5' 7"
Measurements: 36 – 26 - 34

FLORIDA BORN, INITIALLY PLANNING TO PURSUE a career in education, young Faye moved to Boston to study theatre. She was accepted into the National Theatre and Academy in 1961. Perhaps her aura of absolute ferocious femaleness led to early success on the New York stage more than conventional acting skills. Her impossibly high cheekbones and sleek yet lush figure caused Otto Preminger to signed Faye to a five-year contract, beginning with a little-seen (thankfully!) interracial Southern melodrama *Hurry Sundown*. Hostilities between the star and her director flared during the filming process. Faye sued for release. The only part that came her way was as a wicked Beach Bunny in *The Happening*, a dreadful Hippie-era would-be thriller. With such an ugly Biz situation behind her and few offers, Dunaway might have slipped into obscurity. But producer-star Warren Beatty was even then having trouble casting his upcoming controversial *Bonnie and Clyde*. Tuesday Weld, Natalie Wood, and Ann-Margret all said no. Sue Lyon was eager for the part but her limited acting abilities were all too evident. Shortly before shooting commenced, Beatty cast Dunaway, who impressed him with her vitality, wildness, and a willingness to take risks. As *B&C* became a staple of the then-evolving counter-culture, she emerged as a potent radical symbol for young women of the late-1960s and received an Oscar nomination. The film's Bonnie Parker changed the image of femme fatales in commercial cinema. Less a bad-girl than a good-girl gone bad, the work suggests that inside every good girl in some small town, dreaming about a life of adventure, a potential bad-girl desperately hopes for some catalyst to come along and set her free. Clyde doesn't so much take Bonnie along as she insists on accompanying him. Set in the 1930s, and vivid as a period piece, *Bonnie and Clyde* spoke across the decades, reflecting on the Women's Movement then gaining centrality in American ideas. Expecting to be overwhelmed sexually, Bonnie realizes she must teach the sexually confused Clyde how to satisfy her. As the story continues, she ceases to be a gun moll, transforming into the gang's titular leader.

Her best roles were as a frontier seductress out to corrupt Dustin Hoffman in *Little Big Man,* a retro-noir heroine opposite Jack Nicholson in *Chinatown,* luscious femme fatale Milady de Winter in the *Musketeer* movies, and a cut-throat TV executive in *Network* (Faye won an Oscar for the latter). She turned down the ripe role that then went to Jean Seberg in *Paint Your Wagon* opposite Lee Marvin and Clint Eastwood, as well as the charming *Fun With Dick and Jane* (Fonda, 1977) and then *Norma Rae* (Sally Field, 1979) but said 'yes' to *Mommie Dearest,* playing Joan Crawford.. Nothing would ever again be the same. Overnight she had nowhere to go but over-the-top villains in bombs like *Supergirl* and *The Wicked Lady.* Perhaps her fall from acting grace explains why "Cubby"

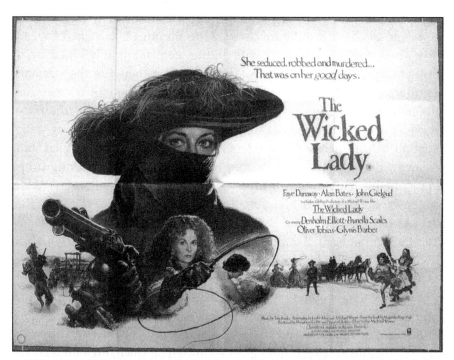

"WHO WAS THAT MASKED LADY?": In one of her increasingly arch villainess roles,
Dunaway played an English highway-woman.

THE WICKED HIPPIE: Early on in her career, Dunaway played a flower child gone bad in *The Happening*.

Broccoli, after considering Faye for the female lead in *Octopussy*, decided against her. She did deliver excellent performances in *Barfly* and the TV drama *After the Fall* as a Monroe type in Arthur Miller's play. Tragically, this proved to be too little, too late.

SELECTED FILMOGRAPHY:

Hurry Sundown (Lou McDowell, 1967); *The Happening* (Sandy, 1967); *Bonnie and Clyde* (Bonnie Parker, 1967); *The Thomas Crown Affair* (Vicki Anderson, 1968); A Place for Lovers (Julia, 1968); *The Extraordinary Seaman* (Jennifer, 1969); *The Arrangement* (Gwen, 1969); *Little*

Big Man (Mrs. Penrake, 1970); *Puzzle of a Downfall Child* (Lou, 1970); *'Doc'* (Katie Elder, 1971); *Oklahoma Crude* (Lena, 1973); *The Three Musketeers* (Milady de Winter, 1973); *Chinatown* (Evelyn Mulwray, 1974); *The Four Musketeers* (Milady, 1974); *The Towering Inferno* (Susan Franklin, 1974); *Three Days of the Condor* (Kathy Hale, 1975); *Network* (Diana Christensen, 1976); *Voyage of the Damned* (Denise Kreisler, 1976); *Eyes of Laura Mars* (Laura, 1978); *The Champ* (Annie, 1979); *The First Deadly Sin* (Barbara, 1980); *Mommie Dearest* (Joan Crawford,1981); *The Wicked Lady* (Lady Barbara Skelton, 1983); *Supergirl* (Selena, 1984); *Barfly* (Wanda Wilcox, 1987); *Don Juan DeMarco* (Marilyn, 1994); *In Praise of Older Women* (Condesa, 1997).

Anulka Dziubinska

aka: ANULKA DUBINSKA; ANULKA
Birthdate: December 14, 1950; Preston, Lancashire, UK
Height: 5'4"
Measurements: 35 ½-23-35

HOWEVER BRIEF (AND LARGELY FORGOTTEN), her career may be, Anulka portrayed a memorable vampire girl in the aptly named *Vampyres*. She and Barbara Morris are lesbian vampires living in an isolated area who prey on a young honeymoon couple tht makes the mistake of camping nearby. A finalist in the Miss United Kingdom beauty pageant

THE LADY IS A VAMP: In one of the more memorable lesbian-vampire films of the 1970s, Anulka turns a Bowie-sized knife on her latest lover (this one male).

in 1970, she then became a Bunny and Blackjack dealer at the London Playboy club, following that up with an appearances in August, 1972 as one of the magazine's "Girls of Munich" in May, then the 1973 Playmate of the Month, as well as one of the "Page Three Girls" in a London tabloids, *The Sun*. Such exposure led to her being cast in *Vampyres*, in which she makes a memorably deadly succubus. Strong film roles were not forthcoming.

Between 1976 and 1984, there were small if glamorous roles on episodic TV in such shows as *The New Avengers*, *The Tomorrow People*; *Hello, Larry*; *Magnum, P.I.:Bare Essence* and, perhaps best remembered, *Falcon Crest*, portraying Sonya Louis-Dreyfus. In 2011, she also appeared as herself in the documentary *On Vampyres and Other Symptoms*. After decades away from the spotlight, Anulka is currently planning a comeback of sorts in the planned film *The Other Side of Love* in which she is supposedly set to play a character named Tanya Leigh. During the long career lull, she has worked as both a florist and a tree vendor as well as a dental nurse. She authored the book *Zen Flowers: Designs to Soothe the Senses and Nourish the Soul*.

CREDITS:

Vampyres (Miriam, 1974); *Lisztomania* (Lola Montes, 1975); *The Likely Lads* (Dawn, 1976).

Shirley Eaton

Birthdate: January 12, 1937; Edgware, Middlesex, UK
Height: 5' 7"
Measurements: N/A

AT AGE TWELVE, SHIRLEY set about conquering the British stage beginning with *Set to Partners*. Live-theatre included "Let's Make an Opera" by the much-esteemed Benjamin Britten. Child-hood ballet training expanded her range beyond that of other lovely hopefuls and Shirley became something of a regular fixture on TV. Legendary producer Alexander Korda signed Shirley to a long-term contract. A popular low-brow comedy series, *Carry On...*, offered a male clown ensemble in various exotic settings. Always there had to be a blonde for for onscreen goofballs (and males in the audience) to gawk at. Eaton more than filled that bill. Shortly she also appeared with the comic genius Peter Sellers, making his first great impression. If movies paid the bills, the BBC beckoned with more lofty TV work on ambitious musical productions. And, again, the play was the thing. The London Prince of Wales Theatre wanted no one but Shirley for their adaptation of Neil Simon's early hit *Come Blow Your Horn*. That's when fate stepped in. An offer to play the female lead in a B-budget film caused Eaton to shoot all day, then head over to the theatre for doing double duty.

The film was *The Girl Hunters,* starring writer Mickey Spillane as his own fictional creation, Mike Hammer. In a cost cutting maneuver, the American-set film was shot in London. Shirley's character, Laura Knapp, offered an intriguing redo of film noir dames from the previous decade. Seemingly a classy rich bitch who falls for the tough-guy anti-hero, she turns out to be the villain(ess) he's searching for. Their intense romance doesn't stop Mickey/Mike from tricking his lover into blowing her head

"YOU INTEREST ME, MR. BOND!": Jill (Shirley Eaton) spends a lovely night with 007, but
pays for it by becoming a goldengirl – in every sense of that term.

off with a shotgun while attempting to dispatch him. Though this was a
minor movie, Eaton's ability to appear clean-cut one moment, a deadly
she-beast the next, caught the note of 007's producer Broccoli. In a tight
decision, he chose her over Shirley Anne Field to play Jill Masterson in
the third Bond film, *Goldfinger*. Though the initially bikini-clad beauty, a
spy for the title bad guy, is only onscreen for about ten minutes (an iconic
moment has her being gilded by innovative assassins), it was Shirley, not
the female lead Honor Blackman, who made *Life* magazine's cover.

The onetime sweet heroine from *Carry On* was now re-typecast as
a deadly Spider Woman. An exploitation item, *The Million Eyes of Su-
Muru*, offered an updating of Sax Rohmer's chestnut about the female

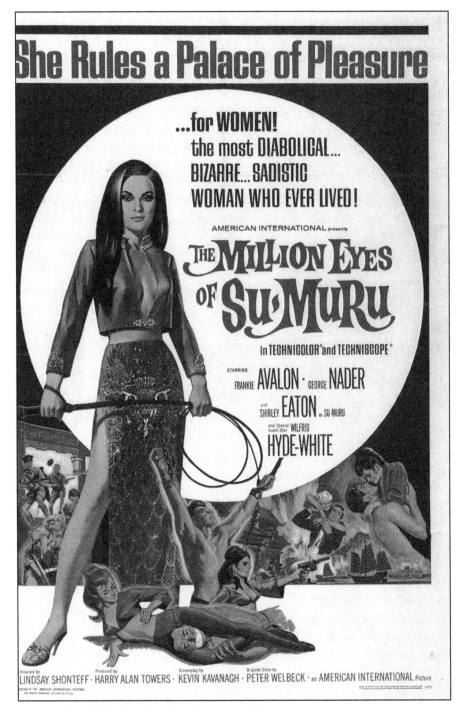

WHEN BLONDES GO BRUNETTE: As her villainess, Sax Rohmer's Su-Maru, was by implication Asian, Shirley Eaton agreed to a darker look for this film only.

equivalent to his Dr. Fu Manchu. The usually blonde Shirley played a dark vamp who amasses an army of Amazons planning to seize control of the world's political structures, using their beauty and sexuality to conquer foolish men. In a low-budget TV imitation of a Bond extravaganza called *The Scorpio Letters* (1967) she enacted the steamy spy-girl once again. There was also a guest-star shot as a Bond-like bad girl in three episodes of TV's *The Saint* opposite future 007 Roger Moore. Eaton shortly chose to retire and live a quiet life, spending much her time in her art studio. She enjoyed a successful long-term marriage to Colin Rowe which lasted

THE BLONDE AS FEMALE VICTIM: Shirley believes herself to be a goner in *Ten Little Indians* until Hugh O'Brian comes rushing to rescue her from a mad killer.

THE MALE GAZE: Sean Connery as James Bond, just visible at the far left of this image, takes long admiring glance at the perfect bedmate, Shirley Eaton as Jill.

from their wedding in 1957 to his passing in 1994, the couple producing two sons. As to her primary loyalty, she has said: "A career is a career, but you're a mother until you die."

SELECTED FILMOGRAPHY:

Doctor in the House (Mill, 1954); *The Belles of St. Trinian's* (Sixth Former, 1954, uncredited); *Sailor Beware* (Shirley, 1956); *Three Men in a Boat* (Sophie, 1956); *Doctor at Large* (Nan, 1957); *Carry On Nurse* (Dorothy, 1959); *In the Wake of a Stranger* (Joyce, 1959); *Nearly a Nasty Accident* (Jean, 1961); *The Girl Hunters* (Laura Knapp, 1963); *Rhino!* (Miss Arleigh, 1964); *Goldfinger* (Jill Masterson, 1964); *The Naked Brigade* (Diane Forsythe, 1965); *Ten Little Indians* (Ann, 1965); *Around the World Under the Sea* (Maggie, 1966); *Eight on the Lam* (Ellie, 1967); *The Million Eyes of Su-Muru* (Sumuru, 1967); *The Blood of Fu Manchu* (Black Widow, 1968); *The Seven Secrets of Sumuru* (Sumuru, 1969).

SHE CAME FROM BEYOND TIME: During her brief stint in films, Julie played one of those goddesses from either the future or the past – or perhaps a combination of the two – in the comedy *Up Pompeii*.

Julie Ege

Birthdate: November 12, 1943; Høyland, Sandnes, Norway
Birth name: Julie Dzuli
Date of passing: April 29, 2008; Oslo, Norway
Height: N/A
Measurements: 36 (C) – 24 - 36

THE UNEXPECTED SUCCESS of *One Million Years, B.C.* starring Raquel Welch as a bikini-clad dinosaur girl initiated a series of such projects for Sir James Carreras at Hammer. Included were *When Dinosaurs Ruled the Earth*, *Prehistoric Women*, and finally *Creatures the World Forgot*, starring Miss Norway, 1962, Julie Ege. Most fans of the genre tend to overlook this one because, title aside, there aren't any dinosaurs on view, though a few Mammoths and wild boars stumble about in the background. Actually, though, the film does have its merits. For one thing, the lack of Thunder Lizards causes the premise to be a bit more realistic, as prehistoric men do struggle with the sorts of beasts that actually were around some 15,000 years ago. Still, there had to be the Money Shot and Julie provides that, looking as elegantly attired in her own animal skin bikini as those previous grunt-and-groan stars did.

Julie qualifies as a Bond girl owing to her small role in the only series entry to star George Lazenby, though that did not lead to bigger and/or better parts. This, despite insistence by Hammer, early on at least, that she would go on to become the most memorable of all the Hammer girls, a claim that attracted the attention of the BBC. That venerable institution actually prepared a special about her called "The Money Programme" in which a panel of experts attempted to assess how much cash was invested in trying to make her an international star. If cult stardom hadn't automatically been assured by her cave girl mini-epic, such status was a natu-

BEWARE THIS BEAUTY!: Julie Ege's alluring face and body are mitigated a bit by
that unpleasant weapon she appears ready to wield.

ral after *The Legend of the 7 Golden Vampires*, an Underground favorite
owing to its striking special effects, bizarre action sequences, tongue in
cheek humor and showing off of Julie in exotic costumes. There is also a
following for the bizarre Brit apocalyptic sci-fi film *The Last Days of Man
on Earth*. Julie also played an ancient-world goddess in the off-the-wall
lowbrow Brit comedy *Up Pompeii*.

For a while, she reigned as part of the glitterati while living, during the 1970s, with Tony Bramwell, a former member of The Beatles' staff and a film as well as record producer on his own. When that ended, she pursued a degree in nursing and worked in that capacity for several years, apparently enjoying the anonymity of a medical professional as much as she had her brief burst of international stardom. Few if any of the women who appeared in femme fatale roles owing to their good looks have ever been so forthright about their careers: "To be honest," Julie once said, "I was never really that proud of my performances in films. But I gave it my best and enjoyed the work very much." She told her own story in Naken (Naked), published in Oslo in 2002. She died of breast cancer, diagnosed as early as 1986, in Oslo, 2008.

Trivia: Though never featured in a *Playboy* celeb layout, Julie did appear as a *Penthouse* centerfold.

SELECTED FILMOGRAPHY:

Robbery (Pretty Girl, 1967); *On Her Majesty's Secret Service* (The Scandinavian Girl, 1969); *Every Home Should Have One* (Inga Giltenburg, 1970); *Up Pompeii* (Voluptua, 1971); *Creatures the World Forgot* (Nala, 1971); *The Magnificent Seven Deadly Sins* (Ingrid, 1971); *Double Take* (April, 1972); *Rentadick* (Utta Armitage, 1972); *Not Now Darling* (Janie McMichael, 1973); *The Last Days of Man on Earth* (Miss Dazzle, 1973); *Craze* (Helena, 1974); *The Legend of the 7 Golden Vampires* (Vanessa Buren, 1974); *It's Not the Size That Counts* (Miss Hanson, 1974); *The Mutations* (Heidi, 1974); *The Amorous Milkman* (Diana, 1975).

THE DANCE OF DEATH: Anita as Terpsichore, seducing Victor Mature in *Zarek*.

Anita Ekberg

Birthdate: September 29, 1931; Malmö, Skåne län, Sweden
Birth name: Kerstin Anita Marianne Ekberg
Date of passing: January 11, 2015; Rocca di Papa, Italy
Height: 5' 6 3/4"
Measurements: 40(D) – 24 - 36

THE MONGOL HORDES RAVAGING EUROPE are lured into a trap by Christian soldiers. Hundreds of barbaric horse-soldiers penetrate a deep swamp and become bogged down in quicksand. Their gorgeous but wicked queen falls from her horse. Horrified of being sucked under, she spots a ray of hope: Young warrior Temujin observes her plight from a hillock. "Save me!" the enchantress screams, believing she might yet live. Though he might easily do so, Temujin prefers to coldly watch as the femme fatale gradually disappears. For fans of cult cinema, this sequence from *The Mongols* defines Anita Ekberg. For those who prefer ambitious arthouse projects, that would be an equally glorious moment when, in Federico Fellini's *La Dolce Vita*, the blonde goddess from Sweden, drunk on moonlight and champagne, wades about in Rome's Trevvi Fountain wearing a sleek black dress. The Iceberg, as Anita was nicknamed, always claimed: "Fellini didn't discover me. I discovered Fellini," by providing an intellectual auteur with the element that allowed him to reach the masses, that being Sex Appeal.

Crowned Miss Sweden in 1950 at age nineteen, Anita headed for the U.S. There she was discovered by Howard Hughes, the aviation entrepreneur who also dabbled in making movies. Soon Ekberg was being hyped as a Scandinavian equivalent to Jayne Mansfield in an era that feminist film historian Marjorie Rosen has described as "Mammary Madness." All set to star in *Sheena, Queen of the Jungle* on TV, Anita bolted (allowing

YOU GET WHAT YOU GIVE: In *The Mongols*, Anita's barbarian queen takes great pleasure in torturing pretty young girls; later, Jack Palance returns such acts with a vengeance.

replacement Irish McCalla her single great success) and went to work for John Wayne's Batjac, scoring a role in *Blood Alley*. There were two Dean Martin/Jerry Lewis films—*Artists and Models*, the team's best, and *Hollywood or Bust*—and a ripe role as Henry Fonda's nymphomaniacal wife in *War and Peace*.

Like Mansfield, the big-busted Anita was always more of a living spoof of sex symbols than an authentic one on the order of Marilyn Monroe. So there would be Peplums, including a large budget item, *Zarak*, opposite Victor Mature. In it, Anita offered international audiences the most

BOUND FOR GLORY: Anita plays an insane stripper who goes the S&M route in her stage performances in *Screaming Mimi*.

daringly exotic onscreen dance. For fans of ultra-low-budget noir sleaze, there has never been anything to even compare with *Screaming Mimi*. She's cast as an innocent (perhaps virginal) girl who works as a stripper, tantalizing men. A hardboiled cop (Philip Carey) becomes one of her admirers, dedicating himself to saving her from an unknown serial killer apparently stalking the beauty. As it turns out, she's the murderer(ess). Here, Anita's dance numbers have her crawling about on a dirty floor in flimsy attire, bound in handcuffs.

THE DEVIL IS A WOMAN: Anita's bad-girl image is enhanced by this Hollywood publicity shot.

Inclusion in the Fellini classic transformed Anita into an icon, not only of sex but of the new decadence of the 1960s. She appears in Fellini's *Boccaccio '70* as a fantasy incarnation of herself, driving male gazers mad with desire. Though she never landed a Bond girl role (Anita lost out on Honey Rider in *Dr. No* to Ursula Andress), her essence is well used in *From Russia With Love* (1963). Connery and Pedro Armenderiz discover a bad guy hiding in Anita's magnificent mouth—or its larger-than-life representation in a poster advertising one of her films. Anita eventually played the exotic Queen Na-Eela in *Gold of the Amazon Women* (1979), a made-for-TV movie, wearing a costume calculated to hide the many pounds she had packed owing to a penchant for pasta. Eventually she starred in a nunsploitation item, *Killer Nun*, none too successfully cast as a woman much younger than her actual age. Though she retired at the beginning of the 21st century to live quietly in Rome, health problems and a fire at her home left her destitute, reaching out to old friends and colleagues for financial aid. This was the former Iceberg's sad situation when she passed away.

SELECTED FILMOGRAPHY:

Abbott and Costello Go to Mars (Amazon of Venus, 1953); *The Golden Blade* (Handmaiden, 1953); *Blood Alley* (Wei Ling, 1955); *Artists and Models* (Anita, 1955); *War and Peace* (Helene, 1956); *Back from Eternity* (Rena, 1956); *Hollywood or Bust* (Actress, 1956); *Man in the Vault* (Flo, 1956); *Zarak* (Salma, 1956); *Pickup Alley* (Gina, 1957); *Valerie* (Valerie, 1957); *Paris Holiday* (Zara, 1958); *Screaming Mimi* (Virginia/Yolanda, 1958); *Sheba and the Gladiator* (Zenobia, 1959); *La Dolce Vita* (Sylvia, 1960); *The Mongols* (Hulina, 1961); *Boccacio '70* (Anita, 1962); *Call Me Bwana* (Luba, 1963); *4 for Texas* (Elya, 1963); *The Alphabet Murders* (Amanda, 1965); *Way... Way Out* (Anna, 1966); *The Cobra* (Lou, 1967); *The Glass Sphinx* (Paulette, 1967); *Woman Times Seven* (Claudie, 1967); *If It's Tuesday, This Must Be Belgium* (Entertainer, 1969); *Fangs of the Living Dead* (Malenka, 1969); *The Blonde Connection* (Sophia, 1969); *The French Sex Murders* (Madame Colette, 1972); *Deadly Trackers* (Jane, 1972); *(The) Killer Nun* (Sister Gertrude, 1978).

TWO BOND GIRLS ARE BETTER THAN ONE: Roger Moore (center) enjoys the company of Maude Adams (right) and Britt Ekland (left) in his first 007 *The Man With the Golden Gun.*

Britt Ekland

Birthdate: October 6, 1942; Stockholm, Sweden
Birth name: Britt-Marie Eklund
Height: 5'5"
Measurements: 34(B)–24- 33

HOW MANY ACTRESSES CAN BOAST that, in addition to being a Bond Girl, they also co-starred opposite Elvis Presley, Peter Sellers, Doris Day, Yul Brynner, John Cassavetes, Michael Caine, and that compleat cult queen, Ingrid Pitt? Britt alone, among the 1960s Scandinavian beauties, survived career-wise into the 1970s, and not only in lower-level movies. In addition to playing the first good-girl opposite then-new 007 Roger Moore, she also appeared in several cult movies. Informed by everyone around her from an early age that her perfect features qualified Britt as a natural for motion pictures, she studied drama, then headed for Italy to appear in junk films. Comedic genius Peter Sellers became enamored, even obsessed, convincing the naïve girl that they were fated for one another. She appeared opposite her then-husband twice, in *The Bobo* and *After the Fox*. She also appeared in one of the first Hollywood movies to feature female nudity, *The Night They Raised Minsky's*, a charming piece of nostalgia about the birth of burlesque. The brief shots of her dancer's breasts were, to the disappointment of Ekland fans, provided by a body double.

She and Maude Adams shared 007 in *The Man with the Golden Gun*. Her on again/off again romance with Rod Stewart gave the gossip columnists spicy material. A dozen and a half fluff films aside, Britt's appearance in two great 1970s films ensured her immortality. One of the original neo-noirs was the Brit-lensed *Get Carter* starring Michael Caine as a notably nasty anti-hero. This tale of cruel vengeance set aside the chintzy glamour of 1960s spy cinema for a cynical tale of London's

PRIMITIVE RHAPSODY: In one of the best movies ever made about Wicca practice in the modern world, Ekland's character performs a Druid ritual with her back to the camera – perhaps to hide the actress' pregnancy!

meanest streets. Ekland effectively played a betraying bitch who gets her just desserts via a glum watery death. Earlier, her sex scene with Caine left little doubt that no body double was employed here. Some three years later, the now-liberated Ekland again went *au natural* again for *The Wicker Man*, directed by Robin Hardy from a script by Anthony Shaffer of *Sleuth* fame. On an all but forgotten Hebredean island, Ekland is the blonde witch who tempts male virgin Edward Woodward in this accurate study of The Wiccan Way.

Ekland claims that she was offered the role of Dwan in the 1977 Dino De Laurentiis *King Kong* remake, turning down the part that went to Jessica Lange. Following her mother's death from Alzheimer's in 2005, Ekland has dedicated herself to helping conquer this disease.

SELECTED FILMOGRAPHY:

G.I. Blues (Britta the Redhead, 1960); *The Happy Thieves* (Mrs. Pickett, 1961); *The Prize* (Blonde Swedish Nudist, 1963); *Advance to the Rear* (Greta, 1964); *Do Not Disturb* (Party Girl, 1965); *After the Fox* (Gina Romantica, 1966); *The Double Man* (Gina, 1967); *The Bobo* (Olimpia Segura, 1967); *The Night They Raided Minsky's* (Rachel Schpitendavel, 1968); *Machine Gun McCain* (Irene Tucker, 1969); *Stiletto* (Illeana, 1969); *The Conspirators* (Princess Spada, 1969); *Year of the Cannibals* (Antigone, 1970); *Tintomara* (Aldolfine, 1970); *What the Pepper Saw* (Elise, 1971); *Get*

"SORRY, WRONG NUMBER": Britt's manipulative villainess makes a final phone call while waiting for Michael Caine in *Get Carter*, one of the finest of all British neo-noirs.

Carter (Anna, 1971); *Percy* (Dorothy, 1971); *A Time for Loving* (Josette Papillon, 1972); *Asylum* (Lucy, 1972); *Endless Night* (Greta, 1972); *Baxter!* (Chris Bentley, 1973); *The Wicker Man* (Willow, 1973); *The Ultimate Thrill* (Michelle, 1974); *The Man With the Golden Gun* (Goodnight, 1974); *Royal Flash* (Dutchess Irma, 1975); *High Velocity* (Mrs. Andersen, 1976); *Some Like It Cool* (Countess Trivulzi, 1977); *King Solomon's Treasure* (Queen Nyleptha, 1979); *The Monster Club* (Busotsky's Mother, 1981); *Satan's Mistress* (Ann-Marie, 1982); *Entrapment* (Penny, 1983); *Erotic Images* (Julie, 1983); *Dr. Yes* (Susannah, 1983); *Love Scenes* (Annie, 1984); *Fraternity Vacation* (Eyvette, 1985); *Scandal* (Mariella, 1989); *Beverly Hills Vamp* (Madame Cassandra, 1989); *Cold Heat* (Jackie, 1989); *The Children* (Lady Zinnia, 1990).

Marianne Faithful

Birthdate: December 29, 1946, Hampstead, London
Height: N/A
Measurements: N/A

IN HER EARLY DAYS, Marianne Faithfull was best known as the beautiful 'bird' who hung out with Mick Jagger of The Rolling Stones. She became so deeply involved with drugs—first cocaine, later heroin—that

THE BIKER BABE, BRIT STYLE: Picking up on the legendary Brigitte Bardot motorcycle poses, as well as an Underground novel presumably inspired by them, Marianne Faithfull roars across the countryside in *Girl on a Motorcycle*.

ALL NEAT IN BLACK STOCKINGS: Few Brit female teenagers embodied the Sexual Revolution of the 1960s, following the musical revolution of The Beatles and The Rolling Stones, as Marianne Faithfull, herself a singer as well as actress and model.

many observers guessed she wouldn't long survive. Meanwhile, Marianne cut several albums which attracted some attention, and "As Tears Go By," co-written by Mick, charted as a single. Still, all of this seemed a comedown for a young woman whose father was a professor at London University's Bedford College, and whose mother had been an anti-Nazi orga-

NAKED UNDER LEATHER: That was the alternative title of this film, one of the first to depict the biker babe not as a Hell's Angels Honey but a respectable upper-class young woman.

nizer as well as a member of Germany's notable Sacher-Masoch family. As such, Faithfull is technically a Baroness. Considerably later in her life, Marianne emerged as an important, critically acclaimed jazz/blues star, thanks to acclaimed albums such as "Broken English" (1979). Her natural abilities as an actress in later life led to several acclaimed stage roles, most notably as 'Pirate Jenny' in *The Threepenny Opera* by Kurt Weill and Bertolt Brecht.

In-between, Faithfull enjoyed a brief movie star career that might have flourished were it not for the destructive drug dependency which decimated her delicate beauty. *Girl on a Motorcycle* (French: *La motocyclette*), also known as *Naked Under Leather*, was based on an underground novel by André Pieyre de Mandiargues. Purportedly, he had been inspired to write the piece after gazing at images of Brigitte Bardot in black leather, alluringly posing by a huge motorcycle, then imagining what such a modern girl's back-story might be like. Too old for the role by the late 1960s, Bebe herself was discounted. When Susan Denberg passed, Marianne won the part of a danger-prone rebel-girl who cruises the countryside in a skin-tight catsuit. The following year, she appeared in acclaimed director Tony Richardson's film *Hamlet*, based on a recent stage play that had also starred Nicol Williamson. In a turnabout from earlier versions, Faithfull was directed to play Ophelia not as an innocent teenager but a manipulative, sexually promiscuous Nymphet; i.e., an Opehlia for the Lolita-driven 1960s. Neither film succeeded with critics or the public, so any hopes for a future as a mainstream actress withered away.

SELECTED FILMOGRAPHY:

Go Go Go Said the Bird (Herself, 1966); *(The) Girl on a Motorcycle* (Rebecca, 1968); *Hamlet* (Ophelia, 1969); *Ghost Story* (Sophy Kwykwer, 1974); *Tripping* (Herself, 1999); *Marie Antoinette* (Empress Maria Theresa, 2006).

Edwige Fenech

Birthdate: December 24, 1948; Bône/Annaba, Algeria
Birth Name: Edwige Sfenek
Height: 5' 9"
Measurements: 34 (C) – 23 - 34

HERE WAS ONE INTERNATIONAL SEX SYMBOL whose origins truly must be considered global. Born in an area called Constantine, then geographically still a part of France, Edwige's father was Maltese, her mother part-Italian, part-Tunisian. Friends of the family insisted the stunning girl enter beauty contests. At 16, she was crowned "Miss Mannequin de la Cote d'Azur." Considerable exposure via photos in continental magazines led to her first movie offer, a sex romp called *All Mad About Him*. For several years, such stuff remained the only material offered to Edwige, her beauty on display in *Sexy Susan Sins Again* and *All Kitties Go for Sweeties*. These items may have been too minor for a U.S. theatrical release, though they did show up in some Canadian venues. A following developed for Edwige, hailed as the most fascinating onscreen icon of eroticism since Bardot.

Cult stardom came knocking, this the era in which the Giallo came into full prominence. Fenech (now her name) incarnated a highly attractive piece of female prey in such violent yet stylish items as *Blade of the Ripper, All the Colors of the Dark* and, most memorably, *Your Vice is a Locked Room and Only I Have the Key*. In due time, Edwige had a chance to work for the master of this form, Mario Bava, in *The Case of the Bloody Iris*. As Bava's reputation continued to grow, in time attracting American audiences for hard-edged horror via the then-new medium of home video in the mid-1970s, Feniche acquired notable femme fatale status.

As smart as she was sexy, Feniche became a talk-show staple in Italy if she remained largely unknown throughout most of the world. In time,

A RECURRING IMAGE: In movie after movie (and not just those of the 1960s and 1970s), beautiful women, including the femme fatales, were often glimpsed while taking a bath – cleanliness, in the case of bad-girls, next to deviltry rather than Godliness.

she revealed her taste as well as intelligence by helping to bring Shakespeare's *The Merchant of Venice* to the screen in 2004. Though by this time she had been forgotten by the mass audience, her status as a cult queen caused Eli Roth to cast Edwige in a cameo (as a university professor) in *Hostel: Part II*. Later she was one of the founders of the Rome-based pro-

SEASIDE SWINGER: However controversial the bikini bathing may have been on its initial appearance, Edwige Fenech proved daring enough to go au natural.

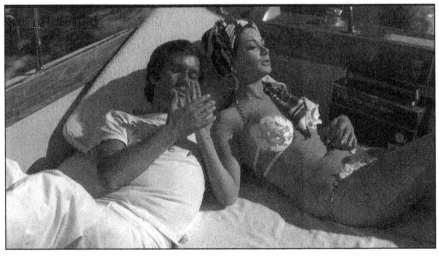

WOMAN AS MASTER, MALE AS SLAVE: In a succession of films, Edwige Fenech employed her sensuality to reduce the men in her life to admiring servants.

duction company Immagine. Today, many fans from her golden era look back most lovingly on *Samoa, Queen of the Jungle*, her Sheena-like mini-epic. The same year that film was released, Edwige appeared with two other Scream Queens, Rosalba Neri and Ewa Aulin, in *Seducers*, a film that owes its lasting reputation to the casting of these three lovelies together.

SELECTED FILMOGRAPHY:

Sexy Susan Sins Again (Céline, 1968); *Samoa, Queen of the Jungle* (Samoa, 1968); *Five Dolls for an August Moon* (Marie, 1970); *The Strange Vice of Mrs. Wardh* (Julie, 1970); *The Case of the Bloody Iris* (Jennifer Osterman, 1971); *All the Colors of the Dark* (Jane, 1972); *Your Vice is a Locked Room and Only I Have the Key* (Floriana, 1972); *Ubalda, All Naked and Warm* (Ubalda, 1972); *(The) Naughty Nun* (Antonia, 1972); *Long-Thigh* (Giovannona Coscialunga, 1973); *Mean Frank and Crazy Tony* (Orchidea, 1973); *Holy God, Here Comes the Passatore!* (Mora, 1973); *Anna* (Anna, 1973); *Poker in Bed* (Eva, 1974); *Innocence and Desire* (Carmela, 1974); *Lover Boy* (Marianna, 1975); *The School Teacher* (Giovanna, 1975); *Strip Nude for Your Killer* (Magda, 1975); *Sex With a Smile* (Emilia, 1976); *Erotic Exploits of a Sexy Seducer* (Gioia, 1976); *Taxi Girl* (Marcella, 1977); *The Schoolteacher Goes to Boys' High* (Monica, 1978); *Sugar, Honey and Pepper* (Amalia, 1980); *Don't Play with Tigers* (Francesca, 1982); *Phantom of Death* (Hélène Martell, 1988); *Hostel: Part II* (Art Class Professor, 2007).

Anitra Ford

Birthdate: January 13, 1942; somewhere in California.
Birth name: Anitra Weinstein
Height: 5' 9"
Measurements: N/A

SO WHAT'S A NICE JEWISH GIRL like Anitra Weinstein doing in a film like *Invasion of the Bee Girls*? Playing the queen of outer space, that's what. A succulent succubus beams down on earth with plans of transforming everyday housewives into Wasp Women, intent on killing men at the moment of climax. "Just imagine," one guy at a sports bar, whose friend recently enjoyed a dreamy death via just such a deadly dame, sighs: "Coming and going at the same time!" That's the most memorable line in a snappy script by cult sci-fi author Nicholas Meyer. Top-billed in this

EVIL EYES: With her icy glare, cruel mouth, and dark hair, Anitra Ford recalled the Vamps of the silent era in *Invasion of the Bee Girls*.

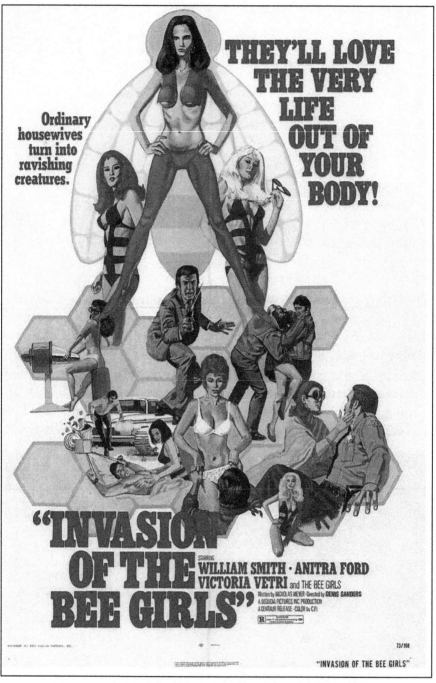

A CULT CLASSIC: The smart script by Nicolas Meyer, as well as the presence of cult queens
Anitra Ford and Victoria Vetri plus the original muscleman action hero,
William Smith, qualified this B-flick as something special.

erotic thriller was blonde Victoria Vetri, cast as the goody-two-shoes secretary who helps our stalwart hero (William Smith) conquer the Amazon women. Memorably evil was Ford as the demure but deadly Queen Bee, whose love—or lust—spells instant death.

Anitra's incidental TV work included appearances on such shows as *The Odd Couple* (1970), *Columbo* (1971), *Love, American Style* (1971), *Mannix* (1971), *Banacek* (1972), and most notably as the original villainess to face off with Wonder Woman (played by Cathy Lee Crosby before Lynda Carter assumed that role) as the evil Ahnjayla in 1974's made-for-TV movie version. That medium's mainstream viewers best recall Anitra as one of the original glamour girls (the other was Janice Pennington) on *The Price Is Right* in 1972. In films, Anitra's cult status was ensured by an appearance in one of the best remembered of all Philippines-lensed women in prison pictures, *The Big Bird Cage*. Director Jack Hill drew a charmingly goofy star turn from Anitra as the sex-crazed member among the mostly bare-breasted beauties who escape into the jungle. When Anitra hit 30 and such ingenue roles dried up, she faced the choice so many flash-in-the-pan starlets must: go with sex, drugs and rock 'n' roll until death arrives at an early age or enjoy an upscale life as a dealer of prime real estate. Wisely, Anitra chose the latter. She now resides in gorgeous Santa Barbara by the sea.

SELECTED FILMOGRAPHY:

The Love Machine (Model, 1971); *The Big Bird Cage* (Terry, 1972); *Where Does It Hurt?* (Beautiful Brunette, 1972); *Messiah of Evil* (Laura, 1973); *Stacey* (Tish Chambers, 1973); *Invasion of the Bee Girls* (Dr. Susan Harris, 1973); *The Longest Yard* (Melissa, 1974).

DEAD RINGER: Scilla Gabel and Sophia Loren might have been twins separated at birth; in this shot, Gabel could easily pass for Loren in one of the former's rare blonde roles.

Scilla Gabel

Birthdate: January 4, 1938; Rimini, Emilia-Romagna, Italy
Birth name: Gianfranca Gabellini
Height: 5' 8 ¾"
Measurements: 38 ½ – 24 - 36

THREE YEARS PREVIOUS TO THE RELEASE of the first James Bond film, *Dr. No* (1962), audiences attending Saturday Matinee Cinema caught a preview of the shape of things to come. From the moment that *Tarzan's Greatest Adventure* began, it was clear this was no ordinary studio-bound series entry. Crisply lensed on convincing locations, the movie featured Sean Connery in a role that soon helped cinch him as 007, here playing the roguish villain. Also on hand: Scilla Gabel, who in retrospect appears to be setting the pace for Bond's beloved bad-girls: openly sexy, no-nonsense about getting what she wants, clearly involved with her partner in crime in a way that no wicked woman in a mainstream action movie had been before. Like a Bond bad-girl, she suffers an unpleasant demise: falling into a trap set for Tarzan, a deep pit with spears pointed upward, while fleeing a jungle cat.

That Scilla never actually played a Bond bad-girl is a shame; also a wonder. She so clearly was born for such a part! She did, however, play parallel roles. *Modesty Blaise*, based on a pop-art comic strip, cast Gabel (opposite good-agent Monica Vitti) as the bikini-clad bad-girl who, at one point, dispatches a desperate victim by strangling him within the vise of her lovely legs, gleefully tossing the body into the Mediterranean below. This, before heading off for a light lunch, champagne, and a casual day of sun-bathing. The titular good girl eliminates her arch enemy in a catfight conclusion that resembles the mano-e-mano final duels in most other 1960s spy films. Many aspiring Italian starlets had cosmetic surgery to make them look more like Sophia Loren. In a fascinating irony, Scilla—born a double for Sophia—went under the knife several times to make her look *less* like the superstar in hopes of forging a unique screen identity. Beginning at age 17, she had worked as Sophia's stand-in during shoots. Producers encouraged Scilla to "go for it" on the merits of her face and body. Photo layouts (she would appear in *Playboy* in 1963) revealed her hypnotic blue eyes and, whenever she was not instructed to "go blonde" for a film, ultra-radiant red hair.

Scilla's definitive screen appearance occurred in what may have been the most ambitious of all Italian-lensed international Peplums, *(The Last Days of) Sodom and Gomorrah*, directed by two top action experts in collaboration, Robert Aldrich and Sergio Leone. The film opens on a moving-camera shot, up and over an orgy that has recently concluded. Women's scantily-clad bodies, draped with near-see-through-veils, came closer to presenting nudity onscreen than mainstream audiences had heretofore seen. Scilla's slave girl rises and slips away, she an ancient-world spy, providing information to Sodom's enemies. Caught, she is tortured to death in a uniquely sadistic manner: forced into a cage with a blind muscleman. He wears a deadly outfit that allows sharp spikes to appear from beneath

RAPE OF THE SABINE WOMEN: A rather non-gallant Roger Moore does precisely as the title says to Scilla, only to abandon her in favor of another beauty.

ALL THIS AND BRAINS, TOO: According to those knew her way back when, Scilla Gabel was not only one of the most beautiful girls in international films of the Sixties but also one of the brightest.

his leather-peplum garment every time he breathes. He has been ordered to pursue Scilla around the cage until he finally corners, and embraces, the girl, dispatching her with a sensuous hug, as the evil queen (Anouk Aimee) and her lover brother (Stanley Baker) gaze on.

In the spring of 1968, at age thirty, Gabel realized and accepted that

Loren-Lollabrigida level superstardom was not going to happen. She married Piero Schivazappa; they had one child and, at the time of writing, remain a couple. She bid goodbye to spy-cinema and the sand-and-sandals epics, opening a business, pursuing theatre work, eventually winning a law degree at prestigious Oxford University in England.

SELECTED FILMOGRAPHY:

Girls of the Night (Lola, 1958); *Legs of Gold* (Gianna, 1958); *The White Warrior* (Princess Maria, 1959); *Tarzan's Greatest Adventure* (Toni, 1959); *Call Girls of Rome* (Patrizia, 1960); *Queen of the Pirates* (Isabella, 1960); *Mill of the Stone Women* (Elfie Wahl, 1960); *The Fruit is Ripe* (Kissa, 1961); *Romulus and the Sabine Women* (Dusia, 1961); *Colossus of the Arena* (Thalima, 1962); *Sodom and Gomorrah* (Tamar, 1962); *La Salamandre D'Or* (Beatrice, 1962); *Knights of Terror* (Cristina, 1963); *Seven Slaves Against Rome* (Claudia, 1964); *The Revenge of Spartacus* (Cinzia, 1964); *Son of Cleopatra* (Livia, 1964); *Modesty Blaise* (Melina, 1966).

Eunice Gayson

Birthdate: March 17, 1928; Croydon, London, UK
Birth name: Eunice Sargaison
Height: 5' 4"
Measurements: 34 (B) – 21 - 34

QUICK: WHO PLAYED THE FIRST BOND GIRL in the 007 movie series? If you answered Ursula Andress, you were wrong. While that Amazonian beauty owns the distinction of being the first "final girl," several earlier lethal ladies preceded her mid-movie entrance. Early-on, there was Sylvia Trench, something of a mystery woman who happens to be "hangin' out" at the upscale casino during the first post-title sequence. Sean Connery is introduced as the continuing lead. Eunice Gayson, the actress playing Sylvia Trench, appears icily elegant, an aristocratic woman who may or may not be married but who goes her own way. She maintains a remote, unattainable image to all men present but Bond. Cougar-like, she notices him at once, drawn by his sense of power, command, self-assurance. When he wins big, she leans close, whispering: "I admire your luck, Mr...." Connery then says, for the first time ever, "Bond. James Bond." Later, when Bond retires to his room, Sylvia Trench is waiting, having decided that he shall be crowned a winner in every sense of the term, including her as the ultimate prize.

In Broccoli's original conception, Sylvia was supposed to appear near the beginning of each following Bond film, the one woman he apparently always returns to. Essentially, this was to have been the 1960s' first onscreen portrait of a post-Sexual Revolution relationship. That seemed the case when *From Russia With Love* appeared, the two picking up pretty much where they'd left off. After that, the concept was scrapped. Why? Several veterans of the series insist Sylvia was eliminated at the insistence

THE ORIGINAL THREE BOND GIRLS: *Dr. No*, the first in the official series, introduced Sean Connery (third from left) as 007 along with, from left to right, Eunice Gayson, Tania Mallet, and Ursula Andress.

of Guy Hamilton when he took over as director. Gayson, who had originally tested for the Moneypenny role, disappeared not only from the series but from sight, so far as films were concerned. She did appear in such Bond-inspired TV series as *The Saint* starring future Bond Roger Moore, and *The Avengers*. As to her background, following a successful stage career, Eunice entered the Brit film industry, mostly appearing in conventional fare that made more extensive use of her exquisite appearance than her acting abilities. Several films qualified her for cult stardom even before Bond Girl. *Down Amongst the Z Men* was the first screen vehicle for The Goons, who had become all the rage on London-based TV. *Revenge of Frankenstein* rates as one of the earliest Hammer horror flicks to be shot in color, creating the atmosphere for which that company would be reknown. And *Zarak*, a sumptuously produced costumer co-starring Gayson with Anita Ekberg and Victor Mature, had been produced by Broccoli, initiating the working relationship.

Eunice had a child with her first husband, Brian Jackson. After the divorce, she married Leigh Vance, though that too fizzled. Later, despite her excellent diction, Eunice was, for reasons unknown, dubbed in *Dr. No* by actress Nikki Van der Zyl. Official records suggest it's her own voice in *From Russia With Love*. Early training had included opera; later in life she appeared in London productions of popular musicals *The Sound of Music* and *Into the Woods*.

FIRST CONQUEST: Early in *Dr. No*, James Bond meets, then beds, Sylvia Trench (Eunice Gayson).

THE SECOND TIME AROUND: Shortly after the opening of *From Russia With Love*, 007's follow-up affair with Sylvia is interrupted by a phoned-in assignment.

SELECTED FILMOGRAPHY:

My Brother Jonathan (Pretty Girl, 1948); *Melody in the Dark* (Pat Evans, 1949); *Dance Hall* (Mona, 1950); *To Have and to Hold* (Peggy, 1951); *Miss Robin Hood* (Pam, 1952); *Down Amongst the Z Men* (Gorgeous Girl, 1952); *Dance Little Lady* (Adele, 1954); *Out of the Clouds* (Penny Henson, 1955); *Zarak* (Cathy Ingram, 1956); *Light Fingers* (Rose Levenham, 1957); *The Revenge of Frankenstein* (Margaret Conrad, 1958); *Dr. No* (Sylvia Trench, 1962); *From Russia With Love* (Sylvia Trench, 1963).

Laura Gemser

aka: MOIRA CHEN
Birthdate: October 5, 1950; Surabya, Java, Indonesia
Birth name: Laurette Marcia Gemser
Height: N/A
Measurements: N/A

ONE EVENING IN 1983, millions of Americans watched the network
TV premiere of *Love Is Forever*, co-produced by Michael Landon (of *Bo-
nanza* and *Little House on the Prairie* fame), he playing the lead. Filmed
on location in Thailand, the movie told the fact-based story of Australian
journalist John Everingham. Following the Pathet Lao takeover of Laos,
Everingham escaped to the West shortly before his planned execution.
But he left behind the Eurasian woman with whom he had fallen in love
and vowed to return, find Keo, and somehow bring her to the free world.
A slender, soft spoken Eurasian actress played Keo. Family audiences fell
under the hypnotic spell of Moira Chen even as much as Everingham had
with Keo. For some viewers, though, a sense of déjà vu set in: Where have
I seen this girl before? In fact, this was the notorious Laura Gemser, who
had appeared in some of the most graphically violent and sexual grindhouse films turned out during the previous decade.

At age four, Laura had traveled from her native Indonesia with her
family to Europe, growing up in Utrecht, a city in the Netherlands. This led
to the false impression that, despite her mixed racial background, Gemser
was a Dutch citizen. Originally she studied at the Artibus Art School in
hope of becoming a fashion designer. Her stunning looks caused her to
be picked for modeling assignments. While in Belgium, she accepted an
offer to appear in a sexually explicit film that was intended to capture the
New Morality of the early 1970s, when young people—particularly young

215

GOING BACK TO THE BOOK: Though the first actress to play Emmanuelle onscreen was a Frenchwoman, the casting of multi-national (and part Asian) Laura Gemser (as 'Emanuelle') came far closer to the novel's central character.

women—would no longer be stigmatized for sexual promiscuity. Sylvia Kristel now appeared in the *Emmanuelle* movies, based on a book by Emmanuelle Arsan, aka Marayat Bibidh, aka Marayat Rollet-Andriane, who happened to be Asian, as was her most (in)famous character. That ethnicity had been eliminated from the Just Jaeckin film. Its success led

THE GENTLER SIDE OF A SEX SYMBOL: Laura Gemser appears more lighthearted and playful than usual in this advertising poster for Eva Negra.

exploitation filmmakers to offer Laura her own franchise as 'Black Emanuelle.' They escaped potential lawsuits by leaving off one of the m's in the character's name. Hardly black, the elegant woman of color (far closer to Arsan's conception of her character than Krystel) not only headlined her own series but joined Kristel for an intense girl-girl lovemaking scene in the second (and best) entry in the official *Emmanuelle* series.

Initially, the *Black Emanuelle* films, like their 'white' parallel franchise, were intended as realistic studies of a young woman finding sexual liberation. By mid-decade, such films had run their course owing to oversaturation of similar stuff. To survive as a series, Black Emanuelle was transformed into a combination of super agent and femme fatale, enjoying outrageous adventures (involving much violence as well as sex) all over the world, particularly in exotic locations. Reaching a mature age, at which Laura was no longer comfortable doing porn, soft or hard, Gemser returned to her original dream of fashion design, working in that capacity for film productions. When her husband, actor Gabriele Tinti, passed away in 1991, Laura settled into a quiet life in Rome, Italy.

DIDN'T ANYONE EVER TELL YOU THAT SMOKING IS BAD FOR YOUR HEALTH?:
Let's at least hope that Laura has something less dangerous than tobacco inside that paper.

SELECTED FILMOGRAPHY:

Black Emanuelle (Mae Jordan/Emanuelle, 1975); *Emmanuelle II* (Masseuse, 1976); *Emanuelle in Bangkok* (Emanuelle, 1976); *Emmanuelle on Taboo Island* (Haydee, 1976); *Voyage of the Damned* (Eurasian Beauty, 1976); *Vow of Chastity* (Maid, 1976); *Black Cobra Woman* (Eva, 1976); *Black Emmanuelle, White Emmanuelle* (Laura, 1977); *Emanuelle in Amer-*

ica (Emanuelle, 1977); *Crime Busters* (Susy Lee, 1977); *Confessions of Emanuelle* (Emanuelle, 1977); *Emanuelle and the Cannibals* (Emanuelle, 1977); *Emanuelle and the White Slave Trade* (Emanuelle, 1978); *Private Collections* (Siren, 1979); *Emanuelle: Queen Bitch* (Emmanuella Brindisi, 1980); *Sexy Nights of the Living Dead* (Luna, 1980); *Love Camp* (The Divine One, 1981); *The Bushido Blade* (Tomoe, 1981); *The Dirty Seven* (Sheila, 1982); *Caligula: The Untold Story* (Miriam, 1982); *Horror Safari* (Maria, 1982); *Ator, the Fighting Eagle* (Indun, 1982); *Love Is Forever* (Keo, 1982); *Women's Prison Massacre* (Emanuelle, 1983); *The Pleasure* (Haunani, 1985); *Eleven Days, Eleven Nights* (Dorothy Tipton, 1987); *Dirty Love* (Massage Girl, 1988); *Reflections of Light* (Chiara, 1988); *Metamorphosis* (Prostitute, 1990); *The Hobgoblin* (Grimilde, 1990); *Quest for the Mighty Sword* (Grimilde, 1990); *Passion's Flower* (Hooker, 1991).

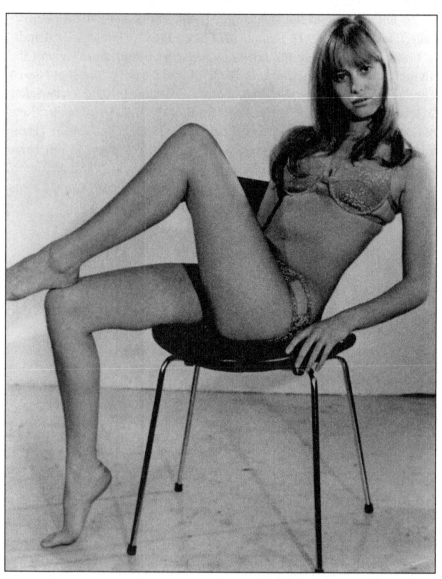

SITTING PRETTY: Susan George shows off The Stuff in an early publicity picture.

Susan George

Birthdate: July 26, 1950; Surbiton/Surrey, UK
Birth name: Susan Melody George
Height: 5' 5"
Measurements: N/A

THERE WAS NEVER ANY QUESTION that this gorgeous teenager would pursue acting. Young Susan went so far as to purposefully flunk herself out of school so as to be available for drama lessons. Early English acting jobs included a continuing role on the TV series *Swallows and Amazons* (Kitty Walker, 1963). Success as a youthful (occasionally underage) sexpot was immediate, though Susan understood that such typecasting would preclude the more serious roles she hoped to land. While such a situation did interfere with her desire to play a variety of three-dimensional roles, which often went to lookalikes Susannah York and Sarah Miles, Susan's bad-girl parts, coming as they did in rapid succession, gained a cult following, something those more mainstream stars did not acquire.

Her edgy image was solidified as early as 1967, when the former child actress appeared in *The Sorcerers* as a wide-eyed Trilby type who finds herself under the cruel domination of a Svengali-like hypnotist (Boris Karloff). In *The Strange Affair* George was cast as a Lolita-like seductress who destroys the life and career of a heretofore straight-and-narrow policeman. A Pretty Baby syndrome was repeated in *All Neat in Black Stockings*, Susan playing a Mod girl who drives London's Teddy Boys mad with desire, and *Lola*, a Nabokovian piece in which her child-woman marries an adult male (Charles Bronson) who writes pornographic novels. *Die Screaming Marianne* offered a Brit variation on the Italian Giallos, with George clad only in a black bikini while undergoing ritualistic torture.

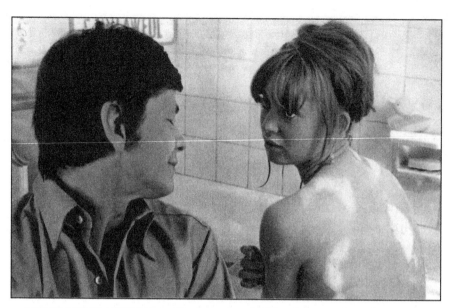

LOLITA LOVES AGAIN: Susan George revives the Nymphet image from the previous decade in this early 1970s film opposite older man Charles Bronson.

On a higher level, there was *Straw Dogs*, Sam Peckinpah's contemporary thriller which critic Pauline Kael dubiously praised as "a fascist masterpiece," Susan playing Amy, the flirtatious wife of an intellectual (Dustin Hoffman). She seduces or is raped by a previous Neanderthal boyfriend; part of the film's horror comes in the viewer's inability to grasp whether the violence is imposed on an unwilling victim or if, as that now politically incorrect phrase would have, 'she was asking for it.' *Dirty Mary, Crazy Larry*, an unexpected phenomenon on the rural Drive-In circuit, teamed her with Peter Fonda in a crime thriller best described as a combination of *Bonnie and Clyde* (1967) and *Easy Rider* (1969). Memorable in the George canon was a period piece (set in 1840), *Mandingo*. Based on a controversial pulp-fiction Bus Station Book from the 1950s by Kyle Onstott, previously deemed unfilmable, this gleefully decadent exploitation flick cast Susan as Blanche, the sex-crazed daughter in law of an Old South plantation owner (James Mason) who, to spite her inattentive husband, not only seduces but becomes pregnant by a strapping slave (Ken Norton).

As the next decade began, Sue appeared in *Enter the Ninja*, one of the first films to present Ninjutsu to the American audience. As to her personal life, romantic relationships included Charles, Prince of Wales and the American pop singer Jack Jones. When she did marry, to actor Simon

AN ANSWER TO GONE WITH THE WIND: The most anti-romantic book written about the Old South, considered unfilmable in the 1950s, reached the screen in the early 1970s as a result of the Motion Picture Production Code finally being scuttled.

THE YOUNG AND THE RECKLESS: Susan George plays a White Trash variation on Bonnie Parker in the irresistibly titled road movie *Dirty Mary, Crazy Larry*.

MacCorkindale, the union was serious, lasting from 1984 until his passing in 2010. Since then, Susan has kept a low profile, breeding horses via her business, Georgian Arabians. She does still accept acting jobs if the quality of a project is worthy of her time. These include the role of Margaret on *Eastenders* (2001). Also, she can be credited as a film producer thanks to *Stealing Heaven* (1988).

Trivia: Her early film *Cup Fever* was not about bra size but race-car driving.

SELECTED FILMOGRAPHY:

Cup Fever (Vicky Davis, 1965); *Davy Jones' Locker* (Susan, 1966); *The Sorcerers* (Audrey Woods, 1967); *Billion Dollar Brain* (Blonde Russian, 1967); *Up the Junction* (Joyce, 1968); *The Strange Affair* (Fred, 1968); *The Looking Glass War* (Susan, 1969); *All Neat in Black Stockings* (Jill, 1969); *Lola* (Twinky, 1970); *Sudden Terror* (Pippa, 1970); *Die Screaming Marianne* (Marianne, 1971); *Fright* (Amanda, 1971); *Straw Dogs* (Amy, 1971); *Dirty Mary, Crazy Larry* (Mary Coombs, 1974); *Mandingo* (Blanche Maxwell, 1975); *Out of Season* (Joanna, 1975); *A Small Town in Texas* (Mary Lee, 1976); *Tintorera: Killer Shark* (Gabriella, 1977); *Tomorrow Never Comes* (Janie, 1978); *Enter the Ninja* (Mary Ann, 1981); *Venom* (Louise, 1981); *The House Where Evil Dwells* (Laura, 1982); *Kiss My Grits* (Baby, 1982); *The Jigsaw Man* (Penelope, 1984); *Lightning, The White Stallion* (Madame Reme, 1986); *City of Life* (Constance, 2009).

LADY IN A TRENCHCOAT: Gila Golan is the spy who loved to thrill and then kill her prey in *Our Man Flint*.

Gila Golan

Birthdate: Unknown; somewhere in Poland
Birth name: Unknown
Height: N/A
Measurements: N/A

GILA GOLAN MAY BE THE ONLY international sex symbol of the 1960s whose greatest on-camera moment appeared not in a movie but on a late night talk show. In 1966, she appeared on *The Tonight Show* with Johnny Carson to plug her new spy comedy *Our Man Flint*. Also on the evening's schedule was James Garner, a tall, dark, handsome actor. In those pre-politically correct days, it was acceptable, almost de rigeur, for a glamour girl to arrive decked in fur. This Israeli beauty took everyone's breath away by strolling onstage in one of the most immense, sleek wraps anyone had seen. "Does it bite?" James Garner, almost at a loss for words, joked. "No," Gila sighed, eyeing the good-looking man as if he were prey, "but *I* do!"

Golan is unique in that the plot of her life took more strange, unpredictable turns than any of the films or TV shows she appeared in during her brief fling with international stardom. The precise date of her birth is unknown, not only to the public but Golan herself. That's true too of her birth name. In 1943, a lost Jewish child of the Holocaust was discovered either wandering in the streets of a small village or packed up in a blanket near a train station (here, details vary with the source). A kind-hearted Catholic man took the little girl home, hid her from the Nazis for the duration of the war, and brought her (now called Zoshia Zavatski) with him and his famly to Krakow when they moved there. Eventually the family was contacted by a group of Jewish nationals, searching for such children in the hope of relocating each with a Jewish family. The girl who would grow up to be Gila Golan, movie star, soon found herself relocated in a Czech refugee center, then spirited away to France. Here, in St. Pierre, she lived in a Jewish boarding school while authorities attempted to track down any still living relatives. That proved impossible, though Gila found herself relocated once again, this time to the land still officially referred to as Palestine, soon to be re-named Israel. Here, she lived with another adoptive family, this time in Haifa. Following her working period on a

IT'S ALL IN THE MIND: As Flint, James Coburn plays mind games with Gila (playing Gila), turning an enemy agent into an ally.

Kibbutz, followed by a move (her choice, this time) to Tel Aviv, she worked as a telephone operator. While going about her humble daily business, the young woman happened to meet an American photographer who asked if he might take several shots of the teenager. Shortly, she found herself entered in the Miss Israel contest, where Gila placed as first runner up to Aliza Gur, who likewise would decorate several 1960s glitz-cinema films. At this time, she picked her own name: Golan is a key site in Israel; Gila in Hebrew means joy.

Shortly, she signed with Columbia Pictures. This was an era in which women with exotic good looks were quickly herded into spy movies. Shortly, she and James Coburn were teamed as a Bond-like glib hero and an impossibly gorgeous enemy agent turned lover and co-conspirator in the first of the notably shallow *Flint* films. Golan's next venture only added to a growing cult status when she was cast as the heroine in *The Valley of Gwangi*, a dinosaur vs. cowboys mini-epic featuring F/X by the master himself, Ray Harryhausen. In addition to her few movies, Gila appeared on network TV several times, playing Constanze 'Tantsy' Lipp on "The Safe House" episode of *Kraft Suspense Theatre* in 1965 and Princess Tarji on *I Dream of Jeannie* a year later. For some time, Golan lived in Seattle, which she thought of as her American home when away from Israel. Her second marriage was to the entrepreneur Matthew B. Rosenhaus. The couple had three daughters: Sarita, Hedy, and Loretta. Gila abandoned her nominal film work to live in style, remarrying after Rosenhaus' passing.

SELECTED FILMOGRAPHY:

Ship of Fools (Elsa, 1965); *Our Man Flint* (Gila, 1966); *Three on a Couch* (Anna, 1966); *Catch As Catch Can* (Emma, 1968); *The Valley of Gwangi* (T.J., 1969); *L'allenatore nel Pallone* (Beautiful Woman, 1984).

QUEEN OF THE URBAN ACTION FLICK: Pam Grier had no competition at all as first lady of those movies that were booked into 'downtown' (i.e., ghetto) theatres.

Pam Grier

Birthdate: May 26, 1949; Winston-Salem, NC
Birth name: Pamela Suzette Grier
Height: 5' 8"
Measurements: 38DD – 29 - 36 ½

BACK IN THE EARLY-TO-MID 1970S, terrible things happened to anyone who made Pam Grier angry. In *Friday Foster*, she played a young black activist hoping to drive the drug dealers out of an inner city. A slick, handsome white businessman (Peter Brown) has been conning Friday into believing he's one of the good guys, also hoping to land her in bed. Then she discovers the superficial charmer is actually a drug kingpin and source of bad vibes in her community. Pam has her back-up boys hold him tight, overseeing his castration. It doesn't end there: Friday then sends his separated parts, in vinegar, to his nymphomaniacal girlfriend. That's justice, Grier style.

A quarter-century earlier, Pam had been an army brat growing up in the South, her family often plagued by illnesses, particularly cancer. Cousin to football great (and sometimes actor) Roosevelt Grier, Pam attended UCLA, supporting her tuition by working as a back-up singer to Bobby Womack. Roger Corman discovered the young beauty contest winner working as a receptionist at his indie American-International. Pam's sexiness combined with an aura of strength was precisely right for the years in which The Women's Movement had its greatest impact on American society. Off she flew to the Philippines, where Pam starred in a pair of the highly popular (with the grindhouse and Drive-In movie crowd) 'women in chains' movies, *The Big Doll House* and *The Big Bird Cage*. Another exploitation filmmaker, Jack Hill, featured Pam in *Coffy* as a young beauty who works as a respected nurse by day, then heads out vigilante style to kill without mercy the drug dealers (black as well as white) who prey on the inner city. By this time, the old Production Code (which until 1967 insisted that at the end of any movie a person must pay for his or her crimes) was gone, so Coffy strutted away from her latest bloodbath (blasting her long-time lover with a shotgun after realizing that he's a dealer himself—and, worse still, two-timing her, and with a blonde at that!).

In follow-ups like *Foxy Brown* and *'Sheba, Baby'*, Pam played similar roles. Feminists chose to honor the obvious strength of Pam's characters by putting her on the cover of *Ms.* magazine, 1975, the first African-American woman to receive that honor. Meanwhile, though, the urban-action film had run its course. Soon Pam was lucky to pick up cameo roles in such 1980s films as *Fort Apache, The Bronx* starring Paul Newman. Then, along came Quentin. Although she auditioned for various female roles in *Pulp Fiction* (1994), Tarantino put off casting Grier until she could play the lead in a large scale thriller that paid homage to the black exploitation he had so loved in his youth, particularly those starring the first lady of urban action. *Jackie Brown* proved a major comeback vehicle, with the

THE ULTIMATE IN BLACK EXPLOITATION FLICKS: The lobby poster for *Coffy* revealed all the elements that its target audience expected in such entertainment.

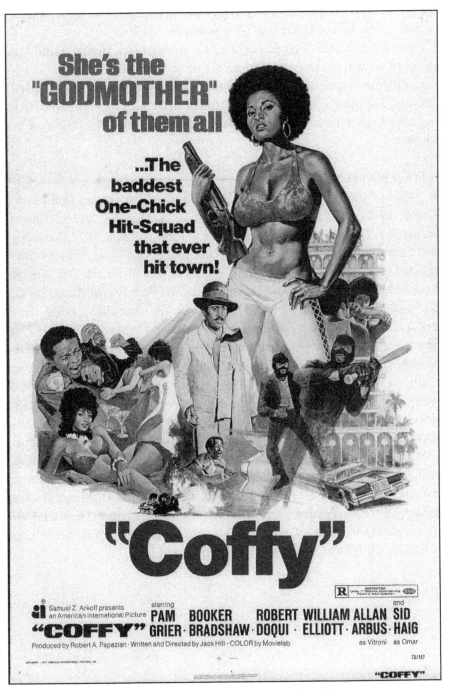

MEET FRIDAY FOSTER: As the decade wore on, Grier played a less intense, more mainstream oriented version of her classic character Coffy.

still unmarried Pam having no trouble finding constant work afterwards, including The White Queen on TV's *Smallville*.

She once stated: "People see me as a strong black (female) and I'm proud of that, but I'm (actually) a mix of several races: Hispanic, Chinese, Filipino. My dad was black, my mom Cheyenne Indian. I was raised Catholic, baptized a Methodist, and almost married a Muslim. So (when you have such a life history) you (learn to) look at things beyond race or religion."

SELECTED FILMOGRAPHY:

Beyond the Valley of the Dolls (Pretty Girl, 1970); *The Big Doll House* (Grear, 1971); *Women in Cages* (Alabama, 1971); *Cool Breeze* (Mona, 1972); *The Twilight People* (Ayesa the Panther Woman, 1972); *The Big Bird Cage* (Blossom, 1972); *Hit Man* (Gozelda, 1972); *Black Mama White Mama* (Lee Daniels, 1973); *Coffy* (Coffy, 1973); *Scream Blacula Scream* (Lisa Fortier, 1973); *The Arena* (Mamawi, 1974); *Foxy Brown* (Foxy, 1974); *'Sheba, Baby'* (Sheba Shayne, 1975); *Bucktown* (Aretha, 1975); *Friday Foster* (Friday, 1975); *Drum* (Regine, 1976); *Greased Lightning* (Mary, 1977); *Fort Apache the Bronx* (Charlotte, 1981); *Tough Enough* (Myra, 1983); *Something Wicked This Way Comes* (The Dust Witch, 1983); *Stand Alone* (Cathryn Bolan, 1985); *The Vindicator* (Hunter, 1986); *On the Edge* (Cora, 1986); *The Allnighter* (Sgt. McLeesh, 1987); *Above the Law* (Delores 'Jacks' Jackson, 1988); *The Package* (Ruth Butler, 1989); *Class of 1999* (Ms. Connors, 1990); *Bill & Ted's Bogus Journey* (Ms. Wardroe, 1991); *Posse* (Phoebe, 1993); *Original Gangstas* (Laurie Thompson, 1996); *Mars Attacks!* (Louise Williams, 1996); *Escape from L.A.* (Hershe Las Palmas, 1996); *Strip Search* (Janette, 1997); *Fakin' Da Funk* (Annabelle Lee, 1997); *Jackie Brown* (Jackie Brown, 1997); *Jawbreaker* (Vera Cruz, 1999); *No Tomorrow* (Diane, 1999); *Slow Burn* (Della, 2000); *Ghosts of Mars* (Braddock, 2001); *The Adventures of Pluto Nash* (Flura, 2002); *Mafia* (Womack, 2012).

Aliza Gur

Birthdate: April 1, 1944; Ramat Gan, Israel
Birth name: Aliza Gurgross
Height: N/A
Measurements: N/A

SOME OF THE GREATEST CAT-FIGHTS in movie history appear in the films of the 1960s. Here was a way to, shall we say, stimulate an audience while remaining within the boundaries of what was then permissible, even as any such line began to dissolve in the dust set flying by ever more edgy screen epics. One of the first, and best, occurs in *From Russia With Love*. 007 (Connery) is the guest at a gypsy camp for a wild celebration where, as its turns out, two of the fiery women present desire the same man. At a show for the dinner guests, they fight it out, scratching and screaming, wrestling, rolling around on the ground—all to determine which girl gets to go to bed the evening's prized male. The dueling gypsy girls are played by Martine Beswick and Aliza Gur. The latter was born in Israel during the World War II years.

Her Jewish-German parents, sensing that the rise of Hitler would soon spell disaster, fled and resettled in Palestine, establishing a home in Mandatory. As a girl, Aliza won the title Miss Haifa while studying at that University, then went on to become Miss Israel in 1960. Eventually she appeared as one of the top fifteen contestants in the Miss Universe pageant. Aliza's earliest film credit reaches way back: She was among the multitude of extras in Cecil B. DeMille's *The Ten Commandments* (1956), with Charlton Heston as Moses. She headed for California, hoping to crash into the Biz and, with those darkly-dangerous looks, picked up undemanding roles as femme fatales in spy-oriented TV shows like *Get Smart* and *The Wild Wild West*, both 1965, as well as the female lead in several

AN EXPORT FROM ISRAEL: A beauty contest winner in her homeland, Aliza Gur
went on to become a minor figure in 1960s spy cinema.

Eurospy flicks. Twice married, twice divorced, Aliza continues to live in
Beverly Hills. Always, she has been active in American organizations that
support and raise funds for the state of Israel.

   Trivia: During the Miss Universe competition of 1960, Gur's room-
mate was Daniella Bianchi, the lead in *From Russia With Love*.

A CLASSIC CAT FIGHT: One highlight of *From Russia With Love* was getting to see Aliza Gur (left) and Martine Beswick (right) attempt to tear each other's hair out.

SELECTED FILMOGRAPHY:

The Ten Commandments (Israeli child, uncredited, 1956); *From Russia With Love* (Vida, 1963); *Night Train to Paris* (Catherine Carrel, 1964); *Agent for H.A.R.M.* (Spy/Agent, 1966); *Kill a Dragon* (Tisa, 1967); *Beast of Morocco* (Mariska, 1968); *Tarzan and the Jungle Boy* (Myrna, 1968).

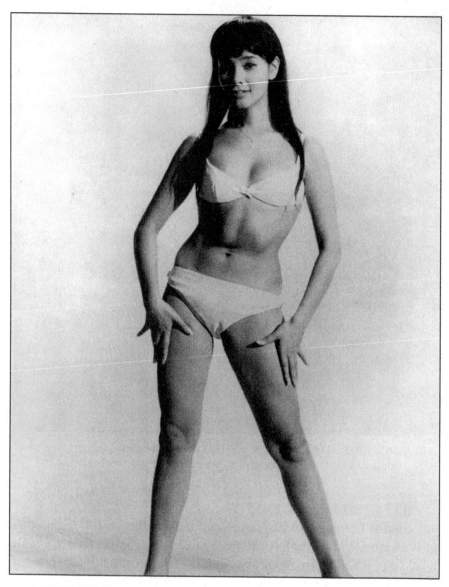

A FRESH BREEZE FROM THE FAR EAST: Mie Hama displays her perfect figure in the de rigeur bikini bathing suit in a publicity still for *You Only Live Twice*.

Mie Hama

Birthdate: November 20, 1943; Tokyo, Japan
Birth name: 浜美枝,
Height: 5' 4'1/2"
Measurements: 35 ½ – 23 - 35

MIE HAMA'S FAIRYTALE-LIKE ENTRANCE into Tokyo's booming post-World War II movie business is fact: The gorgeous girl worked as a fare collector on a city bus when film producer Tomoyuki Tanaka spotted her. Shortly, he installed Mie as the new heartthrob of Toho studios. *Godhira*, re-christened *Godzilla* for American audiences, had been a surprise commercial smash, opening the doors for more. Durable U.S. creation *King Kong* was lured out of retirement. As a man in a monkey suit bouncing around on tabletop models rather than the time-consuming stop-action photography of the 1933 original, the big ape went mano-e-mano with Godzie; Hama was the lethal lovely caught between their pugilistic endeavors. Here she would achieve a moment of screen history: Between Fay Wray and Jessica Lange, Mie was the single woman to be held in Kong's furry paw. Perhaps her most remarkable project was the film that, in the United States, would be known as *What's Up, Tiger Lily?* Woody Allen had just recently been disappointed with the results of his first screenplay, *What's New, Pussycat?* (1965), intended as a small, smart comedy, under producer Charles K. Feldman ballooning into a huge spectacle. Woody backed off mainstream Hollywood to do a small indie film. Employing footage from one of Japan's low-budget 007 imitations, Allen added new plot plus off-the-wall dialogue, performed on the soundtrack by fellow New York hipsters, transforming a run-of-the-mill spy saga into an edgy comedy classic. Mie, paired with Akiko Wakabayashi, is one of two gorgeous double-crossing secret agent girls embroiled in the case of a missing Chicken Salad recipe. Shortly, they would appear together again in *You Only Live Twice*.

The following year, she met up with Kong again (during his attempt at 'escape'), this time playing the bad-girl. Madam Piranha allowed Mie to incarnate onscreen one of the legendary images of an Asian woman as femme fatale, a tradition that ran from Su Maru and The Dragon Lady

GIRLS WITH GUNS: The young beauties of spy cinema, Mie Hama included, made clear that the era of pretty, passive female leads in a film were quickly coming to an end.

in Milt Canuff's Sunday comic strip *Terry and the Pirates*. Nothing lasts forever, and that includes the golden age of Japanese-made sci-fi and spy movies. Mie Hama disappeared along with the films that helped make her famous.

Trivia: During the shooting of *You Only Live Twice*, Mie became seriously ill and could not film an underwater diving sequence. Her double was Diane Cilento, then-wife of star Sean Connery. Originally, Mie and Akiko were cast in one another's roles. They were switched shortly before shooting began as Mie had trouble learning English and the role she eventually played called for less spoken dialogue.

SELECTED FILMOGRAPHY:

Jiyûgaoka fujin (Sachiko, 1960); *Blueprint for Murder* (Kyôko, 1961); *The Merciless Trap* (Setsuko, 1961); *Playboy President* (Yukiko, 1961); *King Kong vs. Godzilla* (Fumiko Sakurai, 1962); *47 Samurai* (Woman 1, 1962); *Attack Squadron!* (Beautiful Girl, 1963); *500,000* (Igorot, 1963); *The Lost World of Sinbad* (Princess Yaya, 1963); *Yearning* (Ruriko, 1964); *The Sandal Keeper* (Kanako, 1964); *The World's Most Beautiful Swindlers* (Geisha, 1964); *You Can Succeed, Too* (Beniko, 1964); *Ankokugai Gekitotsu* (Chikako, 1965); *Key of Keys* (Miichin, 1965); *Ironfinger* (Yumi Sawada, 1965); *Kiganjô no bôken* (The Innkeeper's Daughter, 1966); *What's Up, Tiger Lily?* (Teri Yaki, 1966); You *Only Live Twice* (Kissy Suzuki, 1967); *King Kong Escapes* (Madame Piranha, 1967); *Monsieur Zivaco* (Nana, 1967); *Two in the Shadow* (Teruko, 1967); *Night of the Seagull* (The Woman, 1968); *The Clean-up* (Akiko, 1969).

IS THERE LIFE AFTER THE EISENHOWER ERA? There would be for Joy Harmon, who first appeared in 1950s rock and roll films but would enjoy her brief moment of onscreen immortality in the following decade.

Joy Harmon

Birthdate: May 1, 1940; Flushing, New York
(Note: some sources insist Joy was born in St. Louis, MO)
Birth name: Patricia Joy Harmon
Height: 5' 5"
Measurements: 41 – 22 - 36

IN 1950, GROUCHO MARX was so impressed with this ten-year-old's burgeoning bustline that he invited the pre-teen to be a guest on *You Bet Your Life* so that the whole world might get a peek. Shortly, Joy was appearing in the first wave of teenage youth-films created during the late 1950s to exploit the then-new rock 'n' roll phenomenon. A shot at what might have been the role of a lifetime: The ingenue in Stanley Kubrick's non-exploitive film version of the controversial Vladimir Nabokov novel *Lolita*. Anyone guessing that Joy's stunning torso might win her the role turned out to be wrong. Early on, Kubrick decided that the Nymphet ought to be flat-chested, avoiding any obvious vulgarity. Sue Lyon fit that bill, while the more developed Joy—resembling a young Jayne Mansfield—did not.

Joy did get to play a Lolita-like character in one major film. *Cool Hand Luke* dealt with a group of chain-gang prisoners (Paul Newman played the title character) in the deep South. At one point, the chain gang guys are forced to work on a notably sweltering day. Already on the verge of collapse, things grow worse as a teenage femme fatale (played by Joy, then nearly 27) drives her car close to the staked-off area, then proceeds to wash her automobile, while getting as much sudsy water on her flimsy dress as possible. "Man, she doesn't know what she's doing," one of the guys sighs. Macho Newman/Luke answers: "She knows exactly what she's doing." Her other most iconic moment occurs in the teen fantasy *Village*

I WAS A FUGITIVE FROM A CHAIN GANG: *Cool Hand Luke* (Paul Newman) and his buddies dream about making a break from their prison after a Deep South Lolita (Joy Harmon) "just happens" to wash her car in clear sight of them.

of the Giants when Joy, as one of the title characters, allows normal-sized Tommy Kirk to hang on to her bikini top.

There were roles in minor movies and lots of TV work (*Gidget*, *The Monkees*, *Batman*, *The Man from U.N.C.L.E.*). And even a lead, as a surfer girl who heads to Hawaii to reboot her life in the B-budget beach movie *One Way Wahine*. While shooting her bikini sequences near the surf, production had to close down as men in planes soared preciously low to get a good look. Joy later began baking cakes for the cast and crew while working on the Disney lot. Everyone marveled at how great they were. When offers for window-dressing roles dried up after she hit the age of thirty, she created Aunt Joy's Cakes, a wholesale bakery in Burbank, which supplied sweets for the craft services people working on movies. As one observer put it, she arced from one definition of cheesecake to another. Rare among denizens of Tinseltown, she has been married to one man, Jeff Gourson, since 1968; they have three children.

SELECTED FILMOGRAPHY:

(The) Man in the Gray Flannel Suit (bit, uncredited, 1956); *Let's Rock* (Pickup Girl at Bar, 1958); *Mad Dog Coll* (Caroline, 1961); *Under the Yum Yum Tree* (Ardice, 1963); *Roustabout* (College Girl, 1964); *Young Dillinger* (Gun Moll, 1965); *One Way Wahini* (Kit Williams, 1965); *Village of the Giants* (Merrie, 1965); *The Loved One* (Miss Benson, 1965); *A Guide for the Married Man* (Party Girl, 1967); *Cool Hand Luke* (The Blonde, 1967); *Angel in My Pocket* (Miss Holland, 1969).

THE QUEEN OF A.I.P.: Susan Hart was the surfer girl who caught the eyes, and heart, of producer James Nicholson; he insisted that she become a top-billed star of B-movies.

Susan Hart

Birthdate: June 2, 1941; Wenatchee, Washington
Birth name: Susan Neidhart
Height: N/A
Measurements: N/A

A GORGEOUS BRUNETTE, wearing nothing but a gold bikini, strolls along an upscale avenue. She grins idiotically, never seeming to be aware of people staring or even the cars driving by. Entering a business office, she spots a businessman and, as if everything has been pre-ordained, steps directly toward him. He reacts with panic: She's one of the girl bombs he's heard about, a deviously designed mannequin. Though she appears sexy-sweet, the slightest touch of her pretty lips against his will result in an explosion. Problem is, she's so beautiful that he freezes up, unable to resist, terrified but acceptant of his fate. The film is *Dr. Goldfoot and the Bikini Machine*, first of two in which Vincent Prince chewed the scenery as a lampoon of those larger-than-life villains in the recently popular James Bond films. The actress: Susan Hart.

Once her family moved from the apple capitol of America to Palm Springs for warmer weather, Susan studied dance and drama. She pushed on to Hollywood in search of fame and fortune, soon decorating such early 1960s sitcoms as *The Joey Bishop Show* and *The Bob Cummings Show*, both 1961. The next year Sharon played a date for Dwayne Hickman on *The Many Loves of Dobie Gillis*. Bits in major films led to her being cast in several *Beach Party* spinoffs, a staple of American International Pictures, where founders James Nicholson and Sam Arkoff held the purse-strings. Nicholson fell in love at first sight, casting the shapely brunette in ever larger roles. Hart's inability to convincingly deliver dialogue hadn't mattered in surf-and-sand films, though this did cause obvious problems

THE BIKINI BENEATH THE TRENCHCOAT: Likewise carrying a gun to belie that seemingly sweet surfer-girl smile, Susan Hart falls for teenage spy Frankie Avalon though still in the service of Goldfinger-like super-villain Vincent Price.

when she moved over to more traditional science-fiction items like *City Beneath the Sea*, which required more than merely frenetic frugging.

Some observers believe that Hart served as the catalyst for the Nicholson-Arkoff break-up. Hart married Nicholson in 1964 and they remained together until his passing in 1972, at which point she inherited the rights to many of his projects including such 1950s schlock classics as *It Conquered the World* (1956) and *I Was a Teenage Werewolf* (1957). The continuing cult for exploitation films from that nostalgia-drenched era has ensured that money continues to roll in. Hart's onscreen antics as the faux girl who kisses and kills for *Dr. Goldfoot* likewise ensures that her fans will remain forever loyal, as does her nearly nude romp in *The Ghost in the Invisible Bikini*.

Trivia: Susan cut several records for the MGM label. A diligent fund-raiser, her efforts were essential in creating the James H. Nicholson pediatric Chair at the UCLA Medical Center. Hart was involved in the production of such 1970s exploitation flicks as *The Legend of Hell House* (1973) and *Dirty Mary, Crazy Larry* (1974).

SELECTED FILMOGRAPHY:

Boys' Night Out (Glamour Girl, 1962); *The Slime People* (Lisa Galbraith, 1963); *A Global Affair* (Brunette at Dog Show, 1964); *For Those Who Think Young* (Beach Beauty, 1964); *Ride the Wild Surf* (Lily Kilua, 1964); *Pajama Party* (Jilda, 1964); *City in the Sea*, aka *City Beneath the Sea*, aka *War Gods of the Deep* (Jill, 1965); *Dr. Golldfoot and the Bikini Machine* (Diane, 1965); *The Ghost in the Invisible Bikini* (The Ghost, 1966); *Chrome and Hot Leather* (Singing voice on jukebox, 1971).

BOTTOM OF THE BARREL: By the early 1970s, Hay had plummeted to dubious stardom in the lowest level of lurid junk movies.

Alexandra Hay

Birthdate: July 24, 1947; Los Angeles, CA
Birth name: Alexandra Lynn Hay
Date of passing: October 11, 1993
Height: N/A
Measurements: N/A

ABOUT HALFWAY THROUGH *Guess Who's Coming to Dinner*, Spencer Tracy and Katharine Hepburn drive to an outdoor restaurant. As they discuss the upcoming marriage of their daughter (Katharine Houghton) to an African-American (Sidney Poitier), a car hop smilingly stops by to take their order. Though the sequence barely lasts a minute, everyone wanted to know: Who *was* that *girl*? The press revealed her to be Alexandra Hay. Hollywood, hoping to cash in, insisted that she was The Next Big Thing. At age twenty, Alexandra—a then recent graduate of Arroyo High School in El Monte, California—made her TV debut on *The Monkees* (1967) as Clarisse, one more mini-skirted free-spirited beautiful blonde. She even faked a British accent. When Hay's unsuccessful two-year fling with potential mainstream movie stardom was over, she returned to the small screen to work on such popular early-seventies fluff as *Love, American Style*. One potential breakthrough was her casting as a hippie spy (to attract younger viewers) on *Mission: Impossible* (1969) after sleek Barbara Bain dropped out of the series. Apparently, what Alexandra had to offer didn't satisfy the producers, who did indeed add just such a character but gave the role to Leslie Ann Warren. Hay found work on such police procedurals as *Dan August* (1970) and *Kojak* (1974), as well as a cult made-for-TV movie, *The Screaming Woman* (1972).

During her Warholian Fifteen Minutes, Hay played a small role as a teenage spy in *The Ambushers*, opposite Dean Martin as Matt Helm. Next came several disastrous attempts to transform Hay into a symbol of the Hippie Era Girl. These included *How Sweet It Is!* which, despite the title,

AN AUSPICIOUS PREMERE: Following Alexandra's brief but memorable role as a car hop in *Guess Who's Coming to Dinner*, it briefly seemed as if she would become a major player in movies.

was not a Jackie Gleason vehicle. The Big Bomb was *Skidoo,* which did star Gleason (along with Carol Channing and Groucho Marx). Otto Preminger disastrously attempted to lampoon the Youth Movement though, in what Alvin Toffler would have labeled Future Shock, by the time that film appeared in theatres the scene it punched gags at was long gone. Two more flops followed: *The Model Shop* and *The Love Machine.* But the best/worst was yet to come. Hay starred in a pair of ultra-low budget sexploitation films, first as a teenage nympho (and the prison warden's daughter) in *1,000 Convicts and a Woman*, then as a sleep-around type in *How to Seduce a Woman.* A 1974 nude *Playboy* layout was intended to kickstart her career but Hay's looks had begun to fade; she appeared a tad frumpy. The official cause of her early passing was arteriosclerotic heart disease; friends insist she had long suffered from clinical depression.

SELECTED FILMOGRAPHY:

Guess Who's Coming to Dinner (Carhop, 1967); *The Ambushers* (Quintana's Secretary, 1967); *How Sweet It Is!* (Gloria, 1968); *Skidoo* (Darlene Banks, 1968); *(The) Model Shop* (Gloria, 1969); *The Love Machine* (Tina St. Claire, 1971); *1,000 Convicts and a Woman* (Angela Thorne, 1971); *How to Seduce a Woman* (Nell Brinkman, 1974); *How Come Nobody's on Our Side?* (Brigitte, 1975); *That Girl from Boston* (Blonde, 1975): *One Man Jury* (Tessie, 1978).

Gloria Hendry

Birthdate: March 3, 1949; Winter Haven, FL
Height: 5' 5"
Measurements: N/A

SO... WAS GLORIA HENDRY the first African-American Bond Girl or was she not? That depends on how one interprets the phrase "Bond Girl." In *Diamonds Are Forever* (1971), Trina Parks played Thumper, part of a team of female assassins (the other, Bambi, was played by Lola Larson) who wrestle with Bond until he dumps both into a swimming pool to cool off. But if there was physical interaction there, none was of a romantic nature. Then came Gloria in *Live and Let Die*, playing Rosie Carver, one more of those early beauties who are eliminated shortly after a sexual encounter with 007 (Roger Moore). Like others before her and many more yet to come, she's a seductive enemy agent who allows the secret agent to have his way with her. Then, realizing that he may kill her if she doesn't tell him all that she knows, Rosie nervously inquires: "James, you *wouldn't*! Not after what we just did?" With callous glibness, he smilingly replies: "Well, I certainly would not have killed you *before*!" It isn't our anti-hero who does her in, but yet another assassin working for the forces of evil. Rosie is shot as she attempts to escape.

However difficult it may be to believe today, there were theatres that refused to book the film owing to an interracial love affair in such a commercial undertaking. Still other venues excised the entire sequence involving gorgeous Gloria Hendry. However much the forces of resistance hoped to stem the coming tide, here was an initial bit of courageous casting that would help to create an era in which Halle Berry could decades later play the female lead in a Bond film, with no reference to her race at all required, and no one thinking to make an issue out of it. Gloria's good

AN AFRICAN-AMERICAN BOND GIRL: Though Gloria Hendry in *Live and Let Die* was not the first black actress to be seen in an 007 opus, she was the beauty who made a huge impact with audiences.

looks helped the aspiring actress-model to win gigs as a Bunny at various *Playboy* Clubs during the height of their popularity during the late 1960s. Though she hoped for a mainstream career, premiering in a lighthearted Sidney Poitier vehicle, there were few strong roles for black actresses in most of that era's middle of the road movies. In order to work, she appeared in a string of black-exploitation flicks. Even though the titles of several remain famous today, Hendry never became known as a top-billed performer in such urban action dramas as did Pam Grier. Too ambitious to remain on the sidelines, she opted for a singing career and produced a motion-picture on the life of the African-American Paul Robeson. In

EBONY AND IVORY, TOGETHER IN PERFECT HARMONY: In defiance of racists and racism, Roger Moore and Gloria Hendry flaunt their mutual attraction on the set of *Live and Let Die*.

fact, Gloria is multi-ethnic: her DNA includes Seminole-Creek Indian, Chinese, and Irish as well as African elements.

SELECTED FILMOGRAPHY:

For Love of Ivy (Cocktail Waitress, 1968); *The Landlord* (Gloria, 1970); *Across 110ᵗʰ Street* (Laurelene, 1972); *Black Caesar* (Helen, 1973); *Live and Let Die* (Rosie Carver, 1973); *Slaughter's Big Rip-Off* (Marcia, 1973); *Hell Up in Harlem* (Helen Bradley, 1973); *Black Belt Jones* (Sydney, 1974); *Savage Sisters* (Lynn Jackson, 1974); *Bare Knuckles* (Barbara Darrow, 1977); *Lookin' Italian* (Leon's Mother, 1994); *Man in the Mirror* (Street Hooker, 2008); *Absolute Evil – Final Exit* (Blind Woman, 2009); *Freaky Deaky* (Sgt. Maureen Downey, 2012).

Marianna Hill

aka: MARIANA HILL
Birthdate: February 9, 1941; Santa Barbara, CA
Birth name: Mariana Schwarzkopf
Height: 5' 4"
Measurements: 36 (D) – 23 ½ - 36

AT AN ISOLATED FORT, a beautiful woman (Mariana Hill) lives as the mistress of a military commander (Patrick O'Neal). Late one night, she notices bandidos and their Indian allies are crawling up and over the walls. Swiftly, she makes a decision: As there are too many of them to defeat, rather than alert the drowsy guards she will assist in the takeover, winning esteem in the eyes of mercenary leader Jim Brown. Up on her balcony, in the moonlight, she spontaneously slips into a riveting strip-tease. The guards rub their eyes in amazement and turn away from their assignment to gaze at erotic Terpsichore. As the invaders come over the top they easily slit the throats of these victims of a hypnotic femme fatale, her only concern herself. In *El Condor* that deadly dame is memorably played by Marianna Hill.

The woman born Mariana Schwarzkopf (a cousin of Persian Gulf General "Stormin' Norman") enjoyed a steady if uneven career during the late 1960s and 1970s. The daughter of a building contractor, with no connections to the entertainment industry, her stunning looks and long mane of reddish hair early on allowed her to join the Laguna Playhouse (age 14) and win roles in TV shows such as *My Three Sons* (1960). Even in such conventional fare, it was evident that here was not just one eager young beauty but a true actress of considerable potential. In part owing to her already diverse living situations including Canada, England and

"BOYS, YOU AIN'T SEEN NOTHIN' YET!": As the Contessa, Marianna Hill prepares to enter into her impromptu striptease in *El Condor*.

Majorca, Mariana was able to swiftly offer up an array of international accents. Legendary producer-director Howard Hawks cast her as one of the young cast members of his racing film *Red Line 7000*. She appeared opposite Elvis in his second (and lesser) Hawaii-based musical, *Paradise—Hawaiian Style* and like so many of his co-stars became romantically linked with The King.

So why didn't she become a major star? Mariana arrived on the scene at an awkward moment. The old studios, any one of which might have transformed her into the next Rita Hayworth, were shutting down. In the wake of *Easy Rider,* inexpensive indies were momentarily the way to go, glamour giving way to grit. In this confusing no-woman's land, Hill rolled with the punches as best she could. In a forgotten but worthy film of that era, *Medium Cool,* she played the lover of a contemporary photographer (Robert Forster) busily recording the wild and crazy days of the late 1960s Youth Rebellion. Soon she was too old for ingénue roles, playing attractive older women such as the wife of Fredo in *The Godfather, Part Two.*

Hill studied with Lee Strasberg at New York's Neighborhood Playhouse and later taught at Strasberg's institution's London headquarters, all the while supporting such heady endeavors with work as a fashion model. The uniqueness of her beauty had to do with a rainbow coalition of genetics: Mariana was part English, Spanish, Jewish, and Native American (Iroquois).

Trivia: Her I.Q. is 165, qualifying Mariana as one of the most intelligent starlets in Hollywood history. In her last screen role, as Mrs. Anderson in *Coma Girl,* she chose to be billed as Marianna Renfred. Cult TV appearances include a King Tut two-parter on *Batman* (1955), the classic "Dagger of the Mind" *Star Trek* episode (1955) as Dr. Helen Noel, and a femme fatale on the "Night Train to Madrid" installment of *I Spy* (1967).

MEDIUM COOL: Hill plays the mistress of a documentary filmmaker (Robert Forster) covering the turbulent revolutionary scene in America during 1968 in her finest film.

SELECTED FILMOGRAPHY:

Married Too Young (Marla, 1962); *Black Zoo* (Audrey, 1963); *Wives and Lovers* (uncredited bit, 1963); *Face in the Sun* (The Girl, 1964); *The New Interns* (Sandy, 1964); *Roustabout* (Viola, 1964); *That Funny Feeling* (Kitty, 1965); *Red Line 7000* (Gabrielle, 1965); *Paradise, Hawaiian Style* (Lani Kaimana, 1966); *Medium Cool* (Ruth, 1969); *El Condor* (Claudine, 1970); *The Travelling Executioner* (Gundred, 1970); *Thumb Tripping* (Lynn, 1972); *Messiah of Evil* (Arletty, 1973); *The Baby* (Germaine, 1973); *High Plains Drifter* (Callie Travers, 1973); *The Godfather, Part II* (Deanna Corleone, 1974); *The Astral Factor* (Bambi Greer, 1978); *Schizoid* (Julie, 1980); *Blood Beach* (Catherine, 1980); *Coma Girl* (Mrs. Anderson, 2005).

Jill Ireland

Birthdate: April 24, 1936; London, UK
Birth name: Jill Dorothy Ireland
Date of passing: May 18, 1990
Height: 5' 7"
Measurements: N/A

"YOU BETTER KEEP a real close eye on her," the macho man confides in a combination of Machiavellian cynicism and forthright honesty to the stunned little fellow beside him. The former is hungrily eyeing the latter's impossibly beautiful blonde wife. "I'm gonna steal her away from you." That sounds like the kind of glib, cruel statement one of Charles Bronson's ruggedly individualistic screen characters might make in a movie. In actuality, this was precisely what the star, who in the Third World was referred to only as El Brute, whispered to Brit actor David McCallum on the set of *The Great Escape* (1963) when Bronson first spotted Jill. She, then still a demure English girl, was initially as stunned as her husband that anyone would dare make such a claim. But bit by bit, she felt herself being won over by the force of nature that was Charlie, on and off the screen. By the late 1960s her entourage altered; instead of traveling the world as the wife of McCallum and mother of his three children, she did so as Mrs. Bronson, with their own kids. They would become one of the leading power couples both in Hollywood and of the international set, as her husband's violence-laden vehicles initially made him a top box-office draw in underdeveloped countries, then went over big with the US market.

Ireland played everything from bit parts to female leads in such films. One of their last, *Assassination*, actually focused on her character, the wife of a president who realizes she's been marked for death. Early on, Jill had

LEAN ON ME: Jill Ireland with second husband Charles Bronson, the first couple of
B-action films.

appeared in mid-level Brit films including the role of a blonde in one of
the broadly humorous *Carry On* comedies. Ireland revealed her acting
chops in *So Evil, So Young* as a Lolita-like juvenile delinquent of the type
that become prominent in the early 1960s. Most Americans knew her best
from TV, where she played the female lead (opposite David Carradine) in
the 1966 small-screen adaptation of *Shane*, as the only woman who broke

Mr. Spock's heart (as compared to Captain Kirk) as Leila Kalomi in the "This Side of Paradise" (1967) episode of *Star Trek*, and in five various episodes of *The Man From U.N.C.L.E.* opposite her then-husband McCallum, portraying good and bad-girls. Then came Bronson, and the second phase of her career and life. Two femme fatale roles stand out. *The Family* was a ridiculously inappropriate title for a memorable Eurotrash thriller (apparently the distributors wanted to cash in on *The Godfather's* recent success). Bronson played a hit man, Ireland the remarkable beauty object he finds himself consumed by. A similar if more nuanced Deadlier Than the Male type appears in the American-made *From Noon Till Three*, a nouveau-Western with Ireland as a seemingly respectable girl who has an affair with an outlaw. In due time he, and we, learn that she's not the "nice kid" he originally thought her to be. If Bronson and Ireland had apparently achieved the perfect balance of public career and personal lives, everything changed when, in 1984, Jill was diagnosed with breast cancer. They courageously continued their family/professional existence until the disease claimed her in 1990 at age 54.

SHE SPIES, AND IT'S ALL IN THE FAMILY: Jill (left) joins the men from U.N.C.L.E., Robert Vaughn and then husband David McCallum for the NBC TV series.

A TALE OF TWO HUSBANDS: Jill Ireland appears icily respectable toward first husband David McCallum... AND ALSO ON THE FOLLOWING PAGE: in a state of utter abandonment with second husband Charles Bronson.

SELECTED FILMOGRAPHY:

No Love for Judy (The Other Woman, 1955); *Three Men in a Boat* (Bluebell Porterhouse, 1956); *There's Always a Thursday* (Jennifer Potter, 1957); *Hell Drivers* (Jill, 1957); *Robbery Under Arms* (Jean Morrison, 1957); *The Big Money* (Doreen Firth, 1958); *Carry on Nurse* (Jill Thompson, 1959); *The Desperate Man* (Carol Bourne, 1959); *Jungle Street* (Sue, 1960); *Girls of the Latin Quarter* (Jill, 1960); *So Evil, So Young* (Ann, 1961); *Roommates* (Janet, 1961); *The Karate Killers* (Imogen, 1967); *Villa Rides*

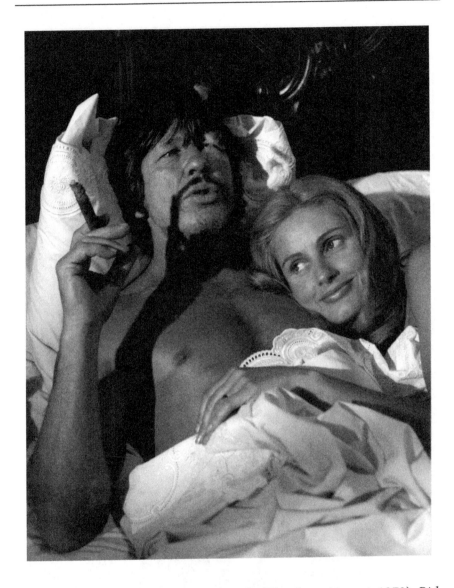

(Pretty Blonde in Restaurant, 1968); *Lola* (Blonde at Airport, 1970); *Rider on the Rain* (Nicole, 1970); *The Family* (Vanessa Shelton, 1970); *Cold Sweat* (Moira, 1970); *Someone Behind the Door* (Frances Jeffries, 1971); *The Valachi Papers* (Maria Reina Valachi, 1972); *The Mechanic* (The Blonde, 1972); *Chino* (Catherine, 1973); *Breakout* (Ann Wagner, 1975); *Hard Times* (Lucy Simpson, 1975); *Breakheart Pass* (Marica, 1975); *From Noon Till Three* (Amanda, 1976); *Love and Bullets* (Jackie, 1979); *Death Wish II* (Geri Nichols, 1982); *Assassination* (Lara Royce Craig, 1987); *Caught* (Janet Devon, 1987).

THE ROLE OF A LIFETIME: Claudia's still popular cult film had her tracking down and doing in the vile men who abused her; 'Gator Bait appealed to men eager to gaze at the redhead and women who perceived it as a feminist statement about fighting back.

Claudia Jennings

Birthdate: February (Some sources say December) 20, 1949;
   St. Paul, Minnesota
Birth name: Mary Eileen Chesterson
Date of passing: October 3, 1979; Malibu, CA
Height: 5' 6"
Measurements: 35 – 23 - 36

AFTER HER PARENTS MOVED to Chicago, the girl born Mary Eileen Chesterson attended Marquette University, majoring in Dramatic Arts. Impressing everyone with strong performances and top grades, Claudia shocked family and friends by suddenly dropping out to take a receptionist's job at *Playboy's* Chicago office. Her "fiery girl from the backwoods" appeal led to an offer to pose for the Centerfold. Redubbed Claudia, she decorated the magazine as November 1969 Playmate of the Month. A favorite of the magazine's fans, Jennings was picked as Playmate of the Year 1970 though she did not boast the large breasts so many of the girls were known for. At the age of 21, Claudia became one more queen of exploitation flicks. Among the most popular, first at Drive-Ins and then, after the mid-1970s boom on pay-cable (uncensored), were *Unholy Rollers* and, better still: *The Texas Dynamite Chase*. The latter focused on a two-girl team of rural bandits, bridging the gap between Bonnie and Clyde and Thelma and Louise, with Joslyn Jones as Claudia's partner-in-crime.

Truck Stop Women featured what sounded like an exploitive title. In fact, the film dealt with girls who frequent such joints and, tired of being treated like trash, turn the tables on redneck men who use them. This was a feminist film disguised as an R-rated bit of exploitation. The role Claudia Jennings will always be remembered for is Desiree Thibodou, the Bowie-knife clutching, scantily-clad swamp girl who tracks down the men who attempt to use her and dispatches hard-edged revenge in *'Gator Bait*, co-written by feminist-inclined filmmaker Beverly Sebastion. Yet Jennings hungered for the respectability that comes with acceptance into the mainstream. Bits in such big films as the musical-comedy *40 Carats* and the soap-opera *The Love Machine* didn't help as both films were awful. The great hope was to land a continuing role on *Charlie's Angels*, which had transformed the T&A type sexploitation flicks from the late 1960s into family style network TV porn (without actual nudity) for the mid-1970s. The show's producers seriously considered Claudia as replacement for Kate Jackson, then broke her heart by picking Shelley Hack instead. Everyone at ABC knew that Jennings was the right girl but some conservative sponsors balked at the *Playboy* exposure.

At age 29, while musing what turn her career might take after she reached the frightful (in Hollywood) age of thirty, she was driving along the scenic Pacific Coast Highway when her sports car became involved in an odd accident. Jennings was pinned inside, still alive, unable to move. The rescue team had a difficult time cutting away the shattered metal. Apparently, Claudia herself at some point realized that, with escape imminent, she was going to die before rescuers could extricate her, one

IT ALL BEGAN WITH PLAYBOY: Claudia was yet another of those Centerfold Girls who set her eyes on a big movie career but had to settle for B-budget exploitation flicks.

WOMEN CAN BE ACTION HEROES, TOO!: Jennings was one of many B-movie babes who set the pace for A-list stars like Scarlett Johannson accepting such roles in the 21st century.

more bitter irony in a life filled with them. Though Claudia had dabbled in drugs, these were ruled out as cause of the accident.

SELECTED FILMOGRAPHY:

The Love Machine (Darlene, 1971); *The Stepmother* (Rita, 1972); *The Unholy Rollers* (Karen Walker, 1972); *Group Marriage* (Elaine, 1973); *40 Carats* (Gabriella, 1973); *The Single Girls* (Allison, 1974); *'Gator Bait* (Desiree Thibodeau, 1974); *The Man Who Fell to Earth* (Peter's Wife, 1976); *Sisters of Death* (Judy, 1976); *The Great Texas Dynamite Chase* (Candy Morgan, 1976); *Moonshine County Express* (Betty Hammer, 1977); *Deathsport* (Deneer, 1978); *Fast Company* (Sammy, 1979).

THE PRIVATE LIFE OF A PREHISTORIC WOMAN: Magda Konopka was one of the
international beauties who donned an animal skin bikini for Hammer's
When Dinosaurs Ruled the Earth.

Magda Kanopka

Date of Birth: 1943 (date unknown); Warsaw/Mazowieckie, Poland
Height: N/A
Measurements: N/A

A REAL-LIFE MYSTERY WOMAN, extremely little is known about the background, life, and current situation of this fetching femme fatale. What *is* known: Magda was descended from nobility, a claim that, unlike most pretenders to some throne, Magda could prove. Her family hailed from high-level Polish nobility, Magda's great grandfather had been a decorated officer during the Napoleonic Wars. Magda's mother was a famed archaeologist, her father a ranking civil servant. Magda's early life was spent on a lavish estate. At age 24, she married into yet more money: Jean-Louis Dessy, a billionaire she had met while employed as a decorative beauty at the Hammer studios in London. Three months after they pledged their love for life in Chelsea, Magda left the stunned Canadian, taking plenty of booty with her. Her darkly exotic looks made her a natural for the spy cycle of the 1960s, including *Satanik!* (one of the first attempts to capture the style of graphic novels on screen) as well as such televised espionage shows as Paula in "The Mindreader" (*Man of the World*, 1962), Conchita in "A Date with Doris" (*Secret Agent*, 1964), and Ingrid in "Read and Destroy" (*The Persuaders*, opposite Roger Moore, 1971). Though she appeared perfect for a Bond villainess, that never happened. Magda did find plenty of work in engaging junk movies, starring opposite Beatle Ringo in a particularly strange spaghetti Western, *Blindman.*

Her best remembered role is as the antagonist in *When Dinosaurs Ruled the Earth.* Magda plays the dark beauty who resents blonde Shell Woman Victoria Vetri's entrance into their primitive village. At the end, Magda suffers a fate similar to that of raven-haired Martine Beswick in

FROM DINOSAUR DAYS TO THE PRESENT TIME: Magda models an ultra-modern outfit; hard to believe this beautiful girl did not go on to achieve stardom.

One Million Years B.C., likewise swallowed up by the earth during a quake. Since her hasty exit from show business, Magda has effectively kept her whereabouts from the press.

SELECTED FILMOGRAPHY:

Becket (Beauty on the Balcony, 1964); *Thrilling* (Luciana, 1965); *Pleasant Nights* (Fiammetta, 1966); *7 Golden Men* (Veronique, 1966); *Top Secret* (Sandra Dubois, 1967); *Code Name Is Kill* (Bibi Randall, 1967); *Satanik!* (Dr. Marnie Bannister, aka Satanik, 1968); *A Sky Full of Stars* (Widow McDonald, 1968); *Night of the Serpent* (Agent Femme Fatale, 1969); *Hell Boats* (Luciana, 1970); *When Dinosaurs Ruled the Earth* (Ulido, 1970); *Quickly!* (Lilian, 1971); *Blind Man* (Sweet Mama, 1971); *Winged Devils* (The Beauty, 1972); *Our Lady of Lust* (Sister Eleonora, 1972); *Canterbury Tales* (Antona, 1972); *Lucky Luciano* (The Contessa, 1973); *Super Stooges vs. the Wonder Women* (Beghira, the Amazon Queen, 1974); *Love Angels* (Mrs. North, 1974); *Reflections in Black* (Contessa Orselmo, 1975); *Diabolical Letizia* (Michaela, 1975); *The Young Bride* (Margot, 1976); *La Casa* (Sharon, 1976).

BATHING BEAUTY: Sylva Koscina began her career in the 1950s, including the role of Steve Reeves' wife in two Hercules movies, but her greatest notoriety would come playing bad-girls in the 1960s.

Sylva (Sylvia) Koscina

Birthdate: August 22, 1933; Zagreb, Yugoslavia/Croatia
Date of passing: December 26, 1994; Rome, Italy
Height: 5' 8 ¾"
Measurements: 39 – 24 ½ - 36 ½

ROME... DURING AN ERA that would come to be known as La Dolce Vita. Moviemaking at Cinecitta studios and decadent night life after hours was chronicled in 1960 by Federico Fellini. If Sylva was not onscreen in that classic, she did garner a brief but notable role in one of that auteur's follow-up films, *Juliet of the Spirits*, also focusing on international filmmaking at that moment in time, when beautiful girls darted about in bikinis, champagne (and drugs) flowed wild and free, rock 'n' roll became accepted as part of the adult mainstream pop-culture now that everyone wanted to be (or pretend to be) young, and a seemingly never-ending party was attended by jet-setters, men with vast fortunes and women with remarkable beauty. Few, if any, were more beautiful than Yugoslavian-born Sylva. A beauty contest winner at nineteen (Miss Da Tapa, 1952), she enrolled as a physics major at Naples University. So distracting were her good looks that Koscina realized she had to pursue movies.

She entered films even as the Peplum became a standard item. Initially, she was the good girl, playing the loyal/lovely wife of Hercules (Steve Reeves) in two epics. Though Sylva was never cast in an actual James Bond film, various spy movies did tap her for the leads. In one, *Agent 8 ¾*, she played a role not unlike Daniella Bianchi's in *From Russia With Love*. Then came her piece-de-resistance: Penelope in *Deadlier Than the Male*, a dumb-dumb/scatterbrained partner of smart, sizzling Elke Sommer. The two beauties murder men for profit and pleasure, appearing near-nude on a beach in skimpy bikinis with spear-guns to first entice, then shoot their prey, or more leisurely drugging a businessman in his high rise apartment, allowing him to gaze down at his oncoming fate before they toss him off the balcony toward the street below. Sylva and Elke would be reunited for a notably different sort of project, the Exorcist rip-off *Lisa and the Devil*.

For a brief period during the late 1960s and early 1970s, Sylva appeared about to emerge as a major-league star on the order of Sophia or Gina thanks to major productions opposite Paul Newman, Kirk Douglas, Yul Brynner, Laurence Harvey, and Rock Hudson. Unfortunately, all those projects were unsuccessful, commercially and critically. Sylva proved unlucky at marriage— her only known such union, to Raimondo Castelli, lasting from late in 1967 to early in 1971. A shrewd businesswoman, she watched other girls invest in clothes and drugs and hot cars, Sylva pouring her profits into a luxury villa in Rome's upscale Marino district. Sadly, such good times did not last. A legal investigation into her tax forms drained away the funds necessary to sustain such a lifestyle. She then returned to *Playboy*, posing at age 42, still looking wonderful.

THE JOYS OF BONDAGE: Sylva certainly appears to be having a great time while tying up her latest victim in this advertising image from her most (in)famous film.

A TOUCH OF CLASS: Sylva (right) and Elke Sommer, as high-priced hitwomen, slip out of their bikinis and into haute fashion halfway through *Deadlier Than the Male*.

BAD-GIRLS WEAR BIKINIS: This image of Sylva Koscina and Elke Sommer was blown up to immense size and appeared over New York's Broadway, as well as many other cities, announcing the coming arrival of this film and also that the Sexual Revolution could no longer be denied as part of the New Normal Mainstream.

The title of one of her films encapsulates the dark appeal of not only this actress but all Deadlier Than the Male types: *A Lovely Way to Die* in which she drew all-too-willing men into her lethal arms.

SELECTED FILMOGRAPHY:

Man of Iron (Giulia, 1956); *Michael Strogoff* (Sangarre, 1956), *Female Three Times* (Sonia, 1957); *Hercules* (Iole, 1958); *Love on the Riviera* (Renata, 1958); *Sabella* (Lucia, 1958); *Hercules Unchained* (Iole, 1959); *Temptation of the Vampire* (Carla, 1959); *(The) Siege of Syracuse* (Clio, 1960); *Trapped by Fear* (Arabelle, 1960); *Ravishing* (Evelyne Cotteret, 1960); *Love, the Italian Way* (Luciana, 1960); *The Iron Mask* (Marion, 1962); *Swordsman of Siena* (Orietta, 1962); *Agent 8 ¾* (Vlasta Simoneva, 1964); *Corpse for the Lady* (Laura, 1964); *Cyrano and d'Artagnan* (Ninon, 1964); *That Man in Istanbul* (Kelly, 1965); *Juliet of the Spirits* (Sylva, 1965); *Deadlier Than the Male* (Penelope, 1967); *Three Bites of the Apple*

(Carla, 1967); *The Secret War of Harry Frig* (Countess Francesca De Montefiore, 1968); *The Last Roman* (Empress Theodora, 1968); *A Lovely Way to Die* (Rena Westabrook, 1968); *The Battle of Neretva* (Danica, 1969); *He and She* (She, 1969); *Hornet's Nest* (Bianca, 1970); *So Sweet, So Dead* (Barbara, 1972); *The Crimes of the Black Cat* (Francoise, 1972); *The Italian Connection* (Lucia, 1972); *Lisa and the Devil* (Sophia, 1973); *Sunday Lovers* (Zaira, 1980).

MEET MRS. ZUBIN MEHTA: Early in her career, Nancy modeled this fantasy wedding outfit; if the great conductor got lucky, maybe she wore it on their honeymoon?

Nancy Kovack

Birthdate: March 11, 1935; Flint, Michigan
Birth name: Nancy Kovack
Height: 5' 8 ½"
Measurements: N/A

PICTURE ONE OF THOSE POSH Manhattan parties most of us will never get to see anywhere but in some elegant black and white movie, maybe by Woody Allen. The men wear tuxedoes; the women are displayed in glamorous gowns owned only by society's upper echelon. Suddenly, the great conductor Zubin Mehta and his lovely wife step into the spotlight: He, genius incarnate; she, the epitome of style. Wait a minute! She looks vaguely familiar. But where might we have seen…? Déjà vu sets in as we realize this is Nancy Kovack, who among other cult roles played the pagan goddess Medea in *Jason and the Argonauts*. Also, a slinky spy woman who tried to murder Dean Martin as Matt Helm (while of course seducing him) before good-girl spy Daliah Lavi arrved in the nick of time. Also, she tried to win Elvis away from good-girl Donna Douglas in *Frankie and Johnny*, playing a legendary temptress, Nellie Blye.

Nancy Kovack: Cult queen then, society matron now. The daughter of a General Motors executive, Nancy set out to conquer the entertainment world in the late 1950s, beginning with an Old Red Barn Theatre appearance on Long Island in a comedy play. Not long thereafter, Nancy offered up another of those memorable 1960s erotic-without-nudity dance sequences in Ray Harryhausen's spectacular rendering of ancient mythology. Here was the first American woman to give serious competition to Scilla Gabel, Eleanora Rossi-Drago, and Chelo Alonso as the great dark beauty of Peplum productions. Indeed, so convincing was Kovack in

281

the part that many viewers assumed she must really be the exotic native of some Aegean island, though in fact the goddess on view was a nice Jewish girl from Flint, Michigan.

That's not Nancy whose voice we hear in the film. So that her character might better fit in with the cast of Brit actors who were chosen to give the production a classy aura, the voice of Medea was dubbed by Honor Blackman, who portrayed goddess Hera in that film. Surprisingly, Nancy never graced a 007 flick, but her brief yet memorable appearance as a gorgeous would-be assassin in *The Silencers* made clear what a fine choice she would have been. Early-on, precocious Nancy took classes at the University of Michigan while only fifteen, went on to become a Deejay a year after, then as a teenager showed up on such TV standbys as *The Jackie Gleason Show* as one of those long-legged hostesses. Her exotic looks allowed her to be cast as a decorative companion to Victor Buono as King Tut on *Batman* and as a jungle queen in a full-color ambitious *Tarzan* epic. She had always hoped for more mainstream stardom, though any chances

A SPACE CADET CALLED NONA: The exotic aspect of Kovack's beauty made her a perfect candidate for a guest-star slot on *Star Trek*.

"ME KIRK, YOU NONA": Well, Shat didn't exactly say that; but he might as well have in the memorable *Trek* episode "A Private Little War."

were dashed after she agreed to appear in a Three Stooges comedy and an awful throwback to 1950s style B-oaters (kiddie-oriented cowboy films) called *The Wild Westerners*. She showed off her considerable acting chops as well as that take-your-breath-away hourglass figure in *Diary of a Madman* opposite Vincent Price, her best femme fatale role. Also there is a standout performance as "Nona," one of those queens of outer space who set their sights on James Kirk on *Star Trek's* memorable "A Private Little War," Nancy and Mehta made their home in Germany after 1998, when he left the Metropolitan in New York to become Music Director of the Bavarian State Opera. The couple shares two children.

SELECTED FILMOGRAPHY:

Strangers When We Meet (Statuesque Brunette, 1960); *Cry for Happy* (Camille Cameron, 1961); *The Wild Westerners* (Rose Sharon, 1962); *Diary of a Madman* (Odette Mallotte, 1963); *Jason and the Argonauts*

(Medea, 1963); *Sylvia* (Big Shirley, 1965); *The Outlaws Is Coming* (Annie Oakley, 1965); *The Great Sioux Massacre* (Libbie Custer, 1965); *Tarzan and the Valley of Gold* (Sophia Renault, 1966); *Frankie and Johnny* (Nellie Blye, 1966); *The Silencers* (Barbara, 1966); *Enter Laughing* (Linda/Miss B, 1967); *Marooned* (Teresa Stone, 1969).

Sylvia Kristel

Birthdate: September 28, 1952; Utrecht, The Netherlands
Birth name: Sylvia Maria Kristel
Date of passing: October 18, 2012; Utrecht, The Netherlands
Height: 5' 9 ¼"
Measurements: N/A

THE ACTRESS WHO CAME to symbolize the sensuality of the modern French woman was actually Dutch. No matter: Sylvia's understated beauty allowed her to emerge as a top model at age sixteen. Even then, her wide-eyed innocent look belied a horrible background. Kristel, whose father had been an inn-keeper, had been abused by one of their boarders when nine. She had been devastated when her parents divorced shortly after she turned fourteen. Her victory in the Miss Europe 1973 contest caused Sylvia to be cast as the lead for the upcoming *Emmanuelle*, based on a once-scandalous autobiographical novel by Emmanuelle Arson, pen-name of Marayat Bibidh. "X was never like this," advertisements in the U.S. announced. This was not some cheap, amateurish item like *Deep Throat* but a slick (if shallow) piece of professionalism that initially played at the arthouse, not the grindhouse, and then went on to bookings in even more mainstream suburban-theatre venues.

Despite limitations imposed on the material by filmmaker Just Jaeckin's at best minor abilities, *Emmanuelle s*cored big-time. Far better was *Emmanuelle, The Joys of a Woman*, delightfully directed by fashion photographer Francis Giacobetti. The series popularized a new paradigm that rejected attitudes of the 1950s, which had held that a man can have as much casual sex as he likes without this impinging on his reputation but a woman who acts similarly is a slut. Kristel became the poster-girl for an emergent

"X WAS NEVER LIKE THIS!": *Emmanuelle* starring Sylvia Kristel represented an important
early attempt to remove the stigma of sleaze from "adult only" movies.

idea, on the continent conveyed by the phrase "emanieru suru": For wom-
en, as well as for men, to have "a casual and extravagant love (i.e., passion-
ate/romantic) affair" could be meaningful and important in and of itself,
an idea that D.H. Lawrence forwarded early in the century. It only made
sense that Kristel would eventually star in a film based on Lawrence's most
famed book, *Lady Chatterley's Lover*. Unfortunately, this too was directed
by Jaeckin, who did not possess the talent to present eroticism intelligently.

SHE SWINGS BOTH WAYS: In *Emmannuelle*, Kristel's heroine discovers why people claim that blondes have more fun; in *Lady Chatterley's Lover*, she embodied D.H. Lawrence's once-controversial heroine who seeks a more natural life.

As the decade moved toward endgame, the international Zeitgeist altered again. In England, there was Thatcher; in the U.S., Reagan appeared on the horizon. Parallel with politics, popular-culture likewise took a sharp pendulum swing in the opposite direction. Appropriately, in the third film, *Goodbye, Emmanuelle*, the symbolic heroine comes to question the Swingin' lifestyle, leaving her long time husband to pursue a quiet old-

SWEET SURRENDER: For many young female viewers of the mid-1970s, Sylvia Kristel's embracement of The Sexual Revolution mirrored their own real life experiments.

fashioned existence with another, more traditional man. In time, there would be other *Emmanuelle* movies for Kristel, as well as a TV version, though now the character was no longer a relatively realistic symbol of the modern female but a superspy type. Kristel did get to play one truly great femme fatale, the exotic dancer turned WWI spy Mata Hari. Sadly, the movie was done in by the same element that destroyed so many of her other films: Just Jaeckin as director. In time, Sylvia would, like such other femme fatales as Sybil Danning and Joan Collins, appear in one of that brief-lived cycle of movies in which gorgeous older women seduce young boys; her own genre entry titled *Private Lessons*. In time, Kristel's smoking habit caught up with her. Informed that she was dying of cancer, the onetime definitive beauty of 1970s cinema, her demure, nuanced face now ravaged, quietly returned home to live her final days in anonymity.

SELECTED FILMOGRAPHY:
Because of Cats (Hannie Troost, 1973); *Naked Over the Fence* (Lilly Marischka, 1973); *Emmanuelle* (Emmanuelle, 1974); *Julia* (Andrea, 1974); *Playing with Fire* (Diana Van Den Berg, 1975); *Emmanuelle II* (Emmanuelle, 1975); *A Faithful Wife* (Mathilde, 1976); *The Streetwalker* (Diana, 1976); *The Last Escapade* (Alice, 1977); *Goodbye, Emmanuelle* aka *Emmanuelle 3* (Emmanuelle, 1977); *Mysteries* (Dany, 1978); *Tigers in Lipstick* (Lady on the Bed, 1979); *The Fifth Musketeer* (Maria Theresa, 197); *The Concorde... Airport '79* (Isabelle, 1979); *The Nude Bomb* (Agent 34, 1980); *Lady Chatterley's Lover* (Constance, 1981); *Private Lessons* (Mallow, 1981); *Private School* (Regina Copuletta, 1981); *Emmanuelle IV* (Emmanuelle/Sylvia, 1984); *Mata Hari* (Mata Hari, 1985); *Red Heat* (Sofia, 1985); *Dracula's Widow* (Vanessa, 1988); *Hot Blood* (Sylvia, 1990); *Beauty School* (Sylvia, 1993); *Emannuele VI* (Emmanuelle, 1993); *Sexy Boys* (Sexologue, 2001).

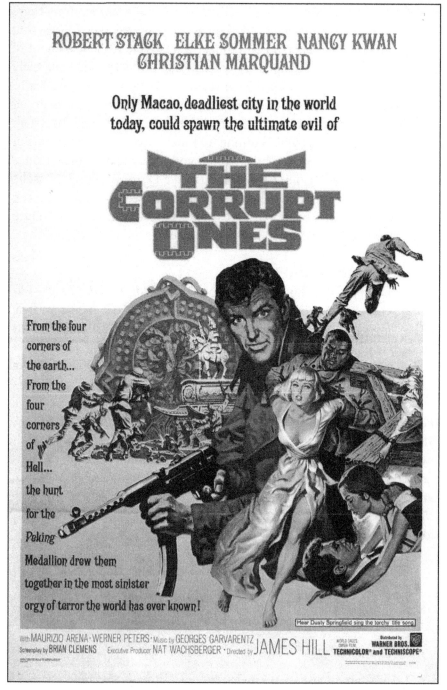

A PRELUDE TO INDIANA JONES: This action-oriented B-flick drew on such legendary pop-culture as *Terry and the Pirates* while looking ahead to the more upscale Steven Spielberg-George Lucas retro-nostalgia entertainments.

Nancy Kwan

Birthdate: May 19, 1939; Hong Kong
Birth Name: Ka Shen Kwan (关家蒨)
Height: 5' 3"
Measurements: N/A

AN ELEMENT OF ACCIDENT propelled Nancy Kwan into the unexpected status of international movie star. The Hong Kong native had, during her childhood, dreamt of another sort of artistic fame: Becoming a world-class dancer. Her talent earned her a spot with the Royal Ballet School in England. She was in the process of mastering her craft when fate stepped in. A major production, *The World of Suzie Wong*, headlined by William Holden, was about to shut down because its female lead, France Nuyen, found herself unable to perform (while steadily losing weight) owing to her tumultuous romance with Marlon Brando. That's when producer Ray Stark recalled a gifted dancer who had also auditioned in a London studio and was now playing the role of Suzie in a touring version of the stage play. Kwan was yanked from that company on a pretext (she had to return home to attend her ill father, or so the lie went) and on February 15, 1960, the upscale girl (her father was a prominent architect) found herself playing a prostitute involved in an inter-racial love affair with an American (William Holden).

In actuality, Kwan was only half Cantonese: Her mother had been Scotch. No matter: From then on, if someone needed an Asian girl for a movie, the first person mentioned for the role would during the Sixties was Nancy Kwan. In the musical *Flower Drum Song*, Kwan played a manipulative Asian-American princess who schemes to win a man she doesn't really love but considers quite a catch as she climbs the social ladder in Chinatown. Memorably, Kwan performed "I enjoy being a girl!" while modeling a bikini in front of a mirror for a sense of total narcissism. Though she never appeared opposite Elvis, Kwan co-starred

THE WORLD OF NANCY KWAN: Her performance as Susie Wong in the once controversial film about an Anglo's deep love for an Asian prostitute set this tiny powerhouse off on a long, successful career.

with Pat Boone in one of his non-singing vehicles, *The Main Attraction*, a tawdry drama with a circus background. Kwan joined the spy genre by appearing in *The Wrecking Crew*, as a Dragon Lady-type trying to stop Dean Martin as Matt Helm. Bruce Lee, unknown at the time, served as stunt coordinator. He and Nancy became close; she later appeared in the Hollywood film version of Lee's life. Kwan returned to the Dragon Lady mode in *The Corrupt Ones*, a half-hearted attempt to revive the glory days of *Terry and the Pirates* and, as such, a predecessor to the Indiana Jones retro-action flicks yet to come. Kwan licked her lips with delight during a sequence in which she threatened to pour acid over the face of the film's good girl (Elke Sommer). Kwan would play a similar character, Dr. Tsu, on TV's *Wonder Woman* (1975).

Married three times, Kwan gave up her still-lucrative Hollywood career to return home and care for her critically ill father. Though her parents had divorced when Nancy was only one, she never forgot that her father risked everything to smuggle Nancy and her young brother out of Hong Kong, to safety, when that city was invaded by the Japanese. Following her return, she created her own production company to turn out TV commercials and low-budget movies in which she starred. In recent years, she has chosen to live a no frills lifestyle in Los Angeles and is the driving force behind the Asian-American Voters Coalition.

SELECTED FILMOGRAPHY:

The World of Suzie Wong (Suzie, 1960); *Flower Drum Song* (Linda Low, 1961); *The Main Attraction* (Tessa, 1962); *Tamahine* (Tamahine, 1963); *The Wild Affair* (Marjorie Lee, 1963); *Honeymoon Hotel* (Lynn Hope, 1964); *Fate Is the Hunter* (Sally Fraser, 1964); *Lt. Robin Crusoe, U.S.N.* (Wednesday, 1966); *Arrivederci, Baby!* (Baby, 1966); *The Corrupt Ones* (Tina, 1967); *Nobody's Perfect* (Tomiko, 1968); *The Wrecking Crew* (Yu-Rang, 1968); *The Girl Who Knew Too Much* (Revel Drue, 1969); *The McMasters* (Robin, 1970); *Fortress in the Sun* (Maria, 1975); *That Lady From Peking* (Sue Ten, 1975); *Project: Kill* (Lee Su, 1976); *Night Creature* (Leslie, 1978); *Keys to Freedom* (Dr. Lao, 1988); *Dragon: The Bruce Lee Story* (Gussie Yang, 1993); *Rebellious* (Joni Mitchell, 1995); *Soul of the Avenger* (Ling Li, 1997); *Murder on the Yellow Brick Road* (Natalie Chung, 2005).

WHEN THAT 'ITSY BITSY TEENY WEENY YELLOW POLKA DOT BIKINI' MET 'THESE BOOTS ARE MADE FOR WALKIN'": Jocelyn Lane models the preferred outfit of most post-Sexual Revolution girls.

Jocelyn Lane

Birthdate: 16 May 1937, Vienna Austria
Birth name: Jocelyn Lane "Jackie" Bolton
Height: N/A
Measurements: N/A

OTHER THAN TUESDAY WELD, who's the only beautiful girl to appear opposite Elvis Presley in a theatrical film and also the faux pretender to rock 'n' roll's throne, Fabian? Jocelyn Lane, that's who. She was matched with The King in one of his least ambitious musicals, *Tickle Me*, then appeared opposite Mr. Forte in his appearance as 1930s gangster Arthur Floyd in a *Bonnie and Clyde* rip-off. (Weld did play opposite Elvis in *Wild in the Country* and Fabian in *High Time*). Jocelyn also appeared in an odd (for this era) throwback to those fantasy costume films of the 1940s, *The Sword of Ali Baba*, which at one point in its genesis was supposedly to be an Elvis musical (Peter Mann assumed the thankless role). There was a Peplum, *The Son of Hercules vs. Venus*; a spaghetti Western, *Land Raiders*; a sci-fi item, *War Gods of Babylon*; and a softcore sexploitation item, *How to Seduce a Playboy*. But the film that established Jocelyn Lane as a standout bad-girl was *Hell's Bells*, among the last of a cycle of biker flicks.

Beginning with *The Wild Angels* (1966), almost all such movies were male-oriented, the biker babe's main function to hang on tight behind her man driving that Harley. Still, the age of social, political, and Cultural Revolution also happened to be the time period during which the Women's Movement continued to gain momentum. Even the lowly biker flick responded. As Cathy, Jocelyn Lane may have looked like Nancy Sinatra opposite Peter Fonda, but all similarity ended there. Here, and for the

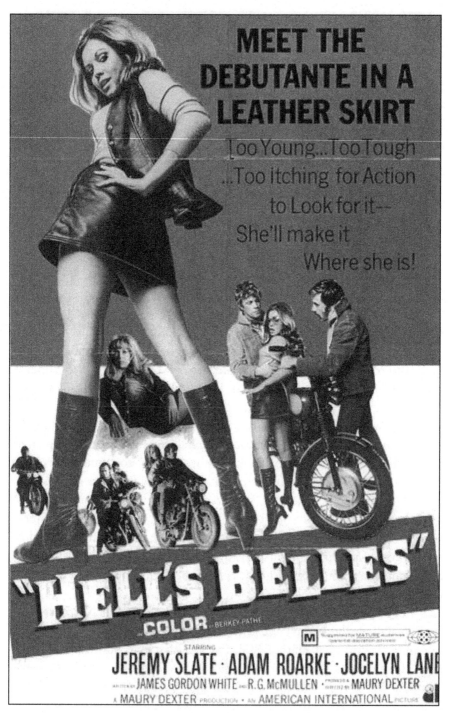

THE BIKER BABE TO END ALL BIKER BABES: Rather than riding on a hog behind a guy, Jocelyn Lane created a proto-feminist all-girl gang of her own in *Hell's Belles*.

first time, a female biker led the pack. A roughhewn sisterhood of girls on choppers followed Lane down the lost highways of the American southwest, and Lord help any biker boy—or anyone else—who didn't take them seriously.

Jocelyn's remarkable beauty ran in the family. While she lived in London (though born in Austria, her mom was Russian, her dad English) before turning eighteen, Jocelyn established herself as a model, her face adorning the covers of U.K. publications. On October 4, 1964, *Life* printed a picture of Jocelyn, claiming that she was among the handful of new beauties who would shortly end what they referred to as Hollywood's "girl drought." *Playboy* featured Lane as a celebrity attraction in the September 1966 issue. Upon entering the movie business, she would have been billed as Jackie Lane were there not yet another London-based actress (later to appear in *Dr. Who*) already going by that name. Some observers insisted that her aristocratic aura and pouty mouth caused Jocelyn to resemble Brigitte Bardot.

Jocelyn also did a great deal of TV, including the all but forgotten *Sailor of Fortune* in 1956, when she was all of nineteen but already so well-developed that she could be cast as a romantic lead. Other small-screen appearances included femme fatales on such cultish shows as *The Man from U.N.C.L.E.* and *The Wild, Wild West* and as herself on *The Dating Game* in 1968. Jocelyn hardly needed help in landing a man; she married Prince Alfonso of Hohenlohe-Langenburg in Marbella, Spain, in February 1971. When she divorced him several years later, Jocelyn would complain that the million dollar settlement (close to fifty million by today's standards) was "Hardly a sum befitting a princess." Today, if you should ever happen to be in Beverly Hills, peek into one of the chichi boutiques and note the feather-adorned necklaces for sale. If one should be labeled as part of the "Princess J. Feather collection," know Jocelyn designed it.

SELECTED FILMOGRAPHY:

Men of Sherwood Forest (bit, 1954); *April in Portugal* (Pretty Travel Guide, 1955); *The Gamma People* (Anna, 1956); *These Dangerous Years* (Maureen, 1956); *The Truth About Women* (Saida, 1957); *The Angry Hills* (Maria, 1958); *Conspiracy of the Borgias* (Young Lucrezia, 1959); *The Magnificent Rogue* (Chou-Chou, 1960); *Robin Hood and the Pirates* (Karin Blain, 1960); *Goodbye Again* (Maisie, 1961); *Operation Snatch* (Bianca, 1961); *The Son of Hercules vs. Venus* (Daphne, 1962); *War Gods of Babylon*

CALL HER PRINCESS: Jocelyn Lane was among those B-movie bad-babes who seized the moment by marrying into royalty.

(Mirra, 1962); *The Sword of Ali Baba* (Princess Amara, 1965); *Tickle Me* (Pamela, 1965); *The Poppy is Also a Flower* (Photographer, 1965); *How to Seduce a Playboy* (Ginette, 1965); *Hell's Belles* (Cathy, 1966); *Land Raiders* (Luisa, 1969); *A Bullet for Pretty Boy* (Betty, 1970).

TWO SIDES OF A SEDUCTIVE KILLER: Whether stripped down for action or looking hot in basic black, Daliah's spy girls almost always had a gun in hand.

Daliah Lavi

Birthdate: October 12, 1940; Palestine/Israel
Birth name: אִיבל הילד (Daliah Levenbuch)
Height: 5' 9"
Measurements: N/A

DALIAH LAVI MAY NOT HAVE starred in the best of the mid-to-late 1960s spy films but she holds the distinction of appearing in more of them, and doing so in rapid succession, than any other lady. Her first, *The Silencers*, introduced Dean Martin in his recurring role as Matt Helm, an Americanized James Bond. Lavi serendipitously shows up at the last possible moment to eliminate a slay girl (Nancy Kovack) employing her female wiles on the agent. Shortly, Lavi moved on to *The Spy with a Cold Nose*, that film's title a spoof of the more serious espionage film *The Spy Who Came in From the Cold*. Lavi's single 007 role, in *Casino Royale*, cast her opposite David Niven and Woody Allen in the only non-official 1960s James Bond film of the Sixties. At one point, Woody holds her in bondage (she's clearly naked if discretely covered by metal bonds that hold her in place), providing one of the few fine moments in a gigantic misfire that sorely needs any help it can get. As the spy cycle concluded, Lavi appeared opposite Richard Johnson, a Connery looka-like who had unwisely turned down the role of 007, in *Some Girls Do*, the lesser known sequel to *Deadlier Than the Male*. At one point, her leering villainess Helga perches in a tree with a long-range rifle, casually picking off distant bystanders as target practice.

Israeli-born Lavi originally hoped to be a ballet dancer, training for that occupation from an early age. Everything changed when Jewish-American Hollywood star Kirk Douglas arrived to shoot *The Juggler* (1953), about Holocaust survivors. He met the ten-year-old while filming a sequence in Shave Ziyyon bei Haifa, her village. Douglas sponsored the child to study dance in Stockholm. Nearly a decade later, Daliah would co-star with Douglas and Edward G. Robinson in *Two Weeks in Another Town*, a kind of "The Bad and the Beautiful Go to Cannes." While in Scandinavian climes, Lavi switched her interest from dancing to modeling, eventually arriving in Italy where she found roles in Giallos such as *The Whip and the Body*, long considered one of the genre's best. Lavi also worked in Germany, appearing in the Teutonic Western *Old Shatterand* opposite former Tarzan Lex Barker. Her last exploitation item was also an oater, *Catlow* with Yul Brynner, shot in Israel. Daliah did appear in one ambitious project, *Lord Jim*, opposite Peter O'Toole. Thereafter, Lavi recreated herself as a smart-set singing sensation. Performing the sort of *schlager* numbers so popular in Germany and her own variations on Israeli folk numbers, Lavi was mentored by Israeli actor Topol (star of the *Fiddler on the Roof* film) to perform first on the BBC. This led to a contract with Polydor and hit records including "Love's Song" in Europe, as well as tours of the nightclub circuit.

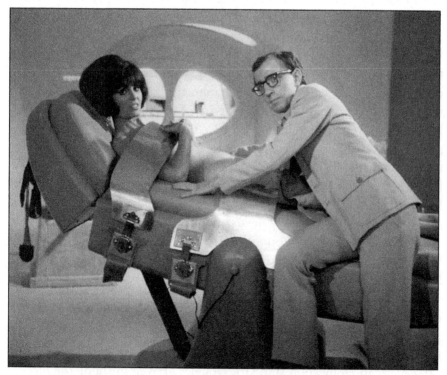

HEY, ISN'T THAT WOODY ALLEN BEHIND THOSE FOSTER GRANT'S?: Daliah's secret agent finds herself in the grip of Little Jimmy Bond in *Casino Royale*.

A bit of trivia: in *Ten Little Indians*, Lavi (not yet a Bond girl) co-starred with Shirley Eaton, already the *Goldfinger* girl.

SELECTED FILMOGRAPHY:
The People of Hemso (The Professor's Teenage Daughter, 1955); *Blazing Sand* (Beautiful Teen, 1960); *Candide* (Cunégonde, 1960); *Violent Summer* (Marie, 1961); *No Time for Ecstasy* (Nathalie Conrad, 1961); *The Return of Dr. Mabuse* (Maria Sabrehm, 1961); *Two Weeks in Another Town* (Veronica, 1962); *Black-White-Red Fourposter* (Germaine, 1962); *The Whip and the Body* (Nevenka, 1963); *The Demon* (Purif, 1963); *Old Shatterhand* (Paloma, 1964); *Cyrano and D'Artagnan* (Marion de L'Orme, 1964); *DM-Killer* (Lolita, 1965); *Lord Jim* (The Girl, 1965); *Shots in ¾ Time* (Irina, 1965); *Ten Little Indians* (Ilona, 1965); *The Silencers* (Tina, 1966); *The Spy with a Cold Nose* (Princess Natasha Romanova, 1966); *Casino Royale* (The Detainer/Ms. James Bond, 1967); *Those Fantastic Flying Fools* (Madelaine, 1967); *Nobody Runs Forever* (Maria, 1968); *Some Girls Do* (Helga, 1969); *Catlow* (Rosita, 1971).

A GIRL TO DIE FOR: Linda Lawson looked properly ethereal for her role as a sea siren come to life in *Night Tide*, her only starring role.

Linda Lawson

Birthdate: January 14, 1936; Ann Arbor, Michigan
Birth name: Linda Gloria Spaziani
Height: N/A
Measurements: N/A

ON SHORE LEAVE, a young sailor happens upon an intriguingly seedy boardwalk. Misfits run such attractions as a broken down carousel; sad-eyed life's losers frequent the area during the off-season. Spotting a jazz joint, the sailor enters and comes in contact with a mysterious girl, Mona. His attraction to her turns into an obsession when he learns Mona is the featured star in a run-down beach-front marina where she plays a mermaid while live fish drift around her. But no one is able to explain precisely how Mora manages to remain underwater for long stretches of time. Then, the sailor hears a rumor: Mona is not an actress but an actual siren, taken from the sea by the establishment's owner. Two previous lovers died in inexplicable ways. As in an Alfred Hitchcock film, the desire for the fall overtakes this young man, now intoxicated by her. Does the sailor hope to prove those rumors wrong, or rather to be her next victim?

Night Tide was one of the first post-studio films to star Dennis Hopper following the termination of his Warner Bros. contract owing to "lack of cooperation" with directors. Hopper luckily met an aspiring filmmaker, Curtis Harrington, who sensed that Hopper's James Dean aura was what he needed for the eerie, edgy, offbeat indie project he was putting together. Despite a miniscule budget, *Night Tide* would be hailed as one of those out of the mainstream items that set the pace for The New American Cinema which developed as the decade wore on. For Mara, Harrington had picked Susan Harrison, a moody actress who'd made a great impression as Burt Lancaster's sister in *Sweet Smell of Success* (1957), but like Hopper

MERMAIDS AREN'T CUTE!: Curtis Harrington's cult thriller revived the notion that the mermaid is actually an undewater vampire, as the advertising made clear.

spoiled her chances at the big time by proving "troublesome." At the last moment, Harrison dropped out to pursue a romantic affair. The director quickly cast Lawson, a former showgirl who had appeared in only one previous film. She proved so convincing in her difficult dual role—sweet, innocent girl by day, the deadly seductress by night—that a cult following ensued, composed mostly of college boys who caught the film at Drive-Ins or saw it on late night TV.

In actuality, Lawson was named Spaziani. She had lived in Michigan until, at age four, her family moved to California. Bitten by the fame-and-fortune bug, she had easily found work as one of the glamorous manques at the Sands Hotel in Las Vegas. Like other stunning actresses who failed to achieve stardom, Linda appeared in episodic TV shows, playing the dark beauty who encountered the noir heroes of *Mike Hammer* (Darren McGavin), *Peter Gunn* (Craig Stevens), and *Man with a Camera* (Charles Bronson) in one year, 1958, later showing up on *77 Sunset Strip, Mr. Lucky, M Squad, Alfred Hitchcock Presents*, and *Richard Diamond, Private Detective*. Her exotic beauty caused Linda to be cast in roles demanding precisely that quality including Lia, the last princess of the Aztecs, on *Wagon Train*. On *Hawaiian Eye*, she played an island native though Linda herself was Italian-American. All of these roles occurred before her brief breakthrough into theatrical films (always of a low-budget order) in the early 1960s. When that dried up, Lawson won recurring roles on numerous series: Wilva in *The Aquanauts* (1961), Renee in *Adventures in Paradise* (1961), Pat Perry on *Don't Call me Charlie* (1962-1963), Betty Lockwood on *The Real McCoys* (1963), Laura Fremont on *Ben Casey* (1965), and Mrs. Farrel on *Saved by the Bell: The New Class* (1994). Though the date of her wedding to producer John Foreman remains uncertain, the two were together until his death in 1992. One of her final film roles, as a member of the Stamper clan in the big-budget film adaptation of Ken Kesey's *Sometimes a Great Notion* starring Paul Newman and Henry Fonda, occurred in one of her husband's productions.

Trivia: In the infamous Beatles misfire *The Magical Mystery Tour* Lawson is one of the bus passengers. Hoping for a singing career, Linda recorded an album, "Introducing Linda Lawson" (1960).

SELECTED FILMOGRAPHY:
The Threat (Gerri, 1960); *Night Tide* (Mora, 1961); *Apache Rifles* (Dawn Gillis, 1964); *Let's Kill Uncle* (Justine, 1966); *Mrs. Stone's Thing* (Woman at Airport, 1970); *Sometimes a Great Notion* (Jan Stamper, 1970).

THE HAUNTED: Something about British beauty Belinda Lee suggested that hers would a short, tempestuous life.

Belinda Lee

Birthdate: June 15, 1935; Budleigh Salterton, Devon, UK
Date of passing: March 12, 1961; San Bernardino CA
Height: N/A
Measurements: N/A

LIVE FAST, DIE YOUNG! That phrase well described James Dean, the youth-cult hero whose September 30, 1955 death in a speeding accident rocked a generation. Less remembered if from the same general era was Belinda Lee, her beauty and talent also lost on a California highway, a little less than six years later. Though newspaper headlines announced "she died too young," within months of her passing Belinda was forgotten. Yet she had been on the verge of star status not unlike that of Brigitte Bardot, likewise representing a new and emergent young woman of the world onscreen: Sultry, pouty, bikini-clad when on the beach, casually assuming the freedoms, including sexual ones, that men had always in the past claimed.

Like Dean, who had hailed from a quiet stretch of America's Midwest, or Bebe, brought up in an upper-middle-class household, Belinda Lee might early-on have seemed an unlikely candidate to embrace, much less embody, La Dolce Vita; i.e., The Sweet Life. Her countryside home, a quaint childhood setting, was followed by stints in Rookesbury Park Preparatory School (Fareham, Hampshire) and St Margaret's (Exeter, Devon). Insisting that she was born to be an actress, Belinda pressured her parents who in time gave in and allowed her to enroll in the Tudor Arts Academy in Surrey. She afterwards appeared as a member of the Nottingham Playhouse company for one year. Had Belinda remained in such environs, she might have matured into a well-known Shakespearean actress. Instead, she slipped off to London, at first pursuing serious stage-actress ambitions at the Royal Academy of Dramatic Art. During a performance of *Point of Departure*, producer Val Guest, in the audience that night, took notice. Shortly, Belinda was cast in *The Runaway Bus*. She married photographer Cornel Lucas, fourteen years her senior, after he shot glamour pics of the girl. When the prestigious Rank organization offered Belinda a seven-year-contract, she accepted. Following a stint as Rosalind at the Open Air Theatre in Regents' Park, Belinda bid farewell to roles like Juliet and Ophelia, opting for quick, easy money.

Like Bardot, Belinda posed in stunning swimsuits at the Cannes Film Festival, soon gracing the covers of international magazines. While in the U.S., Bob Hope expressed his belief that this girl could conquer Hollywood. In 1956, Lee and Marilyn Monroe were, on the same day, introduced to the Queen in London. Yet hints of the horror to come already appeared, as when Belinda's hair caught fire while standing near a candle at the Pinewood studio. A Venice meeting with Prince Filippo Orsini led to dalliances with the married aristocrat; Lee also became involved with co-star Massimo Girotti while filming sand-and-sandles flicks near Rome. Playing the goddess of love Aphrodite ought to have made her an immediate sensation but the film did not attract attention Stateside, nor did her vivid incarnations of such legendary femme fatales as Messalina

SULTRY AND SENSUOUS: The posters for Lee's films, as a pirate girl and a Peplum queen, suggested that here might be the British Bardot.

WALK ON THE WILD SIDE: Belinda Lee gets all tarted up for a downscale
fashion shoot.

and Lucrezia Borgia. Dumping her then-current husband, Lee intensified the affair with Orsino; owing to his high position at the Vatican, an ensuing scandal elicited more interest than any of her B-budget films. Following a suicide attempt in 1958 by overdosing on pills, Belinda embarked on a series of "tempestuous" romances. Rank dissociated itself with the young woman who, only a year earlier, had been the Number Two Box Office attraction in England.

Next, back to L.A. Belinda accompanied Jet Set filmmaker Gualtiero Jacopetti there, the two then driving toward Las Vegas to shoot scenes for his upcoming documentary *Mondo Cane* (1962). Tearing along at over eighty miles an hour, Jacopetti (driving) overturned their car. Unlike Dean, whose death was immediate, Belinda suffered for nearly half an hour, finally expiring from a fractured skull and broken neck. When her final film, *Joseph and His Brethren*, opened the following year, virtually no one recalled who the top-billed girl even was.

SELECTED FILMOGRAPHY:

The Runaway Bus (Janie Grey, 1954); *Blackout* (Phyllis Brunner, 1954); *The Belles of St Trinian's* (Amanda, 1954); *Footsteps in the Fog* (Elizabeth Travers, 1955); *Goddess of Love* (Aphrodite, 1957); *Dangerous Exile* (Virginia, 1958); *Elephant Gun* (Alice Lang, 1958); *Way of the Wicked* (Lina, 1959); *The Nights of Lucretia Borgia* (Lucretia, 1959); *She Walks By Night* (Rosemarie, 1959); *Marie of the Isles* (Marie Bonnard, 1960); *Messalina* (Messalina, Valeria, 1960); *Satan Tempts With Love* (Evelyn, 1960); *Phantom Lovers* (Eileen, 1961); *Constantine and the Cross* (Fausta, 1961); *Joseph and His Brethren* (Henet, 1962).

Janet Leigh

Birthdate: July 6, 1927; Merced, CA
Birth name: Jeanette Helen Morrison
Date of passing: October 3, 2004; Los Angeles, CA
Height: 5' 5 ½"
Measurements: 36C – 23 - 36

JANET LEIGH WAS DISCOVERED by 1930s star Norma Shearer when that grand dame visited a ski lodge where young Leigh's parents labored (her father a desk clerk, her mother a maid). Shearer noticed a single black and white picture of the girl. The sense of sweetness, innocence, and utter purity dazzled Shearer. Yet that quality had to be balanced by the fact that Janet had secretly run off to marry a man (Stanley Reames) when she was barely fifteen. Once established in Hollywood, such a dual quality emanated from the screen whenever Leigh stepped in front of a camera. A sense of blushing virginity in her vulnerable eyes consistently gives way to a hint that a devil in the flesh existed just under that placid surface, likely waiting for an opportunity to slip out. Alfred Hitchcock saw and milked that duality in *Psycho*. Marion Crane cons everyone into believing she's a conventional 'good girl,' trusted at her office. Actually, she's involved in a torrid love affair with a married man and, out of frustration with her secret life, turns into a 'gone girl,' surprising even herself as she steals and then runs off with a large sum of money. In an early scene, the seemingly wholesome blonde wears lingerie that fails to match: her bra and panties are black and white, visually suggesting that there are two distinct personalities inside her. At the legendary moment when she is killed in a motel shower by a knife-wielding assailant, the audience is uncertain whether this girl is a heroine or villainess. In fact, she is neither and both.

A MATURE BEAUTY: Janet Leigh successfully made the difficult transition from 1950s demure ingénue to deadly spy girl in the 1960s, seen here as a femme fatale on TV's *The Man from U.N.C.L.E.*

Previously, Leigh would have seemed an unlikely case for cult stardom. During the early 1950s, she signed a contract with Universal and, for most of the following decade, appeared in mid-level studio fare. There were costume pictures like *The Prince who was a Thief* (opposite Tony Curtis, her husband from 1951-1962), Westerns (*The Naked Spur*, a near-classic with James Stewart); and period drama (*Houdini*) as well as light comedy (*The Perfect Furlough*), both with Curtis. As the Sixties neared, television filled the bill for such programming. Movies had to become events, like Kirk Douglas's shot-on-location *The Vikings* (Leigh again played opposite Curtis) or offbeat, one of a kind projects such as *Touch of Evil*, a noir-nightmare in which Leigh co-starred with Charlton Heston and director Orson Welles. Deserted by husband Curtis for a teenage European starlet, Leigh fought to survive. *Bye Bye Birdie* was a hit but Leigh's role was trimmed down to make room for vicacious newcomer Ann-Margret. Shortly, Leigh was appearing in B-movies like *Kid Redolo*, in which she was encouraged to embrace her dark side, appearing on-screen in then shockingly revealing lingerie. Her next femme fatale role

STAY OUT OF THE SHOWER: After watching Leigh's demise in Alfred Hitchcock's *Psycho* (1960), a great many people decided that they would much prefer baths in the future.

BAD-GIRL GOES WEST: Even in cowboy films like *Kid Rodelo*, Leigh showed off her stuff in the daring 1960s style.

was in the *The Man from U.N.C.L.E.* two parter "The Concrete Overcoat Affair." Later films included junk movies such as *Night of the Lepus*, a rip-off of Hitch's *The Birds* only this time around featuring deadly bunnies. The transition was now complete: From Hollywood princess to aging Scream Queen. The semi-retired Leigh would appear with daughter Jamie

Lee Curtis in 1980 in John Carpenter's *The Fog*. Of course, that director always cited Alfred Hitchcock as one of his prime influences—Curtis had already appeared in Carpenter's *Halloween* (1978), a Hitchcock-inspired film. When Jamie Lee agreed to do a follow up, *Halloween H20: 20 Years Later*, her Mom appeared.

SELECTED FILMOGRAPHY:

The Romance of Rosy Ridge (Lissy, 1947); *Words and Music* (Dorothy Feiner Rodgers, 1948); *Act of Violence* (Edith Enley, 1948); *Little Women* (Meg, 1949); *The Red Danube* (Olga/Maria, 1949); *That Forsyte Woman* (June, 1949); *Holiday Affair* (Connie, 1949); *Strictly Dishonorable* (Isabelle, 1951); *Angels in the Outfield* (Jennifer, 1951); *Two Tickets to Broadway* (Nancy, 1951); *Scaramouche* (Aline, 1952); *The Naked Spur* (Lina, 1953); *Houdini* (Bess, 1953); *Prince Valiant* (Aleta, 1954); *Living It Up* (Wally, 1954); *The Black Shield of Falworth* (Lady Anne, 1954); *Pete Kelly's Blues* (Ivy, 1955); *My Sister Eileen* (Eileen Sherwood, 1955); *Safari* (Linda, 1956); *Jet Pilot* (Anna/Olga, 1957); *Touch of Evil* (Susan Vargas, 1958); *The Vikings* (Morgana, 1958); *Psycho* (Marion Crane, 1960); *The Manchurian Candidate* (Eugenie, 1962); *Bye Bye Birdie* (Rosie DeLeon, 1963); *Wives and Lovers* (Bertie, 1963); *Kid Rodelo* (Nora, 1966); *Harper* (Susan Harper, 1966); *Three on a Couch* (Dr. Acord, 1966); *See You in Hell, Darling* (Cherry, 1966); *Night of the Lepus* (Gerry, 1972); *The Fog* (Kathy Williams, 1980); *Halloween H20: 20 Years Later* (Norma Watson, 1998); *Bad Girls from Valley High* (Mrs. Witt, 2005).

THE WORLD'S MOST GORGEOUS GHOST: Valerie Leon poses for a publicity still in order to enhance her image as the new Queen of Hammer horror.

Valerie Leon

Birthdate: November 12, 1943; Islington, London, UK
Height: 5' 11"
Measurements: 38 – 25 - 36

VAL HAILED FROM MIDDLE to upper-middle class origins, her father an executive at a textile firm and her mother, who had once had aspirations to be an actress, a full time mom. Val and her siblings were treated to private school educations. She originally worked at Harrods Department Store where she aspired to be a fashion buyer. Noting a newspaper ad about an audition for a chorus girl in a variety show, she slipped off, tried out, and won the part. Shortly, she joined the cast of London's *Funny Girl*, headlined by Barbra (then Barbara) Streisand. Her Amazonian height and measurements led to film and television offers. Despite her voluptuous appearance and naughty-girl roles, her life seems to have been very 'proper,' as the Brits like to say. Val remained quietly married to Michael Mills from 1974 to his passing in 1988; the couple had two children. In Britain, one of Val's claims to fame was her appearances as the gorgeous girl in the Hai Karate (aftershave) TV commercials.

Her initial appearance as a spy-girl was as "Therese" in the "To Kill a Saint" (1967) episode of *The Saint*. The following year, Val gave Diana Rigg serious competition for top glamour girl on *The Avengers* as bad-girl Betty in the "Whoever Shot Poor George?" episode. Her ample bosom was exposed as much as the BBC of that era would allow as Dalli in the period-piece comedy *Up Pompeii!* (1970). Even into the 1970s, Leon's edgy femme fatale image remained intact as 'The Queen of Space' on *The Persuaders* (1971), co-starring with a post-*Saint*/pre-Bond Roger Moore, and a similar rule as 'The Thule Girl' in *Space: 1999* (1975). Technically, Val played a Bond girl twice, yet if you'd blinked at the wrong moment during either movie, you'd have missed her. She appeared in the third (and best) of the Roger Moore 007 escapades, *The Spy Who Loved Me*, for a cameo as a Hotel Receptionist. Six years later, when Sean Connery agreed to return (*not*, notably, for Cubby Broccoli) in *Never Say Never Again*, Val momentarily appears onscreen in the Bahamas. She rates as one of the small handful of girls who can claim to have appeared in two 007 films, and the only Bond girl to play scenes with both Moore and Connery.

Today, Leon is better remembered for her work in the *Carry On* series, broad, silly gut-level humor burlesques. Her cult status derives from two roles. The first was for Hammer, which had decided to add The Mummy to the list of Universal Studios' 1930s monsters to be revived from the undead. For a handsome adaptation in *Blood From the Mummy's Tomb*, Hammer relied on an old tried and true technique in which a young modern woman finds herself possessed by the spirit of an ancient Egyptian princess. As these were the early 1970s, nudity was all but required, but Val insisted on a body-double for her brief bedroom

DIE LIKE AN EGYPTIAN: As a reincarnated ancient princess of the Nile, Valerie Leon meets her end in *Blood From the Mummy's Tomb*.

CARRY ON, GORGEOUS: Val went 'Up the Nile' (at least on a studio set recreation) for one of the remarkably popular British 'broad' (in every sense of the term) comedies.

scene. That absolutely is her, though, all but popping out of her remarkably designed Egyptian princess costume later in the story. Val made a brief but memorable appearance in *Revenge of the Pink Panther*, one of the last and least in the Blake Edwards/Peter Sellers series, as a black leather dominatrix.

SELECTED FILMOGRAPHY:

Smashing Time (Secretary, 1967); *The Love Factor* (Atropos, 1969); *Carry On Camping* (Miss Dobbin, 1969); *Carry On Up the Jungle* (Leda, 1970); *Blood From the Mummy's Tomb* (Margaret/Tera, 1971); *No Sex Please: We're British* (Susan, 1973); *Can I Keep It Up for a Week?* (Miss Hampton, 1975); *Queen Kong* (Nabonga's White Queen, 1976); *The Spy Who Loved Me* (Receptionist, 1977); *The Wild Geese* (Car Dealer, 1978); *(The) Revenge of the Pink Panther* (Tanya, 1978); *Never Say Never Again* (Bahamas Beauty, 1983).

Sylvia Lopez

aka SYLVIA SINCLAIR; TANIA KAREN
Birthdate: November 10, 1933; Paris, France
Date of passing: November 20, 1959; Ile-de-France
Birth name: Tatjana Bernt
Height: 5' 9"
Measurements: N/A

FRENCH BY BIRTH, the young beauty modeled for *Vogue* at age nineteen, then moved to Italy to take advantage of the film business in Rome. Her two most memorable roles were in sword-and-sandal flicks. Though Sylvia has gone down in Peplum history as one of the great villainesses, her first part was sympathetic. She played Mariam, aka Miriam, second wife of the title character (portrayed by American actor Edmund Purdom) in *Herod the Great*. Sylvia's role was as a lovely descendant of Israel's Hasmonean dynasty of Judah; Herod, Arabian-born King of the Jews (awarded that position by Rome's hierarchy) banishes his first wife and child in hopes such a union will endear him to the Hebrews. Eventually he goes mad and has Miriam executed, then becomes madder still, believing her ghost haunts the palace at night.

That same year, Sylvia played Onfale in *Hercules Unchained*, the sequel to the mega-hit *Hercules* starring Steve Reeves. She's the gorgeous if evil queen of a remote island who captures handsome men, employs drugs to rob them of their memories, enjoys their 'company' for a month, then executes them (former lovers are transformed into lifelike statues) so as to move on to her next willing victim. This works well enough until she makes the mistake of falling for her latest prey. When young Ulysses helps Hercules regain his memory, the Greek heroes hurry away. Unable to consider another man after him, Onfale commits suicide by diving into

KILLER'S KISS: Something about Sylvia Lopez's face, which resembled Sophia Loren's only with a dark archness, suggested evil incarnate.

a vat of boiling liquid that she previously employed to immortalize her many paramours.

Many reviewers cited her considerable contribution. Momentarily, it seemed as if Sylvia would enjoy a long, fruitful career playing bad girls, thanks to her evil eyes and cruel mouth. Then Lopez visited her doctor, learning that she was suffering from terminal leukemia. She returned to

CIRCE, MOVE OVER: Lopez (with Steve Reeves) as the mythic ruler Onfale in
Hercules Unchained.

her native France and died shortly after, leaving behind Francis Lopez, her grieving husband, a film composer. At the time of her passing, she and Bardot had just begun work on the film *Sexy Girl.*

Trivia: Some sources insist that Sylvia was actually born in Austria. Highly educated (a graduate of Lycée, she was fluent in at least eight languages), friends insist that in person Sylvia Lopez was the precise opposite of her femme fatale image.

FILMOGRAPHY:

Baratin (Patricia Dubois-Dumas, 1956); *Cinq Millions Comptant* (Loulou, 1956); *Mademoiselle et Son Gang* (Marie-Christine, 1957); *Tabarin* (Florence Didier, 1958); *Herod the Great* (Mariam, 1959); *Hercules Unchained* (Queen Onfale of Lidia, 1959); *Son of the Red Corsair* (Carmen, 1959); *Il Moralista* (Woman of the Nightclub, 1959).

TO BED OR NOT TO BED: Presaging the coming style of the 1960s, Tina Louise began posing in a provocative manner in the mid-1950s.

Tina Louise

Birthdate: February 11, 1934; New York, NY
Birth name: Tatiana Josivovna Chernova Blacker
Height: 5' 8 ½ "
Measurements: N/A

BEFORE EMERGING AS A SEX SYMBOL, Tina Louise established herself as a serious actress during the golden age of live TV. She won roles on such prestigious shows as *Studio One* and *Producer's Showcase*, both 1956. Shortly thereafter, the fast-blossoming teen took men's breaths away as the femme fatale Appassionata van Climax in the then-daring Broadway musical version of Al Capp's classic comic strip *L'il Abner*. Here then was the enigma that would haunt Tina throughout her career: Torn between identities as a serious Method actress (she studied at the Actor's Studio) and a glamour girl associated with shallow starlet roles, most notably the marooned movie star Ginger Grant (1964-1967) on TV's *Gilligan's Island* (1964-1967).

Born Tina Blacker, she was the daughter of a hard-working Jewish couple that owned a candy store in Brooklyn. Her movie break came when Carroll Baker refused to appear in *God's Little Acre*, from an Erskine Caldwell story, for fear that she would become typecast in Southern White Trash roles following *Baby Doll*. Tina threw herself into the part and won that year's Golden Globe for the Best New Female Actress. Such a debut ought to have led to stellar parts. Mostly, though, she found herself in B-Westerns, hardly what one would expect from a protégé of the legendary teacher Lee Strasberg. As a result, Tina Louise was one of the first American actresses to head for Italy. There, she became a Peplum queen. Her most notable performance was as Sappho in a film that has been released internationally under various titles including *The Isle of Les-*

FROM THE ISLE OF LESBOS TO THE BACKWOODS OF AMERICA: Louise was equally convincing in a Peplum about the lesbian queen Sappho and as a redneck temptress in *God's Little Acre*.

COOL, CLEAR WATER: Tina Louise always seemed most alluring when heading off to nature and going back to the basics.

bos and *The Warrior Queen*. This marked the first time that the swords-and-sandals genre dared to move away from male-oriented adventures featuring Hercules and Machiste in favor of a focus on the sisterhood of women who hold their own as warriors—and, during fade-outs, retire to what knowing audiences understood to be tender encounters. In due time, Louise played a femme fatale in a spy movie. Along with blonde Elke Sommer and brunette Nancy Kwan, the strawberry blonde was the third female evil musketeer in *The Wrecking Crew* opposite Dean Martin as Matt Helm.

There was plenty of episodic TV work, ranging from top drama (*Route 66*'s "I'm Here to Kill a King," 1963) to a comic turn on *The Red Skelton Show* in 1966. Louise was a regular on *Dallas* during its first season (1978-79). Her only (brief) marriage (1966-1970) was to an ahead-of-his-time abrasive TV talk show host, Les Carne, whose microphone had been mounted on a machine gun. Their daughter is Cheryl Crane.

Trivia: The role of Ginger had originally been created for Jayne Mansfield, who bolted from the series when she closely considered the pilot script and realized that she would be part of an ensemble rather than the series' lead.

SELECTED FILMOGRAPHY:

God's Little Acre (Griselda Walden, 1958); *The Trap* (Linda, 1959); *The Hangman* (Selah, 1959); *Day of the Outlaw* (Helen, 1959); *The Siege of Syracuse* (Diana/Artemide/Lucrezia, 1960); *The Isle of Lesbos* (Sappho, 1960); *Armored Command* (Alexandra, 1961); *For Those Who Think Young* (Topaz McQueen, 1964); *The Seventh Floor* (Dr. Mehr, 1967); *The Wrecking Crew* (Lola Medina, 1968); *The Good Guys and the Bad Guys* (Carmel, 1969); *The Happy Ending* (Helen, 1969); *The Stepford Wives* (Charmaine Wimpiris, 1975); *Death Scream* (Hilda, 1975); *Kentucky Fried Movie* (Voice, 1977); *Mean Dog Blues* (Donna, 1978); *Dog Day* (Blue, 1984); *Hell Riders* (Claire, 1984); *Evils of the Night* (Cora, 1985); *O.C. and Stiggs* (Florence, 1985); *Johnny Suede* (Mrs. Fontaine, 1991); *Welcome to Woop Woop* (Bella, 1997); *Late Phases* (Clarissa, 2014).

BLOODLUST IN A BIKINI: The former good-girl of teen flicks like Blue Denim transforms into a beautiful psycho in *Once You Kiss a Stranger*.

Carol Lynley

Birthdate: February 13, 1942; New York, NY
Birth name: Carole Ann Jones
Height: N/A
Measurements: N/A

A MIDDLE-AGED GOLF PRO (Paul Burke) believes he's stumbled onto an erotic nirvana. There on a West Coast beach is that teenage blonde surfer girl he, and every guy his age, has dreamed about: The bikini-clad beauty (Carol Lynley) who came of age during the 1960s, which he, feeling something of a left-over from the Fifties, sadly missed out on. Amazingly, this gorgeous flower-child throws herself at him. The next morning, however, everything changes. What he took to be charming eccentricity on her part transforms into a darker subtext beneath her bright Hippie-era exterior. First, there's that spear-gun which she had apparently been using on fish, now turned upward and aimed at him. Then, she suggests the two trade murders. Here is the Patricia Highsmith/Alfred Hitchcock *Strangers on a Train* revamped as a jet-set fable.

Carol modeled as a child, and then as a teenager, under the name Carol Lee. Likely she would have employed that as well while acting were it not spoken for with Actor's Equity. Her remarkable face, with those enchantingly ambiguous eyes, appeared on the cover of *Life* magazine's April 22, 1957 issue. This convinced Walt Disney that here was precisely the right person to play an abused Colonial-era girl in *The Light in the Forest* opposite James MacArthur. Two strong roles followed, as the contemporary teenager who discovers that she's pregnant by the boy next door (Brandon DeWilde) in *Blue Denim* and a lass who allows herself to be seduced by a magnetic stranger (Kirk Douglas), neither aware that she's his daughter from a previous fling, in *The Last Sunset*. At age 22, the seemingly demure young woman posed nude in *Playboy* (March 1965) cementing her sex symbol status. Yet Lynley's career would turn out to be one of the oddest in Hollywood history. After playing the lead in *Return to Peyton Place* for director Jose Ferrer, Lynley next appeared in a thankless bit part as yet another boring nice small-town girl in *The Stripper*. Though she headlined two A-list Otto Preminger films, the historical epic *The Cardinal* (playing dual roles) and the Hitchcock-like thriller *Bunny*

GOOD CAROL, BAD CAROL: Lynley proved that nice girls do pose in the nude for *Playboy*, later portraying a beach bunny who employs her spear gun to shoot men.

PEEK-A-BOO!: Like a sprite from some old fairytale, girl-woman Carol Lynley rises from the deep.

Lake Is Missing, Carol also appeared in minor fare opposite pop singers Fabian (*Hound-Dog Man*) and Glenn Campbell (*Norwood*). One of her most bizarre features was *Harlow*, a cheaply thrown together faux film designed to appear before the big budget Joseph Levine film of that title, starring Carroll Baker, could be released. In 1972, she appeared in the B-junk movie *Beware! The Blob* but also in the huge all-star disaster epic, *The Poseidon Adventure*.

One of her most memorable roles came on TV, as the girlfriend of Darren McGavin in *The Night Stalker* (ABC; 1/4/1972), a made-for-television vampire movie penned by the great Richard Matheson, produced by Dan Curtis (*Dark Shadows*). In comparison to many beautifully blonde colleagues of the 1960s, some of whom were done in by such disastrous choices as drugs and men, Lynley appears to have led a relatively quiet (certainly private) life. She married only once, early on, to Michael Selsman (1960-1964), resulting in one (female) child. There was a much-publicized but in no way scandalous long-term affair with Brit interviewer David Frost and another with the considerably older George Burns. During the 1970s she mostly opted for TV, often playing a fantasy femme or neurotic villainess, in such cult shows as *Alfred Hitchcock Presents*, *The*

Invaders, The Man from U.N.C.L.E., The Immortal, and *Rod Serling's Night Gallery.*

Trivia: Though Lynley was one of the first actors hired by producer David Lynch for his *Twin Peaks* series, for the role of Diane, she never appeared on the screen in that part.

SELECTED FILMOGRAPHY:

The Light in the Forest (Shenandoe, 1958); *Blue Denim* (Janet Willard, 1959); *Hound-Dog Man* (Dony, 1959); *The Last Sunset* (Missy Breckenridge, 1961); *Return to Peyton Place* (Allison MacKenzie, 1961); *The Stripper* (Elise, 1963); *Under the Yum Yum Tree* (Robin Austin, 1963); *The Cardinal* (Mony/Regina, 1963); *Shock Treatment* (Cynthia Lee Albright, 1964); *The Pleasure Seekers* (Maggie, 1964); *Harlow* (Jean, 1965); *Bunny Lake Is Missing* (Ann Lake, 1965); *Danger Route* (Jocelyn, 1967); *The Maltese Bippy* (Robin, 1969); *Once You Kiss a Stranger* (Diana, 1969); *Norwood* (Yvonne, 1970); *Beware! The Blob* (Leslie, 1972); *The Poseidon Adventure* (Nonnie, 1972); *The Cat and the Canary* (Annabelle, 1978); *The Shape of Things to Come* (Niki, 1979).

Sue Lyon

Birthdate: July 10, 1946; Davenport, Iowa
Birth name: Suellyn Lyon
Height: 5'3"
Measurements: N/A

APPARENTLY, SUE LYON'S STORY offers a variation on the old plot about a dominating Show Biz backstage mother. The family move from Iowa to California was predicated on the girl-child's remarkable beauty. Suellyn's father had passed away and there was little if any money coming in. Mama rightly guessed that her daughter's perfect features could earn them a considerable income via child-modeling gigs. No sooner had they arrived in L.A. than J.C. Penny picked the budding beauty for print layouts. A guest-shot opposite Jay North on the *Dennis the Menace* TV show would lead to sudden stardom. One of the people watching that Sunday evening was Stanley Kubrick, searching for the right girl to play...

"How did they ever make a movie out of *Lolita*?" ads for the film asked. In fact, 'they' didn't. No sequence more defines the difference between Vladimir Nabokov's novel and the film than the iconic first appearance of Lyon in the title role. The film's Humbert Humbert (James Mason), a college professor in search of a room to rent, is about to turn down the over-eager Mrs. Haze (Shelley Winters) when he spots her teen daughter sunbathing in the back yard in a bikini. No such swimsuit was present in the book; there, Lolita was an innocent, unawares twelve-year-old, obliviously dousing herself with cool water on a hot day. The Lolita of Nabokov's imagination looked four or five years younger than her age; the book's Humbert was a serial child-molester and his seduction of an earlier child was explicit. Here, Lolita is fifteen (like the girl playing her) and might easily have passed for at least two years older than that. More-

THE PICTURE OF INNOCENCE: Lyon, like her screen counterpart Lolita, dares the viewer to guess if she's the sweetest little girl in the world or the harbinger of disaster.

over, the wicked glint in the eyes of the film's Lolita suggests an underage femme fatale: In the film, she does the seducing. That would be the case two years later when Lyon played an almost identical role in John Huston's *(The) Night of the Iguana* opposite Richard Burton.

Lyon proved convincing as well as attractive in both. In hopes of forging a serious career for her daughter, Mama turned down numerous offers, holding out for The Big One. It arrived when John Ford himself cast Sue (with second-billing to Oscar winner Anne Bancroft) in *Seven Women*, his final project. But the film sputtered at the box-office and received lukewarm reviews. The best part that came her way after that was the 1969 TV version of the classic thriller-comedy *Arsenic and Old Lace* with Helen Hayes and Lillian Gish. From then on it was strictly secondary parts in B-movies including George Hamilton's wife in the superior Drive-In flick *Evel Knievel*. Though Sue would not be diagnosed as bipolar until many years later, sudden fits of temper and deep, dark moods did not endear her to producers. A career revival seemed likely in 1967 when Warren Beatty cast her in *Bonnie and Clyde*, though at the last moment, Lyon was replaced by Faye Dunaway. Soon Sue disappeared from public view. When she tied the knot with African-American photographer Roland Harrison, *National Enquirer*-type scandal sheets had a field day. Their move to Spain did not end such problems, which caused so

"HOW DID THEY EVER MAKE A MOVIE OUT OF LOLITA?": That was the log line for the most controversial film of 1962.

TAKE YOUR PICK: Of all the many beachside portraits that Lyon posed for, most fans consider these the two most unforgettable.

THEY CALL HER TWINKLETOES: Humbert Humbert (James Mason) ceases to be the mentor and turns into the slave of underage beauty Lolita (Lyon).

much pressure (along with Lyon's frequent/extreme mood changes) that the marriage did not last. She fell in love with Gary "Cotton" Adamson, a convicted killer, taking such jobs as cocktail waitress in third-rate joints to sustain herself in Colorado, the state in which he was imprisoned. That 'relationship' did not end well either. Finally, Sue Lyon put show business aside to live in anonymity, refusing to grant any interview. What any reporter would likely ask: how did you fall so far, so fast?

SELECTED FILMOGRAPHY:

Lolita (Lolita Haze, 1962); *The Night of the Iguana* (Charlotte Goodall, 1964); *7 Women* (Emma Clark, 1966); *The Flim Flam Man* (Bonnie Lee Packard, 1967); *Tony Rome* (Diana Pines, 1967); *Four Rode Out* (Myra, 1970); *Evel Knievel* (Linda, 1971); *To Love, Perhaps to Die* (Ana, 1973); *Crash* (Kim, 1977); *End of the World* (Sylvia, 1977); *Alligator* (TV Newswoman, 1980).

ONCE WAS NOT ENOUGH: Tania Mallet is the only blonde Bond beauty to never follow-up with another film role following *Goldfinger*.

Tania Mallet

Birthdate: May 19, 1941; Blackpool, Lancashire, UK
Height: 5' 7"
Measurements: N/A

SOME YEARS AGO, I wrote a book called *Once Was Enough*, about people who starred only a single time on the big screen. Or, as the expression goes: One Shot Wonders. Few celebs more perfectly qualify for such status than Tania Mallet, who had a key role in the third (and definitive for the 1960s) Bond film, *Goldfinger*. Tania played "the middle girl," Tilly Masterson, filling in the gap between Shirley Eaton as Jill Masterson during the film's first third and Honor Blackman as Pussy Galore in the final act. Following Jill's demise, Tilly attempts to kill 007 (Sean Connery) during a cat and mouse game as their elegant automobiles tear across a lush green landscape. When she loses the bout, Bond realizes this is indeed the younger sister of the blonde from the opening, out for revenge, wrongly blaming him. Quickly, she's converted, then dies (her head sliced by Oddjob's infamous killer-hat) even as Bond is captured by bad guys and whisked away to Goldfinger's secret lair. Tania's character was one of the few women in a 007 opus who doesn't bed Bond before she expires. Simply, there was no way (however contrived) to get the two in the sack without slowing up the proceedings.

Tania grew up in a seaside resort town and was instantly recognized as a world-class beauty. Classes at the Lucy Clayton School led to a career in modeling shortly after she turned sixteen. Tania auditioned for the role in *From Russia With Love* that went to Daniela Bianchi and made enough of an impression that she was contacted for the next project. When asked why, despite her auspicious debut, she never made another film, Tania insisted she couldn't afford it: Cubby Broccoli had only paid her £150 a week while as a manqué she earned upwards of £2,000 per week. Like other supposed One Shot Wonders, she may actually be visible in another film. Some fans insist that Tania briefly appears in the Swingin' London Beatles-era film *The Girl Getters*. Ultra-private about her off-screen (and

THE BOLD AND THE BEAUTIFUL: Tania Mallet poses with one of Goldfinger's super-power rifles.

GETTING THE DROP ON BOND: Sean Connery, front and present; back row,
Shirley Eaton, Honor Blackman, and Tania Mallet.

off the runway) life, her second marriage succeeded. Gardening occupies
most of her time. Famously, she has said: "If you're only going to make
one movie in life, then why not *Goldfinger*?"

FILMOGRAPHY:

Goldfinger (Tilly Masterson, 1964); *The Girl Getters* (Beautiful Blonde
'Bird', 1964; unsubstantiated/rumored).

CALIFORNIA DREAMIN': Margaret Markov looked likely to become a beach bunny in one of the surf and sand musicals; instead, she became a popular early 1970s action star.

Margaret Markov

Birthdate: November 22, 1948; Stockton, CA
Birth name: Margaret Mary Markov
Height: N/A
Measurements: N/A

FIRST, NOTE THAT THERE EXISTS a discrepancy as to Maggie's (her nickname among friends) date of birth. Some sources give it as 1951; most state 1948. No question that the striking blonde grew up in Stockton. Maggie hungered for a career in The Biz and won a role as a student in *The Sterile Cuckoo*, a charming little film about a pair of college age virgins (Wendell Burton and Liza Minnelli) who decide to go all the way. A mild hit, the film did not propel Markov into a late-studio era career. She slipped into edgy exploitation flicks, virtually guaranteeing a cult following instead of mainstream stardom. While 1970s Second Wave feminists may have expressed dismay at the skimpy costumes Maggie (and frequent co-star Pam Grier) wore in exploitation flicks, the star helped set the pace for what would eventually come to be called Post-Feminism: Those strong, smart female characters, ranging from Lara Croft to Black Widow, who do not feel any necessity to play down their obvious natural beauty to be taken seriously.

Run, Angel, Run was considerably more thought-provoking than the average biker flick, as William Smith, former outlaw, writes an expose about his old chopper gang and is then pursued by them. Maggie was his female lead and also played a gorgeous teenager in *Pretty Maids All in a Row*, Roger Vadim's first American film. Rock Hudson took on the role of a seemingly reliable sports coach who not only seduces but murders pretty co-eds. *The Hot Box* reached beyond the usual limits of Phillipines-lensed Girls in Prison flicks thanks to future A-list director Jonathan Demme's

QUO VADIS, 1970s STYLE: Markov raises her sword in a proto-feminist Peplum, swearing that "We who are about to die salute you."

THE (GIRL-GIRL) DEFIANT ONES: Margaret and Pam Grier redo the old Tony Curtis/ Sidney Poitier teaming from the 1950s Civil Rights classic by Stanley Kramer.

contribution. The durable 1950s Civil Rights melodrama *The Defiant Ones* (1957) provided the paradigm for *Black Mama, White Mama*, in which chain-gang prisoners Markov and Grier were shackled together, fighting one another as often as they did the authorities pursuing them. While working on *The Arena* with Grier (they play female gladiators) she met Mark Damon, a B-movie actor who had moved on/up/over to producing. They co-starred in *There is No 13*, in which he played a doomed soldier in Vietnam recalling the great loves of his life (Maggie was next to last; there would be no thirteen). Once married, she retired.

Trivia: Soap opera fans may recall Maggie as the second actress to play the character Olga on *Days of Our Lives* (1997). Earlier, she appeared on the edgy TV anthology *The Sixth Sense* (1972); this had no relation to the later hit film other than the subject. In a more middle-of-the-road vein, Maggie played a blonde college student on NBC's *The Jimmy Stewart Show* (1971), causing the by-then elderly star's eyes to virtually pop out.

SELECTED FILMOGRAPHY:

The Sterile Cuckoo (Pretty Co-ed, 1969); *Run, Angel, Run* (Meg Felton, 1969); *Pretty Maids All in a Row* (Polly, 1971); *The Hot Box* (Lynn Forrest, 1972); *Black Mama, White Mama* (Karen Brent, 1972); *The Arena* (Bodicia, 1973); *There is No 13* (Eleven, 1974).

Florence Marly

Birthdate: June 2, 1919; Obrnice, Czechoslovakia
Birth name: Hana Smekalova
Date of Passing: November 9, 1978; Glendale, CA
Height: N/A
Measurements: N/A

IN THE EARLY 1990S, an astronaut dozes off in the cabin of his spaceship *Oceano* while traveling from Mars back to Earth. He and his fellow crew members have completed their mission: Pick up the surviving alien in a craft that earlier crashed; bring this queen of outer space home so that hopefully friendly negotiations can occur. While other space travelers sleep, this astronaut awakens, realizing some heavenly body is standing in the doorway, observing him. It's the green girl, smiling seductively, sweetly as she slowly steps close. Concerned, the astronaut rises, grabbing for his ray gun just to be safe. Before he's able to defend himself, the eerily attractive female locks her intense yellow eyes on him, causing the man to fall under her spell, she a siren every bit as much as Circe of myth. Also, a space vampire, embracing her victim, drawing perverse pleasure as well as sustenance while draining every last drop of blood from his body. Finally sated, she slips back to her bunk and falls into deep sleep. Come morning, the other astronauts, unwilling to kill her as that would invalidate the mission's rationale, debate the likeliness any will survive the remaining distance to their home planet. And, if they do, what horror will they bring back?

Alternately known as *Queen of Blood* and *Planet of Blood*, this stylish quickie from Roger Corman and his cohorts at American International Pictures looks to be a true space epic. The shoestring-budget filmmakers employed state-of-the-art F/X footage from two ambitious Soviet sci-

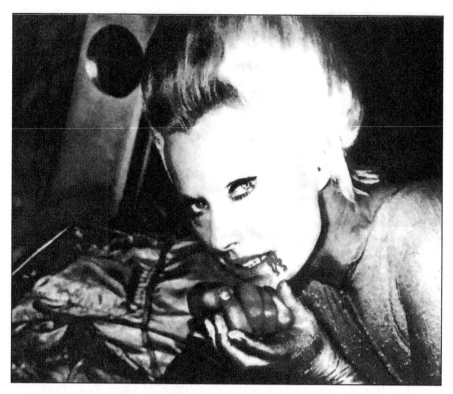

THE ORIGINAL 'GREEN GIRL': Many aficionados of the science-fiction genre believe that Florence Marly's role as the Queen of Blood inspired Gene Roddenberry to create his similar femme fatales on Star Trek.

fi films, *Mechte Navstrechu* and *Nebo Zovyot*, editing grand images with modest closer-shots of stars Basil Rathbone, John Saxon, and Judy Meredith. Florence Marly embodied the title character, who some observers believe inspired those gorgeous green girls in *Star Trek*.

Initially, Corman had planned to cast one of those nubile nymphs even then decorating the studio's *Beach Party* mini-musicals, but director Curtis Harrington convinced the A.I.P. brass that Marly, who had not appeared in a film for nearly a decade, would bring the necessary sense of maturity, sophistication, and worldly (make that galactic) cynicism to this character. Born in Czechoslovokia, the aspiring young opera star of Slavic descent fled to Argentina in 1942, when the Nazis assumed control, to remain with her Jewish husband, himself a filmmaker of note, Pierre Chenal. (He directed his wife in several films including *Sirocco*). Marly continued her career there and, after the war, briefly returned home before imigrating to Hollywood, where exotically gorgeous actresses were

POP CULTURE IMMORTALITY: Florence Marly's green girl proved so memorable that a popular model/toy was created in her honor.

always welcome. Marly picked up the female lead in a major movie, the role of Humphey Bogart's long lost wife in the post-World War II feature *Tokyo Joe*. Not a box-office hit, the film did little for her career. Soon she was accepting smaller parts in inexpensive films. During the 1950s, Marly proved her patriotism by entertaining our troops in Korea, but even this did not save her from being mistakenly blacklisted as a suspected communist during the McCarthy-era madness. Later, Marly wrote (and composed the score for) *Space Boy* (1973), a short in which she played a character named Florence Marly von Wurmbrand. Shortly after, she died of a heart attack. Her most famous line was to the International Hollywood Press Corps when they offered her an award: "I'm speechless in four languages."

SELECTED FILMOGRAPHY:

The Lafarge Case (Emma Pontier, 1938); *Sirocco* (Diana, 1938); *Café de Paris* (Estelle, 1938); *Savage Brigade* (Isa, 1939); *Le Dernier Tournant* (Madge, 1939); *The Damned* (Hilde Garosi, 1947); *Sealed Verdict* (Themis DeLisle, 1948); *Tokyo Joe* (Trina, 1949); *Tokyo File 212* (Steffi Novak, 1951); *Gobs and Gals* (Soyna, 1952); *Undersea Girl* (Leila, 1957); *Queen of Blood*, aka *Planet of Blood* (The Alien, 1966); *Games* (Baroness, 1967); *Doctor Death: Seeker of Souls* (Tana, 1973); *The Astrologer* (Diana, 1975).

Zena Marshall

Birthdate: January 1, 1925; Nairobi, Kenya (Africa);
Date of passing: July 10, 2009; London, UK
Height: 5' 5"
Measurements: N/A

THE FIRST OF THE BOND BAD-GIRLS appeared some forty minutes into *Dr. No.* In Jamaica, 007 (Sean Connery) reports to his contact only to realize the man's seemingly demure, dependable Eurasian secretary (Marshall) has been eavesdropping on their private conversation. Bond makes a date with the girl, driving to her isolated home. On the way he's attacked by assassins working for the title villain. When Bond unexpectedly arrives after all, she's in a state of near-nudity, calling her superiors to learn if her 'date' is dead. Bond sets out to seduce Miss Taro and, after a futile attempt at resistance, she capitulates, appearing to have been won over owing to their wild evening of sex. When Bond suggests they head out for a lovely dinner, she's stunned to realize the arriving limousine is from the authorities, there to whisk her off to prison. Her futile attempt to have the last word (figuratively speaking) occurs when she spits into the face of the man to whom she has totally surrendered. As she's then escorted off into the night, Connery's 007 wipes the spit away, walks back into the building, and awaits the next (male) assassin.

Zena was a surprise choice to play the first of the lethal ladies who would become essential to the series, and then the franchise. Casting of Bond Girls, good and bad, almost always introduced fresh young beauties, often in their initial screen appearances; Marshall was, at the time, a fast-fading glamour star from an earlier era. Following the death of her English/Irish father, young Zena had moved with her remarried French mother from Africa to Leicestershire, England. Her volunteer service en-

THE FIRST BOND BAD-GIRL: Zena Marshall, as Miss Taro, was the first female
enemy agent to try and trap Sean Connery's 007.

A GIRL WHO LOVES HER JOB: In the comfort of her isolated home, Miss Taro invites
Bond to drive by and "see" her, smiling as she does so as thugs are already in place to
kill 007 on the way.

tertaining the troops during WWII led Zena to believe that, when peace-time finally arrived, she might pursue a career in show business. Marshall received a contract from prestigious Rank and, owing to her sultry elegance, often found herself cast as a villainess. When the 1960s ushered in the era of the spy as anti-hero, first on television and shortly in the movies, Zena proved so popular as a femme fatale opposite Patrick McGoohan on the English series *Danger Man* (1961) that she was invited back

SURPRISE!: Miss Taro is shocked when James Bond actually does arrive and, after a moment of panic, decides on sweet surrender as a means of keeping him there until another assassin can arrive.

two more times. Now that her typecasting was a matter of record, it only made sense that Albert "Cubby" Broccoli would hire her for the same sort of deliciously duplicitous role in his first Bond effort.

Trivia: Initially, the role of Miss Taro was to have gone to a considerably younger woman, Marguerite LeWars, at the time reigning as Miss Jamaica. But those in charge of the pageant felt such a naughty-girl

TURNABOUT IS FAIR PLAY: Zena's Miss Taro was the first badgirl to actually fall in love with Bond during sex, planning to go over to the good side; 007, however, turns her over to the authorities the moment they leave her home.

role was inappropriate for her wholesome image. You can glimpse (if you don't blink) LeWars as a photographer who snaps a picture of Bond when he arrives in Kingston. Zena had trepadations as to the archness of her bad-girl. No matter how natural and relaxed director Terence Young helped her appear in the extended (and highly erotic) sequence, the old-fashioned stage actress (Zena had once trained with the prestigious Royal Academy of Dramatic Art) had to justify such (then) graphic sexplay.

SELECTED FILMOGRAPHY:

Caesar and Cleopatra (The Queen's Lady in Waiting, 1945); *So Evil My Love* (Lisette, 1948); *Miranda* (Secretary, 1948); *Good-Time Girl* (Annie, 1948); *Sleeping Car to Trieste* (Suzanne, 1948); *Helter Skelter* (Giselle, 1949); *Operation Disaster* (WREN, 1950); *So Long at the Fair* (Nina, 1950); *Soho Conspiracy* (Dora, 1950); *Dark Interval* (Sonia Jordan, 1950): *Hell Is Sold Out* (Honeychild, 1951); *Men Against the Sun* (Elizabeth, 1952); *Deadly Nightshade* (Ann, 1953); *Scarlet Web* (Laura Vane, 1954); *Three Cases of Murder* (Beautiful Blonde, 1955); *Bermuda Affair* (Chris, 1956); *A Story of David: The Hunted* (Naomi, 1961); *Crosstrap* (Rina, 1962); *Backfire* (Pauline, 1962); *Dr. No* (Miss Taro, 1962); *The Switch* (Caroline, 1963); *The Verdict* (Carola, 1964); *Those Magnificent Men in Their Flying Machines* (Countess Ponticelli, 1965); *The Terrornauts* (Paula Lund, 1967).

THRILL-KILL: In what may be the ultimate femme fatale film, Eiko Makusada can reach full orgasm only while strangling her willing male victim.

Eiko Makusada

Birthdate: May 18, 1952; Yokohama, Japan
Height: N/A
Measurements: N/A

THE VAST MAJORITY OF WOMEN chronicled in this volume are easily accessible. We know where they come from, how they entered the movie business, the people they involved themselves with, and what happened following their golden years. Others are more difficult to track down, keeping their private lives… well… private! Then there is Eiko Makusada, a mystery woman among mystery women. Almost nothing is known as to her early years other than the date and place of birth. There are no records as to how and when she first approached filmmakers or whether she initially believed mainstream stardom might be possible. Following a small handful of films, she appears to have disappeared off the face of the earth. Reports as to whether she remains alive conflict. Adding to the fascination: Eiko must be considered the ultimate femme fatale of her era, arguably the greatest *Deadlier Than the Male* figure ever.

Her small but loyal, intense, and ongoing cult following derives from a single motion picture, Nagisa Oshima's French/Japanese co-production *In the Realm of the Senses* (1976). This project was green-lighted in large part owing to the 1970s syndrome initiated by *Belle de Jour, Emmanuele,* and *The Story of O*: Exquisitely crafted, seriously intended stories involving complex human beings caught in webs of eroticism. Such fare had long been the staple of the upscale arthouse circuit, where graphic sex was presented in the context of social, cultural, or political statements. As such, these were examples of X-rated art rather than porn. This syndrome reached its apex with *In the Realm of the Senses*, based on an actual earlier occurrence.

Eiko plays a variation on Sada Abe, a woman who, in 1936 Tokyo, entered into a bizarre/extreme sado-masochistic tryst with Kichizo Ishida (Tatsuya Fuji), owner of the hotel in which she worked as a maid. The male raped the female, only to discover this was not a repulsive situation for her. She then invited him to continue their sexual liaison, which did a turn-about: She the female master, he the male slave. Obsessed with the ever more degrading acts that Sada suggested, Kichizo dumped his wife. He gradually developed a desire for the fall by becoming at first passionately—then obsessively—aroused by their mutual realization: Completion (and total satisfaction) could only be achieved if Sada were to kill Kichizo at the very height of the sex act, queen B style. Essentially, she becomes a realistic vampire sans fangs, in this real-life varation on "Carmilla" or *Curse of the Spider Woman*. Ultimately, she strangles him, cutting off his penis as the ultimate prize and token of their ongoing (for want of a better term) 'love.' The film's notorious reputation would be enhanced by release of the fact that the sex acts (other than his death) had not been simulated. Such a situation could not be allowed in a Japanese film, explaining why the movie was officially listed as a French production, even though shot in Japan.

The actual incident, as related in 1970 in a book by Roland Barthes, created far-reaching controversies. Many Japanese women came to pe-receive Sada as something of a feminist folk hero. They claimed that she should not be tried as a criminal since she was merely carrying out in-

THIS WOMAN IS DANGEROUS: In this fact based story, Makusada moves in close for the final thrill/kill.

SHE'LL LOVE YOU TO DEATH: The supposed 'fantasy' element of the femme fatale
and her willing victim is belied by the actuality of the case this film was based on.

structions from her all-too-willing victim, and that that this mutual agree-
ment legitimized her action. Likewise, the film's release (it was banned in
many countries, drastically cut in others) led to a firestorm among critics.
Clearly, this was a film about the dark side of human sexuality, not merely
an exploitation of it. What is the line, then, between art and pornography?
Could there be any such line after *In the Realm of the Senses*? Though Oshima spoke at length about such issues, his female star remained mum,
disappearing from sight and, after only a few roles, fading into obscurity
for all but her small yet devoted cult of fans.

SELECTED FILMOGRAPHY:
    In the Realm of the Senses (Sada, 1976); *The General and His Empire
of Joy* (Okoyo, 1977); *Detective Doberman* (Kosode, 1966); *Seibo Kannon
daibosatsu* (Yaobikuni, 1977); *Sochiyo no Kubi* (The Girl, 1979); *Five and
the Skin* (Mari, 1982).

A SWEET SNACK BETWEEN MURDERS: Yvette Mimieux reinvented her innocent beach bunny image from the 1960s by maintaining that persona as a hit-lady.

Yvette Mimieux

Birthdate: January 8, 1942; Hollywood, CA
Height: 5' 4"
Measurements: 34 – 22 1/2 - 35

YVETTE MIMIEUX'S AGE REMAINS a mystery. Some sources insist she was born between 1937 and 1939. No question that her ancestry is French (father) and Mexican (mother). A teenage beauty contest winner, Yvette entered into a hasty early marriage that was shortly jettisoned. She made a vivid first impression in the teen-exploitation flick *Platinum High School* in which Yvette and Terry Moore played the roles that Mamie Van Doren and Tuesday Weld ordinarily essayed for schlockmeister Albert Zugsmith. Yvette had an opportunity to wear her first onscreen bikini, the first of many. Of the four female stars of one of the original surf and sand films, *Where the Boys Are* (Paula Prentiss, Dolores Hart, and Connie Francis were here co-stars), only Yvette sported a skimpy two-piece. From there, it was on to the A-list for MGM. Mimieux appeared opposite Rod Taylor in the George Pal production of H.G. Wells' *The Time Machine*, as the future-blonde pursued by the hideous Morlocks. She and Taylor would reunite eight years later for the African-set tale of mercenaries *Dark of the Sun*.

Yvette's *Time Machine* role as a simple, perhaps simple minded, girl was followed by similar parts in *The Light in the Piazza*, *Diamond Head*, and *Toys in the Attic*. A shot at serious stardom came Yvette's way following a much-admired *Life* cover (again, she posed in a bikini) but her most ambitious vehicle, a contemporary Western called *The Reward*, fizzled with critics and at the box-office. Shortly, she was relegated to television, replacing Inger Stevens (who had committed suicide) on the short-lived *The Most Deadly Game* in 1969. Earlier, Yvette had played a doomed surf-

BLONDE VICTIM: Early on in her career, Yvette was menaced by a Morlock in *The Time Machine* and Charlton Heston in *Diamond Head* (that's George Chakiris looking on).

er girl (she wore a bikini) opposite Richard Chamberlain in *Dr. Kildare*. Shortly, though, she would seize control of her situation and make that bikini image work for her by undermining that much admired sweet, simple image.

First, though, came *Three in the Attic*. Here was another of those late-1960s Groovy Youth films in which three young women, each of whom

NEVER TRUST A BLONDE IN A BLACK BIKINI: Yvette's hit lady celebrates her latest killing with a pleasant swim.

believes herself to be the steady of a campus stud, unite in a sisterhood of vengeance after they meet and realize that he's been using all of them. Yvette went the exploitation route in *Jackson County Jail,* one more of the 'women in prison' pictures, this one set in the rural south. Meanwhile, she wrote a TV script that turned her screen persona upside down and backward. In *Hit Lady* (1974), Yvette played Angela de Vries, a gorgeous, classy artist and illustrator who brings in extra money by moonlighting as a contract killer. (Yes, wearing a bikini on the job.) The film proved to be one of the highest rated, most talked about TV movies of 1974, qualifying as an important entry in the Hit Woman genre.

Though her first marriage to director Stanley Donen (1972-1985) ended in divorce, Mimieux's second, to *National Geographic* photographer Howard Ruby (in 1986), has been a success. Clearly smarter than many of the bubble-headed beach babes (and that one memorable femme fatale) she has played, Yvette re-established herself as an anthropologist, a savvy dealer of real-estate, and (with her husband) owner of an upscale Mexican beach resort.

SELECTED FILMOGRAPHY:

Platinum High School (Lorinda Nibley, 1960); *The Time Machine* (Weena, 1960); *Where the Boys Are* (Melanie Tolman, 1960); *Light in the Piazza* (Clara Johnson, 1962); *The Wonderful World of the Brothers Grimm* (The Dancing Princess, 1962); *Diamond Head* (Sloane, 1963); *Toys in the Attic* (Lily Berniers, 1963); *Joy in the Morning* (Annie Brown, 1965); *The Reward* (Sylvia, 1965); *Monkeys, Go Home!* (Maria Riserau, 1967); *Caper of the Golden Bulls* (Grace Harvey, 1967); *Dark of the Sun* (Claire, 1968); *Three in the Attic* (Tobey, 1968); *The Delta Factor* (Kim Stacy, 1970); *Sky-jacked* (Angela Thacher, 1972); *Jackson County Jail* (Dinah Hunter, 1976); *The Black Hole* (Dr. Kate McRae, 1979).

Soledad Miranda

aka: SUSANN KORDA
Birthdate: July 9, 1943; Seville, Spain
Birth name: Soledad Rendón Bueno
Height: N/A
Measurements: N/A

IN THE LANGUAGE OF THIS femme fatale's native Spain, her birth name—Soledad—refers to a deep sensation of melancholic loneliness. More than one biographer of this breathtaking girl has noted its appropriateness for this strange, haunted, doom-laden young woman. Apparently, Soledad spent her life in search of her own true inner identity only to have her time on Earth suddenly cut short when, not yet thirty years of age, she died in a bizarre accident on the open road not far from Lisbon. Ever since, her ever-youthful if preturnaturally world-weary beauty has been frozen in time on celluloid, allowing an ever-increasing fan base to gaze at this eerie cult queen in hopes of unlocking her Mona Lisa-like sense of mystery.

Soledad began dancing at age eight when her destitute family (she was the first of six children) needed extra money. She was able to secure a position as a flamenco performer thanks to a relative, the popular headliner Paquita Rico. A nationwide tour followed and, bitten by the bug to conquer show business, Soledad moved to Madrid soon after turning sixteen. Her public profile was raised considerably by a tumultuous long-term/on-again-off-again romance with the notorious bullfighter Manuel Benítez ('El Cordobés'). Miranda's striking appearance qualified her as a natural for femme fatales in Peplums like *Ursus*. Sidney Pink, the American producer of low-budget exploitation items, even then churning out a series of junk movies in her native Spain, spotted her in that one and

CHAINS OF LOVE: In *The Devil Came from Akasava*, one of Soledad's most popular
international films, she went the S & M route – perhaps because it worked so well
with her initials?

THE HORIZONTAL SUCCUBUS: In *Vampyres Lesbos*, Soledad's vampire prefers to couple with a real live girl; but in a pinch, a mannequin will do!

signed Soledad for future projects. She soon married José Manuel da Conceiçao Simões, a race-car driver and her sometimes co-star, in 1966. After taking time off to raise their son, Miranda returned to the screen.

In 1961, aspiring Spanish filmmaker Jess/Jessie/Jesus Franco saw the erotically eerie Hammer production *Brides of Dracula* and sensed what kind of film he was born to make. Over the next decade, while working

THE EYES HAVE IT: One common characteristic of most all the vampire stars was an
intense, mesmerizingly irresistible pair of dark eyes.

in Spain and then France, he created his own unique subgenre of horror (occasionally taking time out for spy thrillers) in which the sexual
element was stretched ever further in the direction of pornography. The
eerie link between sex and fear would emerge as Franco's key theme. Recalling Miranda from some minor effort he'd seen her in years earlier,
Franco persuaded the ethereal beauty to take an ever more decadent walk
on the wild side as a contemporary Trilby to his Svengali-like avatar of
her image. They completed half a dozen films in little more than a year.
This collaborative canon began with a *Dracula* interpretation in which
Miranda portayed doomed Lucy. This was followed by *She Killed in Ecstasy*, which solidified her new screen image as a gorgeous combination
of human woman and deadly tarantula; *Vampyros Lesbos*, at the time the
most explicit film to feature two beautiful women in a sex-death struggle;
and *Eugénie de Sade*, in which Soledad proved most adept at portraying
a woman who derives perverse pleasure from inflicting pain on her prey,
transformed her into a legend of darkly desirable sensuality. In most of
these projects, Soledad was billed as Susann Korda in hopes of not dis-
gracing the family name.

Their projects proved so notoriously popular that a major backer of
film projects offered considerable money and total artistic freedom via

a long-term contract, though only if they both agreed. Miranda and her husband were in Portugal on a brief vacation when Franco called with the news. She and her spouse drove together along the Costa do Sol highway near Lisbon (he was behind the wheel) when they collided with a truck. He survived; she did not.

SELECTED FILMOGRAPHY:

La Bella Mimi (First Dancer, 1960); *Ursus* (Fillide, 1961); *The Castilian* (Maria Estévez, 1962); *Pyro* (Liz Frade, 1963); *Eva 63* (Soledad, 1963); *Bochorno* (Piluca, 1963); *Sound of Horror* (Maria, 1965); *Sugar Colt* (Josefa, 1966); *Cervantes* (Nessa, 1966); *100 Rifles* (Naked Woman in Bed in Hotel Room, 1969); *Nightmares Come at Night* (Mystery Woman, 1969); *Vampir* (Herself, 1969); *Count Dracula* (Lucy Westenra, 1969); *The Devil Came from Akasava* (Jane Morgan, 1970); *She Killed in Ecstasy* (Mrs. Johnson, 1970); *Vampyros Lesbos* (Countess Nadine Carody, 1970); *Eugénie de Sade* (Eugénie,1970); *Sex Charade* (Anne, 1970).

GIRL POWER!: Caroline Munro was the most famous and beloved of those B-movie action stars who set the pace for strong if sexy fantasy women in films of the 21st century.

Caroline Munro

Birthdate: January 16, 1949; Berkshire, UK
Height: 5' 6 ¾"
Measurements: 36B – 24 ½ - 35

AS A GIRL, Caroline attended art school at Brighton, quickly discovering that she was not as talented as she had hoped. Meanwhile, her mother noticed that London's *Evening News* was holding a contest to discover the "Face of the Year" (David Bailey, who inspired the character played by David Hemmings in the film *Blow-up*, was the judge) and entered a snapshot. Her daughter's first-place award led to modeling contracts, one for *Vogue* (at age 17). Shortly, she was in demand for movie roles that called for glamorous presence in decorative sequences. Caroline appeared (briefly) in *Casino Royale*; that and her villainess in *The Spy Who Loved Me* qualifies Caroline as a two-time 007 femme fatale. Meanwhile, a high-profile contract promoting Lamb's Navy Rum in provocative commercials led to Munro soon becoming a Peplum queen. She starred for producer Charles Schneer in the second stop-motion animation *Sinbad* film which included monsters by Ray Harryhausen, then opposite Doug McClure in a lower budget fantasy in which she embodied a primitive beauty existing at the earth's core. Full femme fatale status arrived when she co-starred opposite Vincent Price in both the *Dr. Phibes* movies; unaccountably, Munro was not listed as part of the cast. While her provocative teen character was killed off early in *Dracula A.D. 1972* by Christopher Lee, she made a strong impression as a willing victim of his kiss-of-death embrace. Other roles for Sir James Carreras at Hammer included the cult item *Captain Kronos – Vampire Hunter*, an adventure tale involving the supernatural that set the pace for many such films to come once George Lucas and Stephen Spielberg began their *Indiana Jones* franchise.

TV work also tended to be of the cultish variety, including a memorable cat fight between bad girl Caroline and the heroine (Pamela Stephenson, playing Purdey, had replaced Diana Rigg) in "The Angels of Death" episode of *The New Avengers* (1977). She had been the first choice for Ursa, a villainess from Krypton, in *Superman* starring Christopher Reeve. Caroline had to pass on that one as the shooting schedule over-

THE PICTURE OF INNOCENCE: When Caroline Munro first posed for the cameras of fashion photographers, the sweet looking girl-child had no idea that she would eventually become a leading femme fatale.

PEPLUM PRINCESS: Caroline Munro's beauty had to compete with Ray Harryhausen's special effects in *The Golden Voyage of Sinbad*.

lapped with *The Spy Who Loved Me*. Many Bond fans believe her brief role as femme fatale Naomi overshadowed ostensible lead Barbara Bach. Perhaps no shot in the film (other than those employing elaborate F/X) has been cited as often as when Caroline, pursuing Roger Moore's Bond from a helicopter, winks seductively at the man she plans to kill. The tables, of course, were shortly turned.

Munro was offered the lead in what Hammer hoped would be the first in a series based on *Vampirella*, a lurid graphic novel about a scantily clad succubus from space. No mattter how brief Caroline's costumes may have been in previous (and future) films, she refused to strip bare for the camera (also turning down offers from *Playboy*). Rather than recast the role, Hammer eventually gave up on the idea. Caroline passed on *Dr. Jekyll and Sister Hyde* (Martine Beswick did that one) and *Force 10 From Navarone* for the same reason; in the latter, her *Spy* co-star Barbara Bach filled in. On the other hand, Caroline loved to flaunt her body in skimpy, daring outfits. Following *Star Wars* (1977), every film company wanted to throw together and release a sci-fi fantasy to cash in. *Star Crash*, an ultra-low budget item, featured Caroline as a darker version of Barbarella from nearly a decade earlier. The original script called for the lead to wear nothing but a brief black leather bikini and dominatrix boots for the entire running time. While that costume is on view, the producers decided that Caroline would also sport other kinky outfits as well. A bizarre combination of glitz and sleaze, the film did attract an audience owing to Caroline. To this day, the poster artworks for the film remain cherished as collector's items and sell well at Sci-Fi Memorabilia shows, some of which Caroline has attended as a special guest.

Marriages include Judd Hamilton (1970-1982) and George Dugdale (1990-present); she has two childen with the latter.

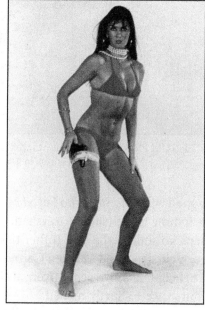

OF GIRLS, GAMS, AND GUNS: Munro came well-armed as a deadly agent in *The Spy Who Loved Me* and as a queen of outer space in *Star Crash*.

STEPPING OUT OF VICTORIA'S SECRET: Caroline poses in kinky attire as one of the dark girls of Hammer horror.

Trivia: The rock song "Caroline Goodbye" by Colin Blumstone was written in a melancholic state by that composer while he was attempting to survive their break-up.

SELECTED FILMOGRAPHY:

Casino Royale (Glamorous Girl Guard, 1967); *Joanna* (Brunette, 1968); *Where's Jack?* (Madame Vendonne, 1969); *A Talent for Loving* (Evalina, 1969); *The Abominable Dr. Phibes* (Victoria Regina, 1971); *Dracula A.D. 1972* (Laura, 1972); *Dr. Phibes Rises Again* (Victoria Regina, 1972); *The Golden Voyage of Sinbad* (Margiana, 1973); *Captain Kronos – Vampire Hunter* (Carla, 1974); *At the Earth's Core* (Dia, 1976); *The Spy Who Loved Me* (Naomi, 1977); *Starcrash* (Stella Star, 1978); *Maniac* (Anna, 1980); *The Last Horror Film* (Jana Bates, 1982); *Slaughter High* (Carol, 1986); *Demons 6* (Nora, 1989); *Flesh for the Beast* (Carla the Gypsy, 2003); *Vampyres* (The Vampire Woman, 2014).

Rosalba Neri

aka: SARA BEY
Birthdate: June 19, 1939; Forli, Ernilia-Romagna, Italy
Height: 5' 7"
Measurements: N/A

THE 1970S WAS THE GOLDEN AGE of female sex-vampire films. Memorable examples hailed from Hammer's House of Horror in England to virtually everywhere on the continent. Despite a plethora to pick from, ask any connoisseur of cult cinema to choose the greatest single sequence in such a film, and chances are, *this* will be the one... at a foreboding castle, far (as Thomas Hardy would put it) from the madding crowd, first one brother (Mark Damon), then his identical twin (also Damon), arrives to visit a legendary aristocrat. She (Neri) bears more than a passing resemblance to Ersbeth Nádasdy Bathory, history's Crimson Countess. This woman is elegant, cultured, refined. But day must pass; night must fall. Then, in the eerie luminescence of a full moon, she rises, naked except for the sweat and blood dripping down from this serpent goddess. The temptress prepares to love the life out of one of the two brothers... though we have long since lost track of which one she's kissing/killing at any single moment.

The film is *The Devil's Wedding Night*. For anyone who might now seek it out, beware the cut/censored versions! In the complete print, Neri's body language is that of a gifted dancer; her eyes mesmerizing. Here is one of those cases where it's difficult to believe, once the film is over, that this was some normal woman simply playing a part. Neri is at one with the role, even as she had been (working under the name Sara Bey) in *Lady Frankenstein*, though that film lacks this thriller's immediate impact and lasting effect on the memory.

QUEEN OF THE NIGHT: Rosalba Neri vividly incarnated the mature female vampire as dominatrix to willing victims in *The Devil's Wedding Night.*

Here (again!) was yet another rural Italian girl whose impossibly perfect appearance allowed her immediate entrance into beauty pageants, modeling, finally a career in junk movies. Early on, she worked for Mario Bava, that director even then proving that sword-and-sandal mini epics and over the top horror items (as well as combinations of the two) could be pumped up via talent, artistry, and style. For Rosalba, a wide array of femme fatale roles opened up in spaghetti Westerns and spy cinema. Still, her cool, calm demeanor while dispatching death to willing male prey caused her horror opuses to stand out as essential to this woman's appeal. Yet another cult director, Jesse Franco, guided Rosalba through *99 Women*, also making the most of her abject immodesty. She also made a strong impression in *The Arena*, a Peplum with Pam Grier.

Trivia: In 2002, a German filmmaker created a documentary about her called *The Italian Sphinx*. She might also have been nicknamed The Garbo of Giallo.

SELECTED FILMOGRAPHY:
Escape by Night (Erika, 1960); *Esther and the King* (Keresh, 1960); *Cleopatra's Daughter* (Slave Girl, 1960); *El Cid* (Harem Girl, 1961); *Conquest of Mycene* (Demeter, 1963); *The Lion of Thebes* (Nais, 1964); *Hercules of the Desert* (Ramhis, 1964); *Angélique* (La Polak, 1964); *I Kill, You Kill* (Santuza, 1965); *The Amazing Doctor G* (Agent 0024, 1965); *Johnny Yuma* (Samantha, 1966); *Electra One* (Silvana, 1967); *OSS 117 – Double Agent*

A WOMAN TO BE RECKONED WITH: Rosalba starred with her husband Mark Damon, a horror-movie actor turned producer, in two of her most memorable roles, as these rare advertising posters make clear.

(Conchita Esteban, 1968); *A Long Ride from Hell* (Incarnacion, 1968); *Sartana Does Not Forgive* (Passenger, 1968); *99 Women* (Zoie, 1969); *Sexy Susan Knows How... !* (Leontina, 1970); *Lady Frankenstein* (Tania, 1971); *The Devil's Lover* (Helga, 1972); *Amuck* (Eleanora, 1972); *Smile Before Death* (Gianna, 1972); *Watch Out Gringo!* (La Ragazza, 1972); *The French Sex Murders* (Marianne, 1972); *Decameron '300* (The Great Beauty, 1972); *Confessioni* (Madonna Lisa, 1972); *The Devil's Wedding Night* (La Contessa Dolingen de Vries, 1973); *A Man Named Invincible* (Miss Pappalardo, 1973); *The Sexbury Tales* (Bona, 1973); *The Arena* (Cornelia, 1974) *High School Girl* (Altomare, 1974); *The Girl in Room 2A* (Alicia Songbird, 1974); *Blood River* (Katherine, 1974); *Libera, Amore Mio...* (Wanda, 1975); *Il Pomicione* (Liliana, 1976).

THE ONE AND ONLY CATWOMAN: No matter how many other actresses essay the role of Selena Kyle, Julie Newmar will always be rated as not only the first but all-time best.

Julie Newmar

Birthdate: August 16, 1933; Los Angeles, CA
Birth name: Julia Chalene Newmeyer
Height: 5' 11"
Measurements: 37 ½ - 23 – 36 ½

TELEVISION FANS HAD NEVER SEEN anything like it. In a medium known for ultra-conservatism about everything, but particularly human sexuality (in order to play to the largest, widest common denominator of possible viewership), here (and in the family hour, no less!) was an S & M fantasy come true. Amazonian actress Julie Newmar strutted into a comic book-like rendering of Gotham City wearing a skin tight black catsuit, augmented by a dark facial mask and sleek, high dominatrix boots. And lest we forget: Wielding a mean cat-of-nine-tails whip. Whenever the plot would allow for some bondage, Selena Kyle (though the character was in truth never addressed by that name on the ABC version) would tie Batman up, threatening to kiss or kill him... perhaps first one, then the other? Wicked smiles passed over what we could see of her gorgeous face; she all but licked her lips at the thought of unleashing pure evil. Actually, on at least one occasion, Julie *did* lick them! Recall: This, in an era when Barbara Eden, playing a sweet fantasy-femme on *I Dream of Jeannie*, was not even allowed to expose her navel.

How did they get away with it? Simple. Because the series was produced and marketed as a Grand Guignol joke which could not be taken seriously. All of this was (supposedly) in good clean (some might say 'dirty,' not necessarily in a pejorative sense) fun—and broadcast during the family hour. Essential to making this tricky bit work was not merely securing the services of a gorgeous woman willing to don such a costume (Lee Meriwether, who played the part in the theatrical film version, failed to click, despite her lovely face and perfect body) but one who truly could act. And do so in a sophisticated manner that made clear she was both deadly serious about the portrayal while mocking her own intensity: i.e., camp, the Susan Sontag defined concept that also included Andy Warhol's latest paintings of soup cans and Roy Lichtenstein's massive renderings of old-time Sunday funnies. With *Batman*, and particularly Julie Newmar as The Catwoman, the American middle-of-the-road medium of entertainment came face to face with the upscale art sensibility of the mid-1960s.

A gifted dancer, Newmar had at age nineteen revealed her talents in the legendary MGM musical *The Band Wagon*. A year earlier, her Amazonian size and take-your-breath-away shape allowed her to portray, in *Serpent of the Nile*, a gilded girl long before Shirley Eaton in *Goldfinger*. Dedicated to proving and furthering her craft, Newmar left the lucrative film business to appear on Broadway in the 1955 Cold War musical *Silk Stockings*. She won a Tony for her devilish intreptation of a sexually-charged Swedish exchange student who attempts to seduce an older married professor in *The Marriage-Go-Round*, repeating that role in the movie version. It almost goes without saying that Newmar was tapped to play the bad girl ("Whatever Lola wants, Lola gets…") in a stage revival of *Damn Yankees!* Still, movie and TV producers weren't precisely sure how to best exploit Julie's unique attributes. A 1964 sitcom, *My Living Doll*, in which

REIGNING FEMME FATALE OF THE SMALL SCREEN: Movie roles aside, Julie Newmar had some of her best parts on the small screen, opposite William Shatner on *Star Trek* and Albert Salmi on *The Twilight Zone*.

WHEN GOOD GIRLS GO BAD: In her early Pin Up photos, Newmar looked sweet and sexy; even here, though, there's a wicked smile on that sensuous mouth.

she played a gorgeous robot, thudded. Then came the perfect timing that led to Catwoman. One memorable TV role was as the soul-stealing Miss Devlin in Rod Serling's "Of Late I Dream of Cliffordsville" episode on *The Twilight Zone*. She later played a villainess Native American in a dreadful A-budget Western, *MacKenna's Gold*. Later still, there was a cameo in *To Wong Foo, Thanks for Everything! Julie Newmar*, a film that set out to fully incarnate in its script Julie's cult status and over-the-top (make that *way* over the top!) appeal.

SELECTED FILMOGRAPHY:

Serpent of the Nile (The Gilded Girl, 1953); *The Band Wagon* (Salon Model, 1953); *Slaves of Babylon*, aka *Love Slaves of Babylon* (Dancer/Assassin, 1954); *Demetrius and the Gladiators* (Specialty Dancer, 1954); *Seven Brides for Seven Brothers* (Dorcas, 1954); *Li'l Abner* (Stupefyin' Jones, 1959); *The Marriage-Go-Round* (Katrin Sveg, 1961); *For Love or Money* (Bonnie Brasher, 1963); *Mackenna's Gold* (Hesh-Ke, 1969); *The Maltese Bippy* (Carlotta Ravenswood, 1969); *Up Your Teddy Bear* ('Mother,' 1970); *Hysterical* (Venetia, 1983); *Evils of the Night* (Dr. Zarma, 1985); *Nudity Required* (Inna, 1988); *Ghosts Can't Do It* (Angel, 1990); *To Wong Foo, Thanks for Everything! Julie Newmar* (Herself, 1995).

Anita Pallenberg

Birthdate: January 25 (Some sources say 6 April), 1944; Rome, Italy
Height: 5' 9"
Measurements: N/A

HAD THE TERM 'GROUPIE' not already existed, someone would have had to create it to describe Anita Pallenberg—the groupie's groupie, according to many observers of the mid-1960s lifestyle. Part of the in-crowd/jet-setter cotillion, Pallenberg hung out with the Rolling Stones. She dated Brian Jones, dumped him for Keith Richards, and by many accounts had a side-fling with Mick Jagger, though to this day Anita insists the latter never happened. The song "Angie" was written specifically for her, as was "You Get the Silver." When the wild days were finally over, and the dust of celeb glamour thuddingly settled, Anita found herself hooked on heroin. In an attempt to recreate her life, she studied fashion design, hoping to semi-cover other manques as gifted designers, in Swingin' London, had with her. Pallenberg received a degree from Central Saint Martins in 1994, then set out to develop her own clothing line.

Her main claim to cult stardom is the role of The Great Tyrant, a Queen of Outer Space in *Barbarella* opposite Jane Fonda. Angie wears a black leather eye patch and garish outfits, as well as frilly feathers and lace. The title character beams down upon this Black Queen's forbidden planet. There, the innocent star-waif finds herself in a myriad of adventures (mostly of an erotic nature). Eventually, Barbarella shares The Great Tyrant's bed. Though versions of the film that exist today on DVD have been toned down, there are many publicity stills yet in existence that suggest in the original director's cut, some hot-and-heavy hanky-panky occurred between the two beauties. The film was one of the earliest interna-

THE GREAT TYRANT: For fans of femme fatales, Anita Pallenberg's queen of outer space stole much of the thunder away from Jane Fonda in *Barbarella*.

tional co-productions to take advantage of the less strict aura in America following the dropping of the old studio Production Code in 1967-1968 in favor of a Ratings System. Also, Barbarella marked the beginning of Hollywood's long overdue realization that contemporary movies could, and should, derive from Graphic Novels, those comic books (so popular in France) created with an adult audience in mind.

Pallenberg's other stand-out part was in *Performance*, directed by Nicholas Roeg, a former cinematographer turned auteur. This bizarre but strangely satisfying phantasmagoria combines elements of Brit neo-noir with the Trip Films briefly popular at that time. James Fox plays a Cockney gangster on the lam who hides out with a faded rock star (Jagger) and his unpredictable female companion (Pallenberg). Anita contributed to Donald Cammell's script, assuming the part of Pherber only when the actress scheduled to play that role had to drop out. Of the era's cinematic femme fatales, Pallenberg was among the few to be accused of being deadlier than the male in real-life. In 1979, she then 37 and still involved with Richards, Anita fell in love (lust) with an apparently normal teenage (17) boy, Scott Cantrell. She initiated the novice into the joys of haute sex, bringing him into her luxurious bed at Richards' eighteenth century estate in St. Salem, New York. One night while Richards was in Paris for a recording session, the police were summoned. On arrival, they found Cantrell dying with a bullet through his temple. The gun, a .38 caliber Smith and Wesson, belonged to Pallenberg, whose ten-year-old son Marlon even then slept in an adjacent room. The rumor mill spread gossip: Anita had handed the boy this gun, then tempted him into playing Russian roulette; she had insulted the youth's masculinity and shamed him

GIRLS WILL BE GIRLS: In the original print of *Barbarella*, as revealed in this European lobby card, the Great Tyrant and the title character (Jane Fonda) got it on; only a hint of the lesbian sexuality remained intact for the American verson.

PERFORMANCE!: In her only other major movie role other than *Barbarella*, Pallenberg seduces a gangster on the run and a rock star (Mick Jagger) in Nicholas Roeg's druggie phantasmagoria.

into suicide; tired of his company, she shot him herself. None of this could be proven. Pallenberg insisted that she momentarily left the room, heard the shot, and returned in shock to discover the boy dying. No one could prove anything other for certain. She faced the relatively minor charges of illegal possession of a hand-gun but not manslaughter. When asked in 1985 about his relationship with Pallenberg, Jagger stated flatly: "She nearly killed me." Independently wealthy today, Anita lives in seclusion with one of her sons.

SELECTED FILMOGRAPHY:

Degree of Murder (Marie, 1967); *Wonderwall* (Party Girl, 1968); *Barbarella* (The Great Tyrant, 1968); *Candy* (Nurse Bullock, 1968); *Dillinger Is Dead* (Ginette, 1969); *Performance* (Pherber, 1970); *Go Go Tales* (Sin, 2007).

Luciana Paluzzi

Birthdate: June 10, 1937; Rome, Italy
Birth name: Luciana Paoluzzi
Height: 5' 6"
Measurements: N/A

GORGEOUS IMPORTS FROM ITALY were all the rage during the mid-fifties; Silvana, Sophia, Gina among them. Despite Paluzzi's unique red-headed appeal, her career didn't spark, at least not immediately. A Rome-based model before reaching the age of sixteen, this child-woman was quickly cast in movies ranging from the Hollywood financed sudsy romance *Three Coins in the Fountain* to the Uber-Peplum *Hercules*. Too swiftly, Paluzzi was relocated to Hollywood and introduced as the female lead on *Five Fingers*, a pre-Bond espionage TV series based on a film that had starred James Mason. The series did not click, nor did Luciana's marriage to actor Brett Halsey, her co-star in the disastrous *Return to Peyton Place*. Simply, demure good-girls weren't her forte. No longer young by Tinseltown standards, Luciana put great hopes into winning the lead role in the fourth 007 film: Domino Derval, elegant mistress of Adolfo Celli in *Thunderball*. Crushed to learn that the part would instead go to younger Miss France, Claudine Auger, she rejoiced at the good news: Luciana had been cast as bad-girl Fiona Volpe. In tight-fitting black leather, she drove a motorcycle, mowing down anyone in her way, setting the pace for femme fatales in so many 1960s action films to follow.

Tough as gun-metal, Paluzzi's cold-blooded female assassin could also appear elegantly feminine, setting dichotomization of women aside to create a truly well-rounded figure in every sense of the term. In one memorable sequence, Connery corners her in the bathtub. Fiona asks James Bond to hand her something to wear. Boyishly, he proffers a pair of

ANCIENT WORLD DREAM-GIRL: Luciana Paluzzi made her first major impact as one of the gorgeous Amazons in *Hercules*.

shoes. After an evening of intense sex, this unforgettable exchange occurs:

James Bond: My dear girl… what I did this evening was for Queen and country. You don't think it gave me any *pleasure*, do you?

Fiona: But of course, I forgot your ego, Mr. Bond. James Bond, the one where he has to make love to a woman, and she starts to hear heavenly choirs singing. She repents, and turns to the side of right and virtue... (viciously, she steps on his foot)... but not this one!

She will, of course, pay a price for that. While the two dance in a public place, Fiona attempts to set Bond up as a target for a hidden assassin. Aware of the trap, 007 turns swiftly at precisely the right moment, causing Fiona to catch the bullet. Pretending his date has passed out, Bond sets her corpse down onto a table, winkingly explaining to the uncomprehending tourists: "She's just dead." Paluzzi's villainess on *The Man from U.N.C.L.E.* dies in a similar fashion while trying to murder Solo (Robert Vaughn). Paluzzi headed back to Rome, soon appearing in fluff/junk movies and, in time, soft-core porn, co-starring with another former Bond Girl, Ursula Andress, in *The Sensuous Nurse*.

A NEW KIND OF BOND BAD-GIRL: Luciana as Fiona set the pace for those bad-to-the-bone enemy agents (as her black leather and motorcycle announce) who don't move it on over to the side of good following a tumble in the sack with 007.

SELECTED FILMOGRAPHY:

Three Coins in the Fountain (Angela Bianchi, uncredited, 1953); *My Seven Little Sins* (Pat, 1954); *The Lebanese Mission* (Michèle, 1956); *Plucking the Daisy* (Sophia, 1956); *Tank Force* (Carola, 1958); *Sea Fury* (Josita, 1958); *Hercules* (Handmaiden, 1958); *Tiger of Bengal* (Baharani, 1959); *Return to Peyton Place* (Rafaella, 1961); *Muscle Beach Party* (Julie, 1964); *I Kill, You Kill* (La Mamma, 1965); *Thunderball* (Fiona, 1965); *The One Eyed Soldiers* (Gava, 1966); *The Venetian Affair* (Giulia Almeranti, 1967); *Chuka* (Veronica, 1967); *The Green Slime* (Dr. Lisa Benson, 1968); *99 Women* (Natalie, 1969); *Captain Nemo and the Underwater City* (Mala, 1969); *Come Together* (Lisa, 1971); *The Italian Connection* (Lalli, 1972); *Black Gunn* (Toni, 1972); *The Klansman* (Trixie, 1974); *The Sensuous Nurse* (Jole Scarpa, 1975); *The Greek Tycoon* (Paola Scotti, 1978); *Deadly Chase* (Rosy, 1978).

Paloma Picasso

Birthdate: April 19, 1949; Paris, France
Birth name: Anne Paloma Ruiz-Picasso y Gilot
Height: N/A
Measurements: N/A

THE DAUGHTER OF PABLO PICASSO played the lead in only one film, but in this case, once was enough. The lurid legend of Ersbeth Bathory had only recently been brought to the post-X international cinema by Hammer. But if their *Countess Dracula* starring Ingrid Pitt pushed the limits of what mainstream moviemakers dared depict, *Immoral Tales* by Walerian Borowczyk went considerably further. Whereas the British film suggested the idea of an aristocrat who bathed in virgins' blood to maintain youth and beauty, this French version vividly depicted such sequences, at considerable length. The historical tale was set against three more contemporary (and fictional) incidents; Paloma's was the one that caught the attention of critics and audiences world-wide. The film was praised and damned, sometimes first damned and then praised by reviewers who couldn't make up their minds whether this was the ultimate proof that art could deal with the darkest areas of eroticism or if the cruelest form of torture-porn were being dressed up by lush cinematography to resemble art. At the film's epicenter stood Paloma: princess-like, embracing amorality in a way that seemed to transcend acting altogether.

Surprisingly, Paloma did not choose to follow up on the loud, often heated controversy, either by taking on other femme fatale roles or attempting to broaden her scope as an actress. Instead, she became a well-known, highly-regarded designer of jewelry. Yves Saint Laurent was among the first to recognize the uniqueness of her work and help Paloma establish herself with connoiseurs. The fabled Tiffany & Co. mar-

THE CRIMSON COUNTESS: In addition to the fictional Carmilla Karnstein, the real-life Ersbeth Nádasdy Bathory would inspire many lesbian vampire films of the 1970s; Paloma Picasso here surveys the lovely young virgins in whose blood she will shortly bathe.

keted not only such creations but also a perfume that bore the stunning (and mysterious, much like the character she once played) beauty's name. Paloma's mother, Francoise Gilot, had been an acclaimed writer with surrealist leanings, so her artistic leanings were familial. In addition to the display of her now immortal beauty in a single dramatic film, Paloma's likeness can also be spotted in several of her father's most famous paintings which include her first name in their titles. When asked to comment on whether the experience of playing a serial killer like Ersbeth/Elizabeth Nádasdy Bathory had been difficult, the Sphynx-like star told one interviewer that she had enjoyed the role immensely. Like herself, Bathory had been a strong woman who made all her own decisions and did not care what others thought.

SELECTED FILMOGRAPHY:

Immoral Tales (Elisabeth Bathory, 1974); *Pablo Picasso: Réminiscences* (Herself, 1980).

A BUCKET OF BLOOD: Having just played Karmilla Carnstein in *Vampire Lovers*, Pitt went on to play that fictional character's historic progenitor: Ersbeth Bathory in *Countess Dracula*, also for the Hammer horror franchise.

Ingrid Pitt

Birthdate: November 21, 1937: Czestochowa, Poland
Birth name: Ingoushka Petrov
Date of passing: November 23, 2010; London, UK
Height: 5' 4"
Measurements: N/A

NO FEMALE STAR OF HORROR can claim to have survived a life of realistic horror as extreme as Ingrid Pitt. Polish-born, half-Jewish on her mother's side, she found herself incarnated in one of the Nazi concentration camps at age five. The child determined that she would somehow see the daylight of freedom and, when World War II ended, the barb wire gates opened. Pitt knew what those who experience more conventional lives can never grasp: Any existence devoid of daily pain would be wonderful after pure Hell on Earth. She set about on a search throughout Europe to hopefully find her missing father, though in time she had to accept that he was among those lost. Journeying to England, the future Hammer star established a serious stage career. Owing to her dedication to live theatre, it did not occur to Ingrid until late in life to employ her beauty to achieve screen stardom. Then, she initially only accepted roles in artistically ambitious projects, working with world-class talents like Orson Welles and David Lean.

Meanwhile, producer Michael Carreras realized during the late 1960s that after more than a decade of Dracula variations, that franchise was running out of steam. Still, he did not want to abandon the vampire genre. Setting Bram Stoker's book aside, the head of Hammer reached for *In a Glass Darkly*, spooky stories from Dublin-based scribe Sheridan le Fanu. "Carmilla" focused on a young vampire who employs her seeming innocent charms to seduce and destroy male and female victims. Hammer produced their first foray into this period-horror subgenre during the early 1970s, when the old rules forbidding female nudity had been abandoned. Yet what had always been most impressive about Hammer in the Sixties—their vivid recreations of historical settings in muted color—was retained. In *Vampire Lovers*, the first in a trilogy (and the only one to star Pitt), Peter Cushing was on hand in a strong supporting role. The film, though, was entirely Ingrid's as, from beginning to end, her Carmilla seethed with irresistible evil, seducing men and more notably some extraordinarily beautiful women. Though Pitt turned down the two follow-ups, *Lust for a Vampire* and *Twins of Evil*, she did shortly thereafter play Ersbeth Bathory, the actual inspiration for Carmilla Karnstein, in *Countess Dracula*. This film avoided supernatural elements, presenting the situation as a dramatic version of the life of the world's first known female serial killer. At about this time, Pitt also appeared on the ninth season of TV's *Dr. Who* as Queen Galleia.

If there was a disappointment, that had to be Pitt's inability to persuade Albert "Cubby" Broccoli to film a novel she had written, *Cuckoo Run*, in which Pitt would have played a female James Bond. Her other

OF FANGS AND CLEAVAGE: Ingrid Pitt may be the most convincing of all the 'mature' vampire girls in the history of Hammer horror.

THEDA BARA REVISITED: With jet-black hair and monstrous make-up recalling the original Vamp, darkly beautiful Ingrid Pitt puts the make (and then the bite) on an innocent blonde virgin in *Vampire Lovers*.

great role in an important horror film was in *The Wicker Man*, arguably the most intelligent studio film ever made about contemporary Wicca. But such edgy stardom does not last for long. Shortly, Pitt found herself reduced to bit parts in second rate films, also providing voice-overs to make a living. She would emerge as a star once again when the horror fan convention cycle began, signing autographs for adoring fans, until her passing at age 73. The story Ingrid most enjoyed relating had to do with her biting gorgeous Kate O'Mara on the neck in *Vampire Lovers*. Pitt's fake vampire teeth would fall out (and disappear deep into Kate's cleavage), so Ingrid borrowed some chewing gun and employed that to hold them in place. The international press once dubbed Ingrid Pitt "the most beautiful ghoul in the world."

SELECTED FILMOGRAPHY:
Falstaff – (The) Chimes at Midnight (bit, uncredited, 1965); *Doctor Zhivago* (bit, uncredited, 1965); *(The) Sound of Horror* (Sofia Minelli,

THE LESBIAN VAMPIRE: In *Vampire Lovers*, Pitt graphically seduced and killed both male and female victims, all of them more than willing to experience the kiss of death.

1966); *A Funny Thing Happened on the Way to the Forum* (Courtesan, uncredited, 1966); *Where Eagles Dare* (Heidi, 1968); *The Omegans* (Linda, 1968); *The Vampire Lovers* (Marcilla/Carmilla/Mircalla Karnstein, 1970); *Countess Dracula* (Countess Elisabeth Nádasdy Bathory, 1971); *The House That Dripped Blood* (Carla Lind, 1971); *The Wicker Man* (Librarian, 1973); *The Final Option* (Helga, 1982); *Octopussy* (Galley Mistress; voice only, uncredited, 1983); *(The) Wild Geese II* (Hooker, 1985); *Underworld* (Pepperdine, 1985); *Hanna's War* (Margit, 1988); *The Asylum* (Isobella, 2000): *Dominator* (Lady Violator, voice only, 2003).

Rossana Podesta

Birthdate: June 20, 1934; Zlitan, Misratah, Libya
Date of Passing: December 10, 2013, Rome, Italy
Birth name: Carla Dora Podestà
Height: 5' 4"
Measurements: N/A

FROM ALL EXISTING EVIDENCE, Homer (man or woman; person or community of artists) wrote *The Odyssey* first, then *The Iliad* as a prequel. In the 1950s, while ancient world epics were all the rage, the first of those two volumes to be adapted to the screen was Homer's tale of the aftermath of Ilium's fall, produced by Dino DeLaurentiis and Carlo Ponti, starring Kirk Douglas. Less than two years later, a grander, more expensive and ambitious Warner Bros. studio film dealing with the earlier siege arrived in theatres, directed by Robert Wise. Though few noticed, a single actress provided a connection between these projects. In *Ulysses,* Rossana Podestà made a brief appearance in the framing device in which the smartest (if not always wisest) of Greek heroes romances Princess Nausicca before arriving home to his isle of Ithaca. In *Helen of Troy*, Podestà embodied the face that launched a thousand ships.

Initially, Warner Bros. had considered a major name star—Lana Turner, Elizabeth Taylor, Rhonda Fleming, or Ava Gardner among the many mentioned—for Helen. Executives sensed something in the wind: Beautiful young European actresses had begun to trickle into Hollywood, many—Sophia Loren, Pier Angeli, Gina Lollabrigida—from Italy. Podestà was picked for the part, though she did not fare well. Partly this was due to her lack of nuance as an actress. Also, she spoke almost no English and had to learn all her lines by rote, then pronounce them slowly so as to be understood. More attention was paid by future star-spotters to an energet-

NATURAL BEAUTY: Though Rosanna Podesta would be transformed into a blonde by Hollywood, her original 'look,' displayed here in her Italian homeland, exerts a strong appeal without any such remodeling.

ic, electric girl playing Helen's handmaiden, Androste: The then-unknown Brigitte Bardot, whom in retrospect might have perfectly incarnated Helen.

At any rate, what could have been a star-making appearance led only to minor work in B-movies. Before the decade ended, Rossana was back in Italy. *Ulysses* had been a hit, bringing in millions in profits internationally. A scramble had begun to find more such ancient-world mighty men of valor to immortalize onscreen, which led to the Steve Reeves *Hercules* hit movies and the Peplum genre. In Rome, films of the low-budget sword and sandals genre were mass-produced. Most were so poor in quality that they failed to win theatrical release in the U.S. (though eventually were shown on TV). Occasionally, a larger internationally funded item would be green-lit. In (*The Last Days of*) *Sodom and Gomorrah*, Podestà plays the older (and more adventurous) of Lot's two daughters. She finds herself unable to resist the advances of Sodom's evil prince (Stanley Baker, Achilles in *Helen of Troy*). Podestà had an opportunity to wear some of the most blatantly exotic costumes imagineable as The Movies inched toward nudity. Even as the Peplum genre slipped into decline, Podestà moved on first to Giallo thrillers, then, still looking terrific if no longer young, those silly sex spoofs that proliferated in Italy during the late 1960s and early 1970s. Allowed to speak in her native tongue, Rossana came across more naturally, oftentimes transitioning from giddish girlishness to intense emotion within a single sequence. In a final farewell to a lengthy if hardly distinguished film career, Rossana was tapped to play the goddess Hera in a 1983 redux of *Hercules* with muscleman Lou Ferrigno in the title role.

THE FACE THAT LAUNCHED A THOUSAND SHIPS: Historically speaking, it was probably closer to 100, but you know how folks love to exaggerate; Podestà went blonde for this immense Peplum produced by Warner Bros., though shot on European landscapes.

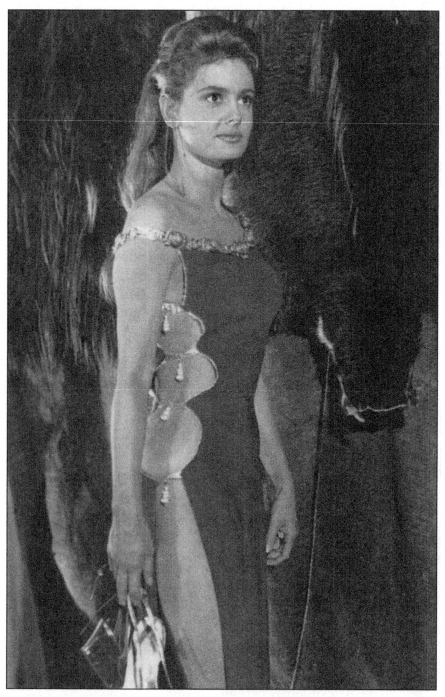

THE COSTUME THAT LAUNCHED A THOUSAND GASPS: As the older of Lot's two daughters in *Sodom and Gomorrah*, Rossana Podestà revealed more skin than had ever been allowed in a post-production code film up to this point.

SELECTED FILMOGRAPHY:

Cops and Robbers (Bottoni's Daughter, 1951); *Don Lorenzo* (Luisa, 1952); *Finishing School* (Pereira, 1953); *Rossana* (Rossana, 1953); *Ulysses* (Nausicaa, 1954); *Helen of Troy* (Helen, 1956); *Santiago* (Isabella, 1956); *The Amorous Corporal* (Bethi, 1958); *(A) Raw Wind in Eden* (Constanza Varno, 1958); *Temptation* (Caterina, 1959); *Fury of the Pagans* (Leonora, 1960); *Slave of Rome* (Antea, 1961); *Alone Against Rome* (Fabiola, 1962); *The Golden Arrow* (Jamila, 1962); *(The Last Days of) Sodom and Gomorrah* (Shuah, 1962); *Horror Castle* (Mary Hunter, 1963); *Intimacy* (Silvia, 1970); *The Sensuous Sicilian* (Lilia, 1973); *Seven Dangerous Girls* (Ivonne, 1979); *Hercules* (Hera, 1983).

THE VAMPIRE AS DOMINATRIX: Janine Renaud as Lorna, a queen of blood....
and dark daylight dreams.

Janine Reynaud

aka: JEANINE REYNAUD
Birthdate: 1930 (?)
Height: N/A
Measurements: N/A

FEW SEDUCTION SEQUENCES involving an enchantress and her female lover, the latter suddenly segueing from sex object to victim of violence, are as memorable as the one that occurs midway through *Succubus*. The film, released under the titles *Necronomicon* and *The Dreamed-of Sin*, focuses on Lorna (Janine Reynaud). A mysterious cabaret performer, Lorna onstage sado-masochistically abuses her latest victims before seemingly killing them. But is this simply a Grand Guignol form of decadent performance art? Or is it possible that she, Lorna, actually *is* a vampire, and that the deaths of her onstage victims are as real as they appear? That's a question many observers would like to solve, also part of the reason why Lorna's 'act' attracts such large, loyal crowds. Eventually, the raven-haired performance-artist takes a pleasant drive through the country with a gorgeous blonde, both in time retiring to Lorna's chateau. Intense lesbian lovemaking occurs in a lavish bed, located in a room filled with mannequins, most adorned in kinky costumes: Leather and lace, feathers and frills. Once the two beauties have brought one another to full orgasm, Lorna turns cold, and witch-like. She commands the lifeless mannequins to move. Slowly, they circle Lorna's lovely companion and murder the screaming girl while The Succubus (bloodsucker) coolly observes.

Though hardly Jess Franco's first film, *Succubus* was his initial project filmed outside of his native Spain. With international money invested, the always erratic Franco had to consider someone other than his favorite actress, Soledad Miranda—who recently died in a car accident—for the

THE ART OF THE SELL: In different markets, Succubus was sold in different ways; as an experimental art film near college campuses and with a come-on promising Narcissistic self-adoration for more general venues.

female lead. Janine came highly recommended, though little was known about this vivacious redhead. Apparently born in 1930, nobody in the industry could ascertain the precise date or whereabouts. That only increased her appropriateness for the part, Reynaud a mystery woman much like Lorna herself. Janine had modeled for fashion designer Jean Patou, her darkly ethereal beauty leading to screen offers. Not surprisingly, these were as bad-girls in sexploitation items, horror flicks, and spy movies. She would soon enact the manipulative Diane (half heroine, half wicked lady) in a series of projects, mostly espionage stories played for laughs. More than a dozen inexpensive indies cast Janine opposite her husband, actor Michel Lemoine, though they did eventually split. Today, her cult status rests entirely on *Succubus*, and the mature, Countess Bathory-like dominatrix character she embodied.

Succubus divided audiences and critics in 1969, continuing to do so today. The late Pulitzer-prize winning reviewer Roger Ebert considered this to be one of the worst films ever made, even speaking unkindly of Reynaud's physical appearance. Most others found her, if not the movie, enticing. Quentin Tarantino, who owns a print, considers this a classic.

REVERSE PENETRATION: Only after one of Lorna's lover/victims has satisfied her does she turn the tables and employ a phallic pin to destroy a guy who thought he 'got lucky.'

Initially, there were complaints that Franco never decided for sure what his movie was supposed to be: An eerie arthouse phantasmagoria about divine decadents on the order of Alain Resnais' *Last Year at Marienbad* (1965) or a hard-edged blood-and-thunder Giallo. Fans of the film (this author included) believe its greatness has to do with the unique blending of those forms.

SELECTED FILMOGRAPHY:

Special Mission to Caracas (Véronique, 1965); *Ypotron – Final Countdown* (Carol, 1966); *Cifrato Speciale* (Sheena, 1966); *Operation White Shark* (Frida Braun, 1966); *La Spia Che Viene dal Mare* (Madame Lina, 1966); *The Seventh Floor* (The English Ambassador's Daughter, 1967); *Succubus* (Lorna Green, 1968); *Run, Psycho, Run* (The Girl, 1968); *Sadist Erotica* (Diana, 1969); *Kiss Me, Monster!* (Diana, 1969); *How Short Is the Time for Love* (Fabienne, 1970); *Libido: Urge to Love* (Murielle, 1971); *Curse of the Scorpion's Tail* (Lara, 1971); *The Chambermaid's Dream* (Adélaïde, 1971); *Blindman* (The Prostitute, 1971); *Pénélope* (Pénélope, 1972); *The Cats* (Maude, 1972); *The Bitches* (Viriane, 1973); *The Little Saint* (Joan of Arc, voice only; 1974).

A RECURRING POSE: Both good girls and bad girls (Rigg's Avenger Emma Peel was a neat combination of the two) often posed with pistol – and a Sphynx-like smile.

Diana Rigg

Birthdate: July 20, 1938; Doncaster, Yorkshire, UK
Birth name: Enid Diana Elizabeth Rigg
Height: 5' 8 ½"
Measurements: N/A

IS THERE LIFE AFTER CULT STARDOM as a leather-clad femme
fatale? There certainly was in the case of Diana Rigg, who went on to
become a great "Dame" of the British Empire for her roles in Shakespearean stage productions. This, despite the fact that she ties Julie "Catwoman" Newmar as the first female to openly play a divinely decadent
dominatrix on the small screen. The strong female hero (or anti-heroine)
played by Rigg in *The Avengers*, a sometimes cartoonish show if never
as removed from reality as the Caped Crusader's, argued that good girls
could be women of action, could lead daring and exciting lives, could
empower themselves by dealing violently with men who attempted to
impose violence on them, and could employ brains as well as beauty;
physical strength augmenting rather than replacing elegance in style.
Also, that she could do so not as a villainess for the hero to conquer, but
as a female hero. ('Heroine' feels a bit anachronistic now, thanks largely
to Rigg). First in England, then in the U.S., there was always a double-vi-
sion as to how Emma Peel was perceived. From a male gaze point of view,
she served as one of the era's top sex symbols. But for members of the
then-emergent Women's Movement, here was a tower of female strength
who refused to play by the old rules. How fascinating that her character
was always identified as "Mrs." Emma Peel. If unattached younger girls
might in the early 1960s dare to live a life of adventure and romance,
here was the first suggestion that a married woman could go off with
another man (precisely what was her relationship with Patrick McNee's

DAMSEL IN DISTRESS: However powerful Emma Steed might be in certain situations, a retro element to the series had John Steed rescuing her in the style of a silent-era chapter play like *The Perils of Pauline*.

John Steed?) to defend the British Isles while also getting to have fun (her eyes were always full of relish when Diana/Emma kicked the baddies around) of a dark nature.

Way back in 1959, a nineteen-year-old Rigg (recently back from India, where her father worked for the railway) played ingénue roles after the the Royal Shakespeare Company accepted her as a member. A graduate of the Royal Academy of Dramatic Art, she overwhelmed critics with her unique combination of talent and attractiveness. Meanwhile, *The Avengers* needed a new star, what with Honor Blackman dropping to pursue movie work. Actress Elizabeth Shepherd had been signed to play the female lead in episodes that would now be filmed to make them easier to sell in American and international markets. Producers sensed that the combination of star and role would not mesh, dropped her, and set about trying to find a replacement without missing a beat. Though an acclaimed young Shakespearean stage actress might have seemed an unlikely choice, someone recalled seeing the shimmering beauty onstage and Rigg was offered the role. She accepted, never (as the cliché would have it) looking back—or apparently, ever pausing to worry whether this was the right career move for a stage star of her growing status. Diana embodied Mrs. Emma Peel in 51 installments, once insisting to the press that she had never even seen

VARIATIONS ON THE DANCE OF DEATH: On several occasions, Emma Peel caught men off guard by performing a Terpsichore, this allowing her to distract and then detroy her enemies.

the original *Avengers*, agreeing to take it on a "whim." The moment that the show concluded, Diana was back on the stage in challenging roles, as if the entire *Avengers* experience had been but a dream.

She did accept a femme fatale role in *The Assassination Bureau* and, that same year, played the woman who wins the hand of James Bond (one-timer George Lazenby) in *On Her Majesty's Secret Service*, only to be killed off at the end so that the series could continue. Albert Broccoli had originally hoped to sign Brigitte Bardot, though in an incredible irony Bebe proved un-available: She was committed to doing a Western, *Shalako*, opposite prevous Bond Connery. One other femme fatale role is worth mentioning. In the offbeat *Theatre of Blood*, Diana played the daughter of a failed Shakespearean actor (Vincent Price) who helps dad to murder the critics who have cruelly reviewed his performances. For once, Diana had an opportunity to combine both aspects of her career—thrillers and the Bard—in a single project.

Always, Rigg balanced a sense of the contemporary woman with a sin-cere appreciation for the classics, as when she played Helena in an experi-mental film version of *A Midsummer Night's Dream* while wearing a mod-ern mini-skirt. As a mature woman she refused to set her sexier antics aside, proving that grown-up ladies could flaunt their stuff as well as pretty girls, by agreeing (some said insisting!) on doing a nude scene in a 1970 stage version of *Abelard and Heloise*. Rigg returned to TV in acclaimed character roles, particularly on the prestigious BBC dramas, though a 1973 American sit-com, *Diana*, swiftly fizzled. She was titled Dame (DBE) in 1994, belying (or perhaps overturning?) the myth notion that that any woman who made a reputation playing kick-ass action babes in her youth would not be able to win acceptance as a 'serious' actress. In 2013 Dame Diana was still offering sound and fury in "The Crimson Horror" episode of the then-current *Dr. Who* incarnation and Lady Tyrell in *Game of Thrones*.

SELECTED FILMOGRAPHY:

A Midsummer Night's Dream (Helena, 1968); *On Her Majesty's Se-cret Service* (Countess Teresa di Vicenzo, 1969); *The Assassination Bureau* (Sonya Winter, 1969); *Julius Caesar* (Portia, 1970); *The Hospital* (Barbara Drummond, 1971); *Theatre of Blood* (Edwina Lionheart, 1973); *A Little Night Music* (Countess Charlotte Mittelheim, 1977); *The Great Muppet Caper* (Lady Holiday, 1981); *Evil Under the Sun* (Arlena Marshall, 1982); *King Lear* (Regan, 1983); *Snow White* (The Evil Queen, 1987); *A Good Man in Africa* (Chloe, 1994); *Parting Shots* (Lisa, 1999); *Heidi* (Grand-mamma, 2005); *The Painted Veil* (Mother Superior, 2006).

Maria Rohm

aka: MARIE ROHM; MARIA ROHN
Birthdate: August 13, 1945; Vienna, Austria
Birth Name: Helga Grohmann
Height: N/A
Measurements: N/A

STARING OUT AT THE AUDIENCE from the big screen in one of
her films, mostly low-budget thrillers in which she was cast as a sensuous
succubus or demented (if desirable) serial killer, with penetrating, merciless eyes, Maria Rohm might well have been secretly thinking: I was not
always as you see me now! As a child, growing up in postwar Vienna, she
began her career at age three in productions at that city's well-respected
Burgtheatre. Young Maria (then Helga) performed child roles in works by
Shakespeare and Tolstoy. Then she teamed up artistically with Jess (Jesus)
Franco, creator of some of the most groundbreaking horror and thriller
films of the 1970s, and American schlockmeister Harry Alan Towers, who
married Rohm. They were together from 1964 until his passing in 2009.

Several of her films are considered classics of their kind. *Venus in
Furs* (aka *Paroxismus*, aka *Schwarzer Engel*) is one of Franco's best-re-
membered sex thrillers. The director combined elements of Hitchcock's
psychological studies of sexually obsessed males and the dead females
they adore (most notably in *Vertigo*) and Federico Fellini's dazzling experiments with time and space, dream and reality, sense and sexuality,
i.e. *8 ½* (1963). Audiences were thrilled or aghast (or in some cases a bit
of both) by bloody/sensual romps that initially played the extremes of
arthouses and Drive-Ins but never, ever at mainstream movie palaces. Indeed, the term para-cinema, implying a daring project that combines the
highs of art and the lows of pornography, was largely created to at least

417

SOME CALL IT 'CATHARSIS': Maria Rohm washes off the blood of her latest victim
in order to get clean on the outside – and, hopefully, inside as well.

attempt to describe Franco's collaborations with Maria Rohm. The plot of
Venus in Furs was drawn from a novel by Leopold von Sacher Masoch,
he of the family that brought masochism to the world's attention. Franco
was also the auteur of *99 Women*, a bizarre women-behind-bars film that
teamed Rohn and fellow 1960s Sex Siren Luciana Paluzzi with heavy-
weight actresses Maria Schell and Mercedes McCambridge. Here again
viewers experienced a vivid and artistic presentation of the most lurid

AN ARTIST'S RENDITION: That's Maria, usurping center stage of the poster for a film known as *House of 1,000 Dolls* in the U.S., even though she received only fourth billing—and co-star status, at that!

VENUS IN FURS: As the title character in a classic thriller, Maria Rohm awaits her next victim (note his reflection in mirror) and then takes him into her bed – first for sex, then for... you guessed it!

sort of material, in a *Caged Heat* cat-fightin' yarn. With *Eugenie*, Franco adapted a disturbing tale by the Marquis de Sade about two beautiful women who became involved with a witchcraft cult, with Marie Liljedahl in the lead, Rohm as her companion. Sans Franco but for Towers, Rohm played Diane, a beautiful young bride kidnapped by white slavers pretending to be cabaret performers, in the marvelous/memorably titled *House of a Thousand Dolls* with Vincent Price and Martha Hyer. Both stars emphatically insisted later that they had no idea quasi-pornographic scenes would be added to the mix once they had finished their roles. After retiring, Maria assumed the producer's chair, overseeing the production of such films as *Edge of Sanity* (1989), *She* (2001), and *Sumuru* (2003).

SELECTED FILMOGRAPHY:
   Teufel im Fleisch (Prostitute, 1964); *Twenty-Four Hours to Kill* (Claudine, 1965); *City of Fear* (Maid, 1965); *The Million Eyes of Su-Muru* (Helga Martin, 1967); *The Vengeance of Fu Manchu* (Ingrid, 1967); *Five Golden Dragons* (Ingrid, 1967); *House of 1,000 Dolls* (Diane, 1967); *Eve* (Anna, 1968); *The Blood of Fu Manchu* (Ursula Wagner, 1968); *99 Women* (Marie, 1969); *Rio 70* (Lesley, 1969); *Deadly Sanctuary* (Juliette, 1969); *Venus in Furs* (Wanda Reed, 1969); *The Bloody Judge* (Mary Gray, 1970); *Eugenie... the Story of Her Journey Into Perversion* (Madame Saint Ange, 1970); *Count Dracula* (Mina, 1970); *Dorian Gray* (Alice, 1970); *Black Beauty* (Lady Anne, 1971); *Treasure Island* (Mrs. Hawkins, 1972); *The Call of the Wild* (Mercedes, 1972); *Ten Little Indians* (Elsa, 1974); *The Killer is Not Alone* (Teresa, 1975).

HAVEN'T WE SEEN THIS BEFORE?: As yet another sensuous succubus, Lina Ronay proves that women are anything but 'the weaker sex' by using her brains and beauty to lure yet another willing male slave into her bedroom.

Lina Romay

aka: JEAN COLLINS; CANDY COSTER; JANE MORGAN
Birthdate: June 25, 1954; Barcelona, Spain
Birth name: Rosa María Almirall Martínez
Date of passing: February 15, 2012; Málaga, Spain
Height: N/A
Measurements: N/A

SEVERAL DARKLY FASCINATING WOMEN played non-blonde
Trilbys to that frightful auteur of evil and eroticism, Jess Franco. How
deeply he was involved with any or all has always been a subject of fascination among the cultists who closely study his out-of-the-mainstream
work. But one thing's for sure: Only one deadly dame can claim to have
been married to him in a long-lasting relationship that would end only
upon her death at age 57 of cancer. That was Lina Romay, a macabre muse
of terrifying cinematic sonnets. Yet early on, Romay seemed likely to become a mainstream member of the arts establishment in Barcelona. She
studied a great many visual and performing art venues and, for a while,
was married to a photographer, Raymond Hardy. In 1971, with the new
freedom of the screen sweeping across the continent, Lina met Franco,
and neither person's life would ever be the same. She inspired him to
want to make progressively more daring films; he set the girl afire with a
sense of unbridled exhibitionism that the moviemaking world has seldom
known. Of the more than 100 films Lina starred in, a great many directed
by Franco, she willingly/willfully moved from R to X-rated entertainer. It
was as if, once she started her journey down this dark career road, only
more intense and outrageous sensationalism could satisfy her growing
appetite to be sensually deadly on the screen.

LOVE 'EM AND LEAVE 'EM: The succubus finishes off her latest prey and then leaves without regret.

The word most often employed by film historians to describe her is "uninhibited." Lina's stage name derived from a well-regarded jazz and mambo performer (a member of Xavier Cugat's band) of the 1950s. Like Ingrid Pitt, Dephine Seyrig, and Martine Beswick, Lina was hailed, during the 1970s, for what one reviewer neatly tagged as her "aggressive sexuality." Feminists could complain that the dominatrix countess in *Female Vampire* embodied every negative stereotype ever devised by men about the female of the species. On the other hand, there was no question that here was a femme fatale who controlled situations, empowering herself, and who, Bathory-like, lived precisely as she wished, lording it over men and other women. Her hard, tough, dominating onscreen women seemed to take a particular pleasure in seducing but also hurting girly-girls, as if to show her contempt for all such recessive behavior on the part of women. Always, Franco's camera, when pointed at Lina, snapped some switch deep inside, because those who knew her best insist that, whenever she was not busily shooting another torture-porn piece, Romay would grow silent, even withdraw, downplaying her beauty when forced to step out in public. It was as if there were two people living inside that luscious body: a nice, normal kind of girl who existed most of the time and an electrifying alter-ego that would in a split second displace that demure lady the moment that a camera could be heard whirring.

Trivia: She is the only woman ever to play Dr. Van Helsing in a movie.

SELECTED FILMOGRAPHY:

The Daughter of Dracula (Young Beauty, 1972); *The Erotic Rites of Frankenstein* (Esmeralda, 1972); *The Sinister Eyes of Dr. Orloff* (Innocent Girl, 1973); *Tender and Perverse Emanuelle* (Greta, 1973); *Les gloutonnes* (Bianca, 1973); *Female Vampire*, aka *Erotikill* (Countess Irina Karlstein, 1973); *The Lustful Amazons* (Yuka, 1974); *Pleasure of Three* (Adèle, 1974); *Night of the Assassins* (Rita, 1974); *Maid at Your Service* (Célestine , 1974); *Lorna the Exorcist* (Linda, 1974); *The Perverse Countess* (Silvia, 1974); *Women Behind Bars* (Shirley, 1975); *Rolls-Royce Baby* (Lisa Romay, 1975); *Marquise von Sade* (Doriana Gray, 1976); *Barb Wire Dolls* (Maria, 1976); *Jack the Ripper* (Marika, 1976); *Wanda, the Wicked Warden* (Juana, 1977); *Kiss Me Killer* (Moira Ray, 1977); *Swedish Nympho Slaves* (Madame Arminda, 1977); *Women Without Innocence* (Margarita, 1978); *Justine and the Whip* (Justine, 1979); *Wicked Memoirs of Eugenie* (Sultana, 1980); *White Cannibal Queen* (Ana, 1980); *Pick-Up Girls* (Suzy, 1981); *Blood on My Shoes* (Paquita, 1983); *Hotel of Love Affairs* (Eva, 1983); *Macumba Sexual* (Alice Brooks, 1983); *Night of 1,000 Sexes* (Irina, 1984); *Bangkok* (Aminia, 1985); *Fury in the Tropics* (Marga, 1986); *Amazons of the Gold Temple* (Mrs. Simpson, 1986); *Faceless* (Mme. Orloff, 1987); *Tender Flesh* (Mrs. Radeck, 1997); *Broken Dolls* (Tona, 1999); *Vampire Junction* (Mados, 2001); *Killer Barbys vs. Dracula* (Camarada Irina, 2002); *Snakewoman* (Dr. Van Helsing, 2006).

THE SHAPE OF THINGS TO COME: Tura Satana kicks male butt in a film that was dissed as sexist exploitation for male audiences by Second Wave feminists, then hailed as a worthy portrait of a strong woman fighting back by post-feminist women.

Tura Satana

Birthdate: July 10, 1938; Hokkaidō, Japan
Birth name: Tura Luna Pascual Yamaguchi
Date of passing: February 4, 2011; Reno, Nevada
Height: 5' 7"
Measurements: N/A

TO SAY THAT *FASTER, PUSSYCAT! KILL! KILL!* received at most
an inauspicious debut is to put the situation mildly. The movie opened at
Drive-Ins and downtown grindhouses. Only rarely did any 'serious' critic
(Roger Ebert was one) deign to review what was widely considered to be
indefensible trash. An exploitation flick by writer-director Russ Meyer,
who had established a reputation several years earlier with mild nudies
like *The Immoral Mr. Teas*, this supposed piece of junk didn't even feature
nudity. What *Pussycat* did boast was a trio of scantily clad bad-girls (Tura,
Lori Williams, Haji) frugging about on the Mojave desert. They beat up
anyone, man or woman, who happened by. Would anybody have dared
suggest that, in half a century, the logo for this exploitation item would
be featured on T-shirts, a popular band would draw its name from that
title, while the film would play retrospectives at leading museums around
the country? A shaking out process exists in the popular arts, allowing
what are perceived as marginal items to be reconsidered as classics once
the cultural context alters. This proved to be the case with Meyer's movie,
which illustrates a radical adage: Everything our parents taught us was
bad for us is actually good. True of the film, and its star, Tura Satana.

At a time when martial arts were just beginning to appear in male-
dominated action movies, Satana ruled the roost owing to her knowledge
of aikido and karate. She also drew on her acclaimed abilities as an exotic dancer, something she'd been practicing since age thirteen. Likewise,

her considerable acrobatic talents were integrated into the mix, along with a bizarre sense of over-the-top humor that lent a camp sensibility to her self-determined onscreen image. Lest we forget, this was the year of Woody Allen's *What's New Pussycat?* and TV's spoof of the James Bond self-spoofing films, *The Man from U.N.C.L.E.* Early on in that series' send-ups, Tara played a Dragon Lady. At the time, what Satana offered was perceived as an amalgam of sleazy bits and pieces from lowbrow enter-

IT'S A WOMAN'S WORLD: Tara (right) relaxes with co-stars Laurie Williams (left) and Haji (center, top) on the set of Russ Meyer's *Faster, Pussycat! Kill! Kill!*

tainment. Today, she can be appreciated as an early example of the avant-garde Performance Artist, who purposefully combines elements of low brow pop culture together in order to artistically represent the Zeitgest.

While no middle-of-the-road offers came Tara's way, she was approached by ulta-low budget filmmaker Ted. V. Mikels to appear in his sleaze-cinema efforts like *The Astro Zombies*. In the late 1960s and early 1970s, Second and Third Wave feminists turned up their noses at Satana and *Pussycat* as the ultimate male-chauvinist nightmare-scenario of bad-girls as objects of male heterosexual desire. More recently, post-feminists perceive something quite different. Varla is, in the words of some, "aggressive," "self-determined," "highly sexual in a purposefully dominating manner"; a strong female role model, as such predecessor to the plethora of such onscreen females in our own age of super-hero cinema and its violent-prone femmes including Lara Croft and Black Widow. No screen character more perfectly set the pace for such thinking as Tara's Varla! If she were still around, likely Quentin Tarantino would revive her career.

Trivia: Raised in Chicago, Satana was a one-woman rainbow coalition, claiming such varied ethnic descendancies as Japanese, Filipino, Cheyenne Native American, and Scots-Irish. She claims to have not only dated Elvis Presley but to have turned down a proposal of marriage from the King. Cause of death: Heart failure.

SELECTED FILMOGRAPHY:
Irma la Douce (Suzette Wong, 1963); *Who's Been Sleeping in My Bed?* (Asian Stripper, 1963); *Faster, Pussycat! Kill! Kill!* (Varla, 1965); *Our Man Flint* (Asian Stripper, 1966); *The Astro-Zombies* (Satana, 1968); *The Doll Squad* (Lavelle Sumara, 1973); *Sugar Boxx* (Judge #1, 2009); *The Haunted World of El Superbeasto* (Varla, voice only; 2009); *Astro Zombies: M-3 – Cloned* (Malvina, 2010).

THE GODDESS SYNDROME: Like so many of the beautiful international sex stars of the 1960s, Rosanna Schiaffino began her movie career in Italian-lensed Peplums.

Rosanna Schiaffino

Birthdate: November 25, 1939; Genoa, Italy
Birth Name: Rosa Anna Schiaffino
Date of passing: October 17, 2009; Milan, Italy
Height: N/A
Measurements: N/A

SO! JUST HOW GORGEOUS was Rosanna Schiaffino? Let's put it this way: Early in *Romulus and the Sabines*, aka *Romulus and the Sabine Women*, aka *Rape of the Sabine Women*, the male hero (Roger Moore) conquers the title tribe. Following less than friendly persuasion, he seduces (to put it mildly) their princess, played by the amazing Scilla Gabel. Later in that film, he meets Venus, as incarnated by Rosanna, and from that moment on can't stand the sight of his previous paramour. The point is, *we believe it*, even though Scilla Gabel was herself drop dead lovely. Like Gabel, Schiaffino bore a notable resemblance to already established Sophia Loren. While neither of these hopefuls for mainstream stardom would win such world-wide attention, both did decorate Peplums, horror, and spy cinema, emerging as cult queens.

When Schiaffino won the Miss Genoa title at age fourteen, she attracted the attention of movie producers eager to cast the stunning girl in ancient-world adventure flicks. As a proper young lady, Rosanna insisted that her mother and her sister accompany her to Rome for the initial auditions. Soon P.R. people were hyping her as "The Italian Hedy Lamar" owing to a similar exoticism and fiery sense of imminent danger. When *Life* magazine featured Schiaffino on its cover, Hollywood took note. Her shot came when, in the early 1960s, she appeared in two hyped 'big' films. One was *Two Weeks in Another Town*, based on an Irwin Shaw novel about maverick American moviemakers filming abroad, with Kirk Douglas and Edward G. Robinson. Rosanna played precisely what she was: One of many beauties wearing bikinis at the Cannes Film Festival in hopes of becoming the next Sophia or Brigitte. Also, *The Victors*, an ambitious anti-war epic by the long-blacklisted Carl Foreman. Focusing on a typical rifle squad, the film allowed a bevy of up-and-coming international beauties (Elke Sommer, Melina Mercouri, Jeanne Moreau, etc.) to play lovers of various soldiers. Schiaffino fared well as the initially demure, later sluttish girl who attracts the attentions of nice guy Vincent Edwards only to fall into the clutches of shallow heel Michael Callan. Unfortunately the film was not a hit; Schiaffino returned to the Peplum genre, occasionally in a bigger than usual project such as *The Long Ships* with Richard Widmark.

In time, movies became less important to her than a jet-set lifestyle. For several years, Rosanna embodied the very idea of La Dolce Vita. With a failed marraige behind her, she became deeply involved with wealthy playboy Giorgio Enrico Falck. Living the sweet life came to an abrupt end when she was diagnosed with breast cancer. A long, reportedly painful period finally came to a halt with Schiaffino's passing at age 69.

SELECTED FILMOGRAPHY:

Roland the Mighty (Angelica/Angélique, 1956); *Piece of the Sky* (Marina, 1958); *The Bid Night* (Rossana, 1959); *Danger in the Middle East*

From the moment that Rosanna Schiaffino appeared in Rome, photographers went quite wild in an attempt to capture that haunting face and perfect body.

ONE MORE BABE IN BONDAGE: American athletic great Bob Mathias must kill the title monster and then undo an obviously stressed Rosanna Schiaffino.

(*Flora*, 1960); *Minotaur, the Wild Beast of Crete* (Princess Fedra/Arianna, 1960); *Lafayette* (Comtesse de Simiane, 1961); *Blood on His Sword* (Jeanne de Beauvais, 1961); *Romulus and the Sabines* (Venere/Venus, 1961); *Two Weeks in Another Town* (Barzelli, 1962); *The Victors* (Maria, 1963); *The Long Ships* (Aminah, 1964); *The Cavern* (Anna, 1964); *Arrivederci, Baby!* (Francesca, 1966); *The Rover* (Arlette, 1967); *Hector the Mighty* (Elena, 1972); *The Man Called Noon* (Fan Davidge, 1973).

DON'T BE TAKEN IN BY THAT WHOLESOME APPEARANCE: Though Jean Seberg
would begin her career playing Joan of Arc, swiftly she moved onto femme fatales.

Jean Seberg

Birthdate: November 13, 1938; Marshalltown, Iowa
Birth name: Jean Dorothy Seberg
Date of passing: August 30, 1979; Paris, France
Height: N/A
Measurements: N/A

IN THE HISTORY OF MOVIES, was there ever a career (and concurrent life) quite so strange and unsettling as that of Jean Seberg? Of all those mystery women whose actual existences outdid their screen projects in terms of bizarre incidents, impossible relationships, too weird to believe coincidences and, in the end, horrible fates (and there were many!), Seberg's seems to take the proverbial cake. A woman of remarkable beauty but also talent, intelligence, and deep-seated commitment to social causes, her rise and fall (several times over, in fact) rates as a full-blown tragedy worthy of Sophocles or Shakespeare or a Grand Opera so over-the-top in its appeal that one can hardly believe this tale might have been imagined. Or a combination of the two. Yet it all began as a variation of the American Success Story about a smalltown girl whose dreams all come true. Sadly, in Jean's case, every one of them turned into a nightmare.

Born in Marshalltown, Iowa to a pharmacist father and a teacher mother, with strong Lutheran-leanings and a mostly Swedish background, Jean's early years resembled a William Inge play such as *Picnic*: The prettiest girl in a small town puts aside any opportunities to marry the local boy of her choice to pursue some romantic dream of success in the wide world. Joan's plan to study drama at the University of Iowa was interrupted when a neighbor saw a newspaper story about a talent hunt. Producer-director Otto Preminger wanted a scintillating unknown for the lead in

435

LOLITA GOES TO PARIS: Seberg's waif-like Nymphet plots the murder of her father's (David Niven) fiancée (Deborah Kerr) in *Bonjour Tristesse*.

Saint Joan. This woman mailed in a picture of Jean without informing anyone and the girl won. Whisked to Hollywood as the new young star of the future, Jean nervously completed the film only to be savaged by the critics. She might have become a bitter L.A. hanger-on, or headed home to lick her wounds. Instead, Seberg turned chin up. She accompanied Preminger to France, starring in his next venture, *Bonjour, Tristesse*. This time her kittenish appeal was employed for reverse typecasting as Jean played a spoiled teen whose obsession with her own father (David Niven) leads her to successfully plan the murder (which appears to be an accidental death) of that man's mature fiancée (Deborah Kerr). While in Paris, Seberg was noticed by Jean-Luc Godard, even then moving from intellectual-critic to director-auteur with *Breathless*. Godard persuaded Seberg to play hoodlum Jean-Paul Belmondo's on-again, off-again girl-friend: A youthful American expatriate in Paris, Patricia ekes out a living by selling the *Herald Tribune* on street corners, also pursuing a career as a celebrity journalist. She wears her hair boyishly short, in an anticipation of the style Mia Farrow would make mainstream five years later on TV's *Peyton Place*. After a bout in bed with her boyfriend, she callously betrays him to the police to serve her shallow self-interests. Before expiring, the hood calls her a "bitch." The placid look on her face, accompanied by a hint of a smirk, suggests that she takes this as a compliment. A new kind of amoral woman had just been born onscreen and in real-life for the upcoming 1960s.

For the next several years, Seberg darted back and forth from Europe (where she starred in offbeat arthouse productions) to America, managing to maintain a dubious star status if often in offbeat vehicles. These included *Let No Man Write My Epitaph*, about drug addiction in the nation's slums. A more definitive role came in *Lilith*, starring Seberg as a lovely madwoman who sucks her young psychiatrist (Warren Beatty) into an alternative inner-world. She married and later left a French director, Francois Moreuil, eventually taking the edgy novelist Romain Gary as her second husband. He would direct her in one of the oddest movies ever made, *Birds in Peru*. As Adriana, Seberg's Grace Kelly sense of swanlike elegance would be photographed from every angle, as if Gary were desperately attempting not only to understand the fictional character but

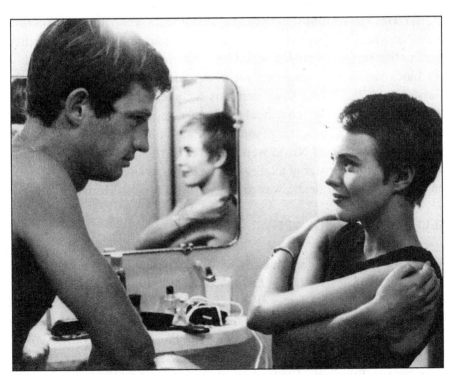

"BITCH!": That's the final word Jean-Paul Belmondo's anti-hero mutters, while dying, to the American girlfriend who betrayed him to the Paris police in *Breathless*.

his real-life wife as well. Adriana is an initially frigid married woman who while in the title place (elements recall Tennessee Williams' *Suddenly, Last Summer*) surrenders to the primitive aura hovering around her. She becomes a masochistic nymphomaniac who (from what we can gather) murders her mates on the beach if they fail to satisfy her sexually. Lesbian lovers are also included. Rare viewers who saw the piece wondered if Gary had modeled Adriana on Jean, who shortly divorced him.

A huge Hollywood comeback seemed imminent when Seberg won the roles that were originally intended for Faye Dunaway and Lana Turner in *Paint Your Wagon* and *Airport*. But if at long last she came to seem a conventional movie star, her personal life remained something else. A huge supporter of the Black Panthers during those radical days, Seberg came to believe the FBI was not only stalking her but also creating wild rumors to ruin Jean's newfound status, leading to her virtual blacklisting. At age 40, Seberg was found dead in Paris (she had recently returned in search of work); the official word went out that this was due to a barbiturate overdose owing to constant depression. Others believe Jean was murdered for her political beliefs.

Trivia: The relationship between Seberg and Gary had been so complex that when he decided to commit suicide late in 1980, Gary felt the need to first scribble a note in which he swore that the act was due to writer's block rather than lingering memories of their unique relationship. Gary's novel *The Talent Scout* contains a character clearly modeled on Jean Seberg. To this day, continual talk in L.A. suggests an eventual biopic that might reveal a conspiracy (some claim that FBI head J. Edgar Hoover and President Richard Nixon were involved) which had been formed to silence the strangest star of all. *Legion*, the film that she had been working on at the time of her death, was completed with actress Mimsy Farmer.

SELECTED FILMOGRAPHY:

Saint Joan (Joan of Arc, 1957); *Bonjour Tristesse* (Cecile, 1958); *The Mouse That Roared* (Helen Kokintz, 1959); *Breathless* (Patricia Franchini, 1960); *Let No Man Write My Epitaph* (Barbara Holloway, 1960); *In the French Style* (Christina James, 1963); *Backfire* (Olga Celan, 1964); *Lilith* (Lilith Arthur, 1964); *Moment to Moment* (Kay Stanton, 1966); *A Fine Madness* (Lydia West, 1966); *Who's Got the Black Box?* (Shanny, 1967); *Birds in Peru* (Adriana, 1968); *Pendulum* (Adele Matthews, 1969); *Paint Your Wagon* (Elizabeth, 1969); *Airport* (Tanya Livingston, 1970); *Macho Callahan* (Alexandra, 1970); *Dead of Summer* (Joyce Grasse, 1970); *This*

Kind of Love (Giovanna, 1972); *Kill! Kill! Kill! Kill!* (Emily, 1972); *Gang War in Naples* (Luisa, 1972); *L'Attentat* (Edith Lemoine, 1972); *The Corruption of Chris Miller* (Ruth Miller, 1973); *Ballad for Billy the Kid* (La star, 1974); *Mousey* (Laura, 1974); *Bianchi Cavalli d'Agosto* (Lea, 1975); *The Big Delirium* (Emily, 1975); *The Wild Duck* (Gina Ekdal, 1976).

DR. QUINN, MEDICINE WOMAN… IN BONDAGE? Indeed, Jane Seymour got all
tied up with Roger Moore's 007 in *Live and Let Die*.

Jane Seymour

Birthdate: February 15, 1951; Hayes, Middlesex, UK
Birth name: Joyce Penelope Wilhelmina Frankenberg
Height: N/A
Measurements: N/A

TODAY, THE PUBLIC'S ONGOING IMAGE of Jane Seymour derives from her TV series *Dr. Quinn, Medicine Woman* (1993-1998). In this feminist Western, she projected strength, sincerity, and a wholesomeness underlined by a touch of class. Nonetheless, earlier in her career, Jane played a Peplum princess, a Bond girl, and several memorable femme

JANE... SEE MORE?: The glamour and elegance that had to be kept hidden in *Dr. Quinn, Medicine Woman* is shared by the actress in a bathing beauty back-to-nature pose.

THE ARABIAN NIGHTS NEVER HAD IT SO GOOD: Jane Seymour as Princess Farah in the Ray Harryhausen ancient-world-epic *Sinbad and the Eye of the Tiger.*

fatales on TV mini-series. Her parents were involved in the medical profession. Though she studied at the Arts Educational School in Tring, Hertfordshire, the girl set her sights on an acting career and borrowed her moniker from the third wife of King Henry VIII, indicative of the elegant roles she aspired to. So in an age of flower-power Nymphets, Jane Seymour consciously offered an alternative: a return to traditionally regal women. In Roger Moore's second Bond outing, *Live and Let Die*, Seymour essayed Solitaire, one more mistress of a super-villain who, after meeting 007, goes over to the good side. *Sinbad and the Eye of the Tiger*, third in a series featuring special effects by Ray Harryhausen, cast the half-Jewish actress as an ancient Persian aristocrat.

Though never a *Star Trek* green-girl, Jane did go the TV sci-fi route with a role as Serina in the original *Battlestar Gallactica*. Her first great Evil Beauty was Bathsheba in *The Story of David*, a TV mini-series. She soon emerged as a true queen of that narrative form. What may be her finest performance appears in a three-part 1981 adaptation of John Steinbeck's *East of Eden*. Whereas Cathy had, in the 1954 film with James Dean, been a supporting role (played by Jo Van Fleet as an elderly woman), here

TODAY, THIS IMAGE MIGHT BE CONSIDERED RACIST: The bondage and torture of Jane Seymour's Solitaire likely would not meet politically correct standards of today.

the approach was to tell the full story over many decades, concluding with those final chapters that were employed for the movie. Now, viewers could witness the stunning transformation of a young girl, seemingly without a past, into a female monster of epic proportion. Jane's four husbands include Michael Attenborough (1971-1973), Geoffrey Planer (1977-1978), David Flynn (1981-1992), and James Keach (1993-2013). She has four children, two with each of the latter. Seymour remains very much committed to social causes, particularly providing aid to abused children. Like Margo in *Lost Horizon* or the fabled queen in *She*, Jane does not appear to have aged one bit, still as strikingly gorgeous as ever.

SELECTED FILMOGRAPHY:

The Best Legs in the Business (Kim Thorn, 1972); *Live and Let Die* (Solitaire, 1973); *Sinbad and the Eye of the Tiger* (Princess Farah, 1977); *Somewhere in Time* (Elise McKenna, 1980); *Jack the Ripper* (Emma Prentiss, 1988).

Delphine Seyrig

Birthdate: April 10, 1932; Beirut, Syria (aka Lebanon)
Birth name: Delphine Claire Beltiane Seyrig
Height: 5' 7"
Measurements: N/A

THE EARLY 1970S was the era of the female (and invariably bisexual) vampire, with one classic following another from diverse international film production centers. Few if any cast as hypnotic a spell as *Daughters of Darkness*. Mood-drenched, able to effectively draw the legend of Elizabeth Bathory from its medieval setting into our own contemporary moment, this Belgian masterpiece owes much to the visual approach of director Harry Kümel. Also, star Delphine Seyrig brought to her performance a sense of the great femme fatales that Marlene Dietrch had played during the 1930s and 1940s. The deadly countess and her recessive dark-haired secretary (Andrea Rau) involve themselves, at an old seaside inn during the off-season, with a young, seemingly 'normal' heterosexual couple (Danielle Ouimet, John Karlen). Their honeymoon turns out to be a haunted one after encountering these gorgeous ghouls. The purposeful resemblance of Seyrig to Dietrich and Rau to Louise Brooks, another strange beauty from cinema's past, allows the knowing interpreter to grasp that this is not merely one more horror film about femme fatales but a statement addressing the idea of deadly female beauty as it appears in motion pictures from their earliest incarnations.

Delphine hailed from a notably upscale family. Her father at one point served as France's cultural attaché in Manhattan. Raised there, in Greece, and also in Paris during her early years, it's hardly surprising that Seyrig developed a cosmopolitan point of view during her teenage years. Quickly, she set her sights on the legitimate stage, studying the art of act-

YET ANOTHER BISEXUAL SUCCUBUS: Having just seduced her young husband, Delphine Seyrig's Countess Bathory sets her sights on the honeymooning blonde wife in *Daughters of Darkness.*

ing with such luminaries as Tania Balachova. Her interpretation of Ariel in Shakespeare's *A Midsummer Night's Dream* attracted critical attention. She was married at the time to Jack Youngerman, a painter. Movies beckoned when Alain Resnais picked Delphine for *Last Year at Marienbad*, the semi-surreal phantasmagoria that successfully transferred Sigmund Freud's concept of Dream States to the international cinema. By this time, friendships with such Beat Generation figures as Greg Corso and Jack Kerouac had created something of a mystique around Delphine, who would also be sought out by another world-class filmmaker, Spain's Luis Buñuel, for his own out of the ordinary projects. Though she did appear in several commercial vehicles like *The Black Windmill* and *Day of the Jackal*, Seyrig's image was set as an inscrutable woman of mysterious origins… perhaps a ghost, whose touch could spell instant death but whose allure could not be resisted. A key part of the appeal was her one-of-a-kind voice, simultaneously husky yet invitingly warm. In her later years, Delphine concentrated on stage work, appearing in classics by Henrik Ibsen and also experimental pieces from Samuel Beckett.

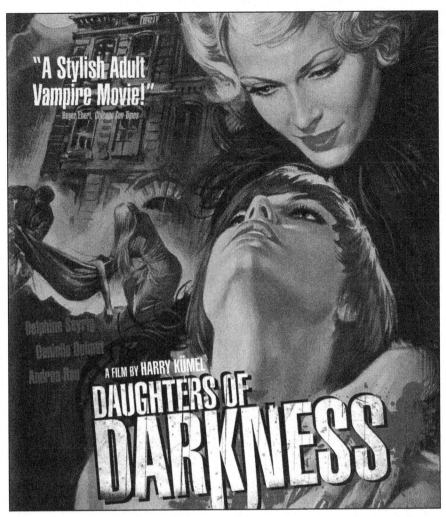

ADVERTISING AS ART: The poster work heralding this film's entry into theatres has become a collector's item owing to the spectacular manner in which it captures the essence of what director Harry Kümel was attempting to portray.

SELECTED FILMOGRAPHY:

Last Year at Marienbad (Brunette Beauty, 1961); *Muriel* (Hélène Aughain, 1963); *Accident* (Francesca, 1967); *La Musica* (Elle, 1967); *Stolen Kisses* (Fabienne, 1968); *The Milky Way* (A Prostitute, 1969); *Donkey Skin* (Lilas, 1970); *Daughters of Darkness* (Countess Bathory, 1971); *The Discreet Charm of the Bourgeoisie* (Simone, 1972); *The Day of the Jackal* (Colette, 1973); *A Doll's House* (Kristine Linde, 1973); *The Black Windmill* (Ceil, 1974); *The Last Word* (Simone, 1975); *India Song* (Anne-Marie,

A DOUBLE HOMAGE TO MARLENE DIETRICH: In *Last Year at Marienbad*, Delphine Seyrig wore fashions that recall that great glamour star of the 1930s and 1940s; in *Daughters of Darkness*, Seyrig appears to be offering a reference to her earlier tribute.

1975); *Faces of Love* (Julie, 1977); *I Sent a Letter to My Love* (Yvette, 1980); *Grain of Sand* (Solange, 1983); *Letters Home* (Aurelia Plath, 1986); *Joan of Arc in Mongolia* (Lady Windermere, 1989).

Cornelia Sharpe

Birthdate: October 18, 1943; Selma, AL.
Height: N/A
Measurements: N/A

THE HIT-WOMAN MADE HER FIRST significant appearance as a
screen icon during the 1960s, in the guise of beautiful, seductive, cold-
blooded killing machines played by Luciana Paluzzi and Karin Dor in
Thunderball and *You Only Live Twice*, also assuming center-stage in
Deadlier Than the Male with Elke Sommer and Sylva Koscina. But these
were merely beautiful monsters, as was Susan Hart in the *Dr. Goldfoot*
films. By the 1970s, though, feminism had taken hold as a social issue and
entered the mainstream. It only made sense that the hit-woman had to be
re-imagined. Yvette Mimieux's script for her TV starring vehicle *Hit Lady*
continued the idea of an amoral beauty using charm as well as brains in
her career as a paid assassin. Now, though, she was an entirely sympathetic character, the audience rooting for her to get away with it. It didn't
take long for The Movies to follow suit. The plot for *The Next Man* was
almost identical to that of *Hit Lady*, only with international-geopolitical
implications. A moderate Arab leader (Sean Connery) hopes to negotiate
a lasting peace with Israel. Meanwhile, he becomes romantically involved
with a spectacular beauty, Nicole Scott (Cornelia Sharpe), who accompa-
nies him on his round the world negotiations. We know what he cannot,
as the film opened with her seductive murder of a previous assigned hit,
portrayed in an unsettlingly graphic sequence that has naked Nicole bedding while suffocating (with a plastic bag) her all too willing victim. The
choice of a costar seems significant, as Adolfo Celli played Bond's near-
nemesis in *Thunderball*. Connery, however, chose to portray his character
as the opposite of cynical 007, and did so without his usual hairpiece. He's
idealistic and deeply caring.

SEPARATED AT BIRTH FROM FAYE DUNAWAY?: Model turned actress Cornelia Sharpe was almost inseparable from that already established star who, according to some sources, had been the original choice for *The Next Man*.

Sharpe, as Nicole, must deal with the fact that she's falling in love with her intended victim. But if the audience thinks she'll do a turnabout, they are in for a surprise. The day when strong catwomen melted into merely pussycats while in the arms of such a virile male (think of Honor Blackman in *Goldfinger* a decade earlier) were gone. Nicole is an independent woman and, despite their great sex and mutual respect, she offs her lover according to the hard contract that she signed. "Soft brown eyes," she muses one final time before coolly shooting Connery. If there is a flaw here, it's that in the final sequence, Nicole appears to be on the verge of annihilation herself. As with Mimieux's *Hit Lady*, it would have been more scintillating as well as satisfying to see her get away with it. Still, this set the pace for Zoe Saldana in *Columbiana* (2011).

DISHONEST ADVERTISING: In some markets, an attempt was made to sell *The Next Man* as a Bond-like spy thriller; in fact, this was a highly intelligent political project featuring Cornelia as one of the first hit-women in mainstream rather than B-movies (other, of course, than the 007 bad-girls).

Cornelia's stunning looks (there was a notable resemblance to Faye Dunaway, who by some reports was considered for Nicole) led to modeling and then small if ripe parts in such A-films as *Serpico*. There, she shares a memorable bathtub sequence with Al Pacino as the real life cop. Unfortunately, the critics were not kind to *The Next Man* (aka, *The Arab Conspiracy*) or to Cornelia. Alone among influential reviewers, Ebert praised her performance; others dismissed Sharpe as one more lifeless manque, going through the motions listlessly. In fact, that was the key to understanding her character: Existential ennui underlined by a hint that there might just be a glint of humanity left, somewhere deep down inside. It would be four years before she would win a lead role in a TV movie called *S+H+E: Security Hazards Expert*, also about a strong, capable, gorgeous contemporary woman, this time working for The Good Guys. Sharpe settled in for the good life as wife of famed Hollywood producer Martin Bregman.

SELECTED FILMOGRAPHY:

Kansas City Bomber (Tammy O'Brien, 1972); *The Way We Were* (Party Guest, 1973); *Serpico* (Leslie, 1973); *Crazy Joe* (Blonde, 1974); *Busting* (Jackie Faraday, 1974); *Open Season* (Nancy Stillman, 1974); *The Reincarnation of Peter Proud* (Nora Hayes, 1975); *The Next Man* (Nicole Scott, 1976); *Cover Girls* (Linda Allen, 1977); *Venom* (Ruth Hopkins, 1971); *Table One* (Fan, 2000); *The Adventures of Pluto Nash* (Fan, 2002); *Vote and Die: Liszt for President* (Mrs. Neil Liszt, 2008).

Barbara Shelley

Birthdate: February 13, 1932; Marylebone, London, UK
Birth name: Barbara T. Kowin
Height: 5' 8"
Measurements: N/A

LONDON-BORN BARBARA'S stunning appearance allowed her to become a sought-after professional model at age sixteen. With that job came financial freedom, so shortly she was off and running on a continental vacation. It was in Italy that Barbara was spotted by filmmakers and encouraged to appear in several Rome-based projects, including a memorable turn as a ravishing young beauty in *Nero's Mistress*. Timing proved perfect to set her off on a course that would eventually cause fans to hail Barbara as "The First Leading Lady of British Horror." In those days, Hammer was still in the process of redefining its image, in the past mostly a purveyor of middling black-and-white melodramas rarely seen outside the British Isles. A U.S. producer, Lou Rusoff of American International, became intrigued by the idea of shooting thrillers in England to save on production costs. Barbara was tapped to play the lead in *Cat Girl*, a rip-off of the old R.K.O. classic *The Cat People* (1942) starring Simone Simon. Several years later, Barbara would appear in an unofficial sequel, *Shadow of the Cat*. In retrospect, Barbara might be thought of as the precursor to Bond's Pussy Galore, and it would be easy to picture this actress in the role that went to fellow Brit Honor Blackman. Though never a Bond girl (what a pity!) Barbara did guest on TV's equivalent, *Danger Man* in England with Patrick MacGoohan and, in Hollywood, *The Man From U.N.C.L.E.*

Not all of Barbara's villainy contained a supernatural element. Several London-based film noirs allowed her to reveal a cut-throat quality in

THOSE LIPS, THOSE EYES, THOSE... TEETH!: in *Dracula, Prince of Darkness*, Barbara Shelley picks up where the title character/paramour left off.

more realistic situations, including her role as an unfaithful wife in *Blind Corner*. As the advertising copy for the film boldly announced, "She loved one man for kicks... one man for luxury... and one man for murder!" To be fair, there were several good girls along the way. Barbara starred in two offbeat Hammer items in their retro-World War II series, both concerning English victims of the Japanese in the South Pacific. The second, *The Secret of Blood Island*, is the more interesting; Barbara plays a British secret agent whose plane is shot down over enemy territory. The only way that prisoners in the hellhole can help her character is to disguise her as a boy and pass her off as one of their own. She was also sympathetic as the wife of George Sanders who gives birth to a Midwich Cuckoo (a strange child from outer space) in the science-fiction classic *Village of the Damned*. Always, though, audiences loved to watch Barbara perform villainy, as in the modern retelling of an ancient myth, *The Gorgon*. One claim to fame: she was the only one woman to be seduced and abandoned by Christopher Lee in two films shot the same year, 1966. In Terence Fisher's stylish *Dracula, Prince of Darkness*, Barbara is an upper-class prim and proper wife who falls under the Count's spell and transforms into a wild, shrieking, sex-craved succubus. Supernatural elements were not present in *Rasputin, the Mad Monk*, in which Barbara plays Sonia, a hand-maiden to Russia's Tsarina and Rasputin's helper in conquering the court. In one of her final films, she played the matron of a haunted house that's visited by young people (Marianne Faithfull one of them) in *Ghost Story*, not to be confused with a later film of the same name. When movie roles were no longer forthcoming, Shelley went on to enjoy a long career in British TV including *Dr. Who – Planet of Fire* (1984). Onstage, she has performed with the Royal Shakespeare Company and, after retiring, Barbara began a second career as an interior decorator.

THE TIME HAS COME: Barbara's crazed vampire girl cannot employ her deadly beauty on the dedicated monks who lead her to execution.

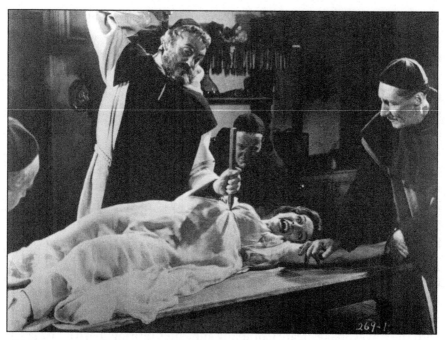

"THIS WILL HURT YOU MORE THAN IT WILL ME!": Barbara's terrified vampire awaits
that great threat, the stake through the heart.

SELECTED FILMOGRAPHY:

New Moon (Ingenue, 1955); *Nero's Mistress* (Seductive Virgin, 1956); *Cat Girl* (Leonora Brandt Johnson, 1957); *The End of the Line* (Liliane Crawford, 1957); *The Camp on Blood Island* (Kate Keiller, 1958); *Bobbikins* (Valerie, 1959); *Village of the Damned* (Anthea Zellaby, 1960); *Shadow of the Cat* (Beth Venable, 1961); *Postman's Knock* (Jean, 1962); *Blind Corner* (Anne Gregory, 1963); *The Secret of Blood Island* (Elaine Hamer, 1964); *The Gorgon* (Carla Hoffman, 1964); *Dracula, Prince of Darkness* (Helen, 1966); *Rasputin, the Mad Monk* (Sonia, 1966); *Quatermass and the Pit,* aka *Five Million Years to Earth* (Barbara Judd, 1968); *Ghost Story* (Matron, 1974).

Elke Sommer

Birthdate: November 5, 1940; Berlin-Spandau, Germany
Birth name: Else (Baronesse) von Schletz
Height: 5' 7"
Measurements: 36 – 23 - 37

FILM HISTORIAN GARY BRUMBURGH once summed up the uniqueness of Elke's beauty thusly: "her trademark pouty lips, high cheekbones and sky-high bouffant hairdos proved irresistible to American audiences, whether adorned in lace or leather, or donning lingerie or lederhosen." But why ignore those tantalizing blue-green eyes! When, in 1942, Elke's Lutheran father and his wife necessarily evacuated their home in Erlangen owing to threats from ongoing war, the two-year-old found herself living in a near-pastoral setting, not far from a university, in the south of Germany. In this quiet enclave, Else (later Elke) was introduced to the arts; she was particularly fascinated with painting. Thoughts about pursuing such a career were soon sidetracked owing to modeling and movie offers, though Elke never stopped painting—and, when her film career eventually wound down, returned to it on a passionate level.

At age fourteen, Elke headed for England. Following work there as an au pair, she returned home and, now fluent in English, took college courses while considering a possible career as a diplomatic translator while paying the bills by modeling. During a vacation in Italy, she was awarded the title of "Most Beautiful Tourist" and spotted by actor-director Vittorio de Sica. He hired Elke to play an example of the new sexually free teenagers who were becoming a reality across Europe and had already been incarnated onscreen by Brigitte Bardot.

In 1963, Elke's career exploded thanks to Hollywood's casting her in several important international productions. In *The Victors*, an episodic

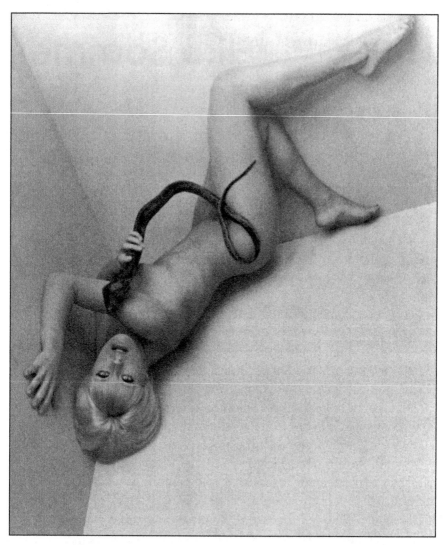

IT ALL STARTED WITH EVE: Shortly after Elke's first great success in *The Prize* opposite
Paul Newman, as a sweet Scandanavian girl with a healthy appetite for sex,
she switched over to bad-girls, as symbolized by a Biblical snake.

epic about the war years, she portrayed (opposite George Hamilton) a
teenage German girl who attempts to hold on to her dignity and values
despite post-WWII chaos. Far more successful with audiences: *The Prize*,
in which she embodied the free-loving Swedish girl of the 1960s who has
no constraints about old-fashioned morality, particularly after meeting
the irresistible Paul Newman. A year later, Elke began her transition from
wholesome (if always overtly sexual) young-woman-of-the-moment to

femme fatale opposite Peter Sellers in *A Shot in the Dark* (1964), the second (and best) of the Inspector Closseau films. Throughout the story, his bumbling detective cannot determine if her character is as sweet and innocent as she appears or actually a cold, calculating murderess. By film's end, he's so swept up in her charms that he (and the audience) could care

SEX AND DEATH: Elke's hit-woman offers first one, then the other to her targeted prey, in *Deadlier Than the Male*.

less. A *Playboy* layout that year established Elke as the reigning sex goddess with American, and international, men.

All the same, her career then took a downward spiral. There were big (but not very good) Hollywood dramas like *The Oscar* and lame comedies including *Boy, Did I Get a Wrong Number!* The next step down the status-ladder was the B-movie route, though these did allow Elke to embody boldness and badness onscreen. Though she never did play a Bond girl, Elke crystalized the essence of one of 007's bad-girls (teamed with brunette Sylva Koscina) in *Deadlier Than the Male*. Richard Johnson, a Connery lookalike, played a resuscitated Hugh 'Bulldog' Drummond, now a secret agent of course, attempting to track down a pair of gorgeous female assassins. Whether it's setting a bomb on a plane before skydiving to safety, shooting one man with a spear-gun or tossing another off a high-rise, Elke's once-innocent eyes blaze with abject evil—adding, of course, to her sex appeal as femme fatale. Shortly, she played an almost identical role opposite Dean Martin as Matt Helm, cinching her new onscreen identity. A third spy 'caper,' *The Venetian Affair*, set Elke opposite *The Man from U.N.C.L.E.*, Robert Vaughn.

SWEET ECSTASY: Before Elke's sudden shift into international stardom, she appeared as a European Lolita, seducing and destroying older men with money.

READY FOR ACTION: In *Deadlier Than the Male*, Elke's hit-girl sets a bomb to go off on and kill all the passengers on a plane (in order to eliminate one man) before parachuting to safety, then relaxes with a pleasant sunbath before beginning her next assignment.

Some of the most interesting tightly-budgeted films then being shot internationally were Italian-lensed horror films, the best directed by Mario Bava. Elke won the leads in *Baron Blood* and *Lisa and the Devil*. There were also several record albums and stage performances. Though a long-term marriage (1964-1981) to photographer Joe Hyams (who shot her second *Playboy* spread) eventually failed, she did forge a working relationship with her second husband, hotel manager Wolf Walther (1993-present). An interesting side-note: When Zsa-Zsa Gabor cattily suggested that Elke was merely a second-rate Zsa-Zsa imitator, Elke sued and won millions, all-but bankrupting Gabor.

Trivia: Elke had been second choice (just behind Juliet Prowse) for the female lead opposite Elvis Presley in *G.I. Blues* (1960).

SELECTED FILMOGRAPHY:

Men and Noblemen (Caterina, 1959); *Jukebox Girl* (Giulia, 1959); *The Warrior Empress* (1960); *Love, the Italian Way* (Greta, 1960); *Daniella by Night* (Daniella, 1961); *Why Bother to Knock* (Ingrid, 1961); *Sweet Ecstasy* (Elke, 1962); *The Victors* (Helga, 1963); *The Prize* (Inger, 1963); *A Shot in the Dark* (Maria Gambrelli, 1964); *The Dolls* (Ulla, 1965); *The Art of Love* (Nikki, 1965); *The Money Trap* (Lisa, 1965); *The Oscar* (Kay, 1966);

Boy, Did I Get a Wrong Number! (Didi, 1966); *The Venetian Affair* (Sandra Fane, 1967); *The Corrupt Ones* (Lilly, 1967); *Deadlier Than the Male* (Irma Eckman, 1967); *The Wicked Dreams of Paula Schultz* (Paula, 1968); *The Wrecking Crew* (Linka, 1968); *Percy* (Helga, 1971); *Zeppelin* (Erika, 1971); *Baron Blood* (Eva Arnold, 1972); *Lisa and the Devil* (Lisa Reiner, 1973); *It's Not the Size That Counts* (Clarissa, 1974); *Ten Little Indians* (Vera, 1974); *The House of Exorcism* (Lisa Riner, 1975); *Carry on Behind* (Anna, 1975); *The Prisoner of Zenda* (The Countess, 1979); *The Double McGuffin* (Kura, 1979); *Lily in Love* (Alicia Braun, 1984); *Severed Ties* (Helena, 1992); *Flashback* (Frau Lust, 2000).

Barbara Steele

Birthdate: December 29, 1937; Birkenhead, Cheshire, UK
Height: 5'6"
Measurements: N/A

AS THE SIXTIES BEGAN, Italy's Mario Bava set about reinventing the horror film, *Black Sunday* prominent among his early work. Likewise, Roger Corman created vividly colorful adaptations of the old Poe classics at Hollywood's American International, *The Pit and the Pendulum* among the most atmospheric. One woman headlined both films: Barbara Steele. At age 20, she had played for Bava foil-like roles, an innocent virgin and a corrupt if lovely witch/vampire, impressing audiences with her "skull under the skin" beauty; Steele seemingly existing midway between a lovely flesh-and-blood woman and a walking/talking skeleton. *Black Sunday* opens with Steele's succubus burned at the stake, as a death-mask is hammered against her horrified face, allowing her fascinating eyes to speak to something deep and dark in the heart of every horror fan. The following year, those eyes dominated the final shot of Corman's film as her adulterous character is locked away forever in an Iron Maiden, the dark eyes wide with terror at the thought of her oncoming long, slow death. Though most of her later films could not compare to these, they set into place a legend of cinematic wickedness.

The British-born beauty more or less stumbled into acting. Hoping to earn quick money so that she could head for Paris and become a painter ("the female Picasso"), this bold girl marched into a Brighton Pier rep company, asked for a job, and was hired on the spot. Shortly, talent scouts from prestigious Rank spotted and hired her. Hollywood wanted a piece of the action. Initially, Steele went the starlet route via

463

THE SKULL BENEATH THE SKIN: That's a phrase many critics employed to describe Barbara's unique, almost skeletal beauty in *The Pit and the Pendulum*.

glamorous window-dressing appearances in mainstream movies like the romantic comedy *Houseboat* (1958) with Sophia Loren and Cary Grant, *The 39 Steps* (1959, a London-shot remake of the Hitchcock classic), and the erotically-charged *Sapphire* (1959). When an actor's strike shut down L.A. production, Steele flew to Italy, filming not only Bava's *Black Sunday* but Federico Fellini's masterwork *8 ½*. Six months later, she was back in Tinseltown and the mainstream career Steele hoped for almost happened.

She was cast opposite Elvis Presley in *Flaming Star*, a serious Western for Fox, but made the mistake of walking off the set in disappointment over the conventional way in which her female lead was to be played. Barbara Eden stepped in; Steele was shown the (rear) door.

Back to Europe. The cult audience for grisly/sexy horror unofficially crowned Steele their first true Scream Queen thanks to outrageous items

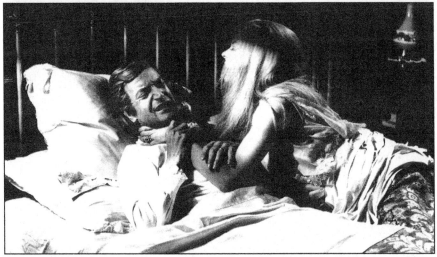

AN OBSESSION WITH DEATH: In *Black Sunday*, Barbara's brunette considers crawling into a coffin with a recently victimized male; in *Nightmare Castle*, her blonde does in a man who was expecting an engaging night of lovemaking.

like *The Horrible Dr. Hitchcock*, *Castle of Blood*, and *Nightmare Castle*. There was an interesting arthouse item, *Young Torless*, but mostly her work consisted of being bound and gagged in old castles. After a decade of such stuff, Steele announced her imminent retirement, stating: "I'll never have to crawl out of a coffin again!" It's rumored that for *She Beast*, Steele was paid a measly $1,000 at a time when most stars of Euro-trash cinema were making upwards of $25,000 per picture. Barbara might have made a perfect bad-girl in a James Bond movie though that never did happen.

SILENCING A SUCCUBUS: In the medieval prologue to *Black Sunday*, Barbara's vampire stands helplessly in bondage, awaiting her unpleasant fate.

"I'LL NEVER HAVE TO CRAWL OUT OF ANOTHER COFFIN AGAIN!": So said Barbara Steele when she retired from gothic horror flicks like *Black Sunday*, aka *Mask of the Demon*, and *Nightmare Castle*.

She did play a beautiful assassin in "Bridge of Spies," a memorable episode of TV's *I Spy*. In time she enacted older evil women, like the sadistic warden in the women's prison picture *Caged Heat* and a demented doctor in *Piranha*. And, once in a while, she also was allowed to do serious character roles in such upscale movies as *I Never Promised You a Rose Garden* and, most memorably, an aging prostitute in Louis Malle's exquisite *Pretty Baby*, the first starring role for Brooke Shields.

One French admirer suggested that if Christopher Lee and Cyd Charisse were to conceive a daughter, the offspring would have been Barbara Steele. Her big dark eyes conveyed a bizarre if seductive combination of lust, terror, repression, carnal hunger, girly-girl vulnerability, female empowerment, anger and fear, and a desire for the fall. Film historian Danny Peary caught Steele's essence in words in *Cult Movies*: "The most fascinating actress ever to appear in horror films with regularity... Her beauty is mysterious and unique: her large eyes, high cheekbones, jet-black hair, thick bottom lip, and somewhat knobby chin don't seem synchronized, and as a result her face can be looked on as being either evil... or sweet."

LINGERIE: During the 1960s, black bra, garter belt, and seamed stockings became associated with the female vampire for the first time; such a trend continues into the 21ˢᵗ century.

SELECTED FILMOGRAPHY:

Your Money or Your Wife (1960, Juliet); *Black Sunday* (Katia/Vajda, 1960); *The Pit and the Pendulum* (Elizabeth Medina, 1961); *The Horrible Dr. Hitchcock* (Cynthia, 1962); *8 ½* (Gloria, 1963); *The Ghost* (Margaret,1963); *Castle of Blood* (Elisabeth Blackwood, 1964); *The Monocle* (Valérie, 1964); *The Long Hair of Death* (Helen/Mary Karnstein, 1964); *Nightmare Castle* (Muriel/Jenny, 1965); *Young Torless* (Bozena, 1966); *She Beast* (Veronica, 1966); *An Angel for Satan* (Harriet/Belinda, 1966); *Caged Heat* (McQueen, 1974); *I Never Promised You a Rose Garden* (Idat, 1977); *Pretty Baby* (Josephine, 1978); *Piranha* (Dr. Mengers, 1978); *Her Morbid Desires* (Vanessa, 2008); *Lost River* (Belladonna, 2014).

Yutte Stensgaard

Birthdate: May 14, 1946; Thisted, Jutland/Denmark
Birth name: Yutte Stensgaard
Height: N/A
Measurements: N/A

DIANETICS/SCIENTOLOGY OR BORN-AGAIN Christian: those are the alternative routes taken by many people who briefly enjoy stardom/celebrity only to hopelessly watch as the years pass and, for reasons difficult to explain, nothing happens following that momentary burst of fame. Yutte Stensgaard chose the latter path after her bubble burst. She was watching a TV show called "Advice Line," hosted by Jesus-oriented self-help guru Roy Masters, and saw the light. In short order she ceased all attempts to follow up on her one great claim to fame, adopting a straight-and-narrow path while condemning the sex-drenched, violence-laden horror film that briefly established her as a cult sensation. Nonetheless, there are few images in the lesbian subgenre of vampire cinema to compare with Yutte, as Carmilla Karnstein, rising up nude, her lithe body covered only by a fast-slipping sheet and layer after layer of faux blood, from a coffin. Her Nymphet appearance as a nubile girl is countered by a zombie-like glaze hanging over those big, beautiful eyes as Hammer's second incarnation of Carmilla, this time more in line with the child-demon that Sheridan Le Fanu created, makes ready to charm victims (male and female) before fulfilling each brief-encounter's death wish.

The film: *Lust for a Vampire*, a hurriedly thrown together sequel to the surprisingly successful *Vampire Lovers* of one year previous. Owing to what she considered a shabby script, Ingrid Pitt passed on the project. Right or wrong about that, this allowed a hopeful starlet from Denmark the shot she'd been hungering for. As a bored teenager, Yutte had

CARMILLA KARNSTEIN IN THE FLESH: No actress ever more fully captured Sheridan Le Fanu's literary conception of his half-child, half-woman vampire than Yutte Stesngaard in Hammer's *Lust for a Vampire*.

abandoned her homeland, hoping to find fame and fortune in Swingin' London during the height of Beatle-mania. Odd jobs as a stenographer and au pair paid the bills until her photos (in a mini-skirt) led to employment as a model. Stensgaard's brief marriage to a British film-biz art designer named Tony Curtis (no relation to the American actor) allowed

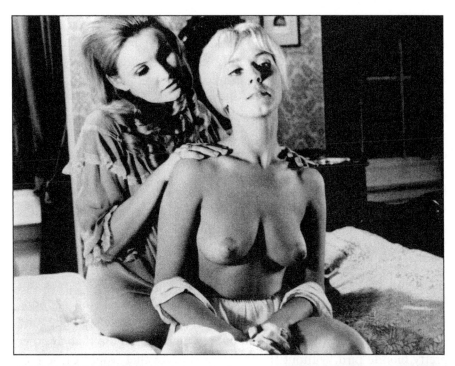

THE TROUBLE WITH GIRLS: As Carmilla, Yutte enters into gentle friendships with some of her boarding school associates, then viciously murders others for their blood.

Yutte to make connections with those in the industry who could help her land auditions. Shortly, she found herself romping about in period-piece costumes, softly seducing, then coldly killing any attractive person she happened to meet. While Stensgaard did not possess Pitt's acting chops, she does tie Annette Stroyberg Vadim in *Blood and Roses* as the most accurate onscreen incarnation of vampire literature's most important female character, a little girl whose seeming innocence masks her inner evil. Essentially Lolita, only with fangs. Surprisingly, her *Lust* role would not be followed-up by a celebrity-spread in *Playboy*, considered more or less *de rigeur* at the time. Though *Lust* was trounced by critics (this author happens to be a huge fan) as an unworthy follow-up, some took note of Stensgaard's radiant presence, predicting major-league stardom on her horizon.

That didn't happen. She won roles as beautiful bad-girls in several Bond imitations, *Some Girls Do* and *Zeta One*, as well as in TV knock-offs like *The Saint* and *The Persuaders*, both starring future 007 Roger Moore. In all truth, and with that remarkable initial starring role set aside (and fangs removed), Stensgaard turned out to be nothing more than another pretty blonde bird, without the thespian abilities that would cause loo-

BISEXUALITY AS THE NEW NORMAL: However much Carmilla enjoys the company of women, she does leave time to casually kiss, then cruelly kill, attractive men as well.

DO NOT GO GENTLE INTO THAT BAD NIGHT: Unwisely, a teacher (Ralph Bates)
attempts to use the cross to place Carmilla under his power; the irresistible succubus
convinces him to throw it away, then takes cruel pleasure in dismembering this unattractive
victim who naively hoped to become her servant through eternity.

kalikes Susan George and Jill Ireland to achieve full stardom; London's
film industry had, at the moment, more such lovely 'birds' than producers
knew what to do with. Yutte followed in the paths of Brigitte Bardot and
Shirley Eaton as The Blonde in several *Carry On...* comedies. In time she
hosted, for half a year, a British TV game show, *The Golden Shot.* A failed
audition for the coveted role of 'Jo Grant' in *Dr. Who* only added to her
growing disappointment. Marriage to an NBC executive brought her to
Hollywood; despite newfound status (until that coupling also came crashing down), juicy roles didn't come her way. Born-again, Yutte found work
as Account Director for a radio-network that brought the likes of ultra-
conservatives Rush Limbaugh, and Glenn Beck to the airwaves.

For years Yutte would recoil in... well... *horror!*... should someone
dare mention her naughtily-nice days. More recently, Stensgaard has
acquiesced, granted retrospective interviews, even agreed to appear at
fan-cons, hailed as the guest of honor at one such gathering—apparently
reconciling her (in)glorious days with the current crusading approach to
Christian values.

STENSGAARD BY STARLIGHT: Carmilla waits patiently, by a roaring fire, for the next willing victim, male or female, to enter her lair.

SELECTED FILMOGRAPHY:

The Girl With a Pistol (Girl, 1968); *Zeta One* (Ann Olsen, 1969); *Some Girls Do* (Sexy Robot 1, 1969); *If it's Tuesday, This Must Be Belgium* (Museum Guide, 1969); *Carry On Again Doctor* (Blonde Nurse, 1969); *Scream and Scream Again* (Erika, 1970); *Doctor in Trouble* (Eve, 1970); *The Buttercup Chain* (Ullah, 1970); *Lust for a Vampire* (Mircalla/Carmilla, 1971); *Burke & Hare* (Janet, 1972).

Annette Stroyberg

aka: ANNETTE VADIM
Birthdate: December 7, 1936; Fyn, Denmark
Birth name: Annette Susanne Strøyberg
Date of passing: December 12, 2005; Copenhagen, Denmark
Height: N/A
Measurements: N/A

FOLLOWING HIS SPLIT from Brigitte Bardot, French filmmaker Roger Vadim needed to quickly find another beautiful young blonde to appear in the artsy soft-core arthouse/sex films he had planned for the woman who had been both wife and star. Vadim chose Annette Stroyberg (they were soon married) and introduced her in a scintillating if in truth shallow contemporary version of the famed novel *Les Liaisons Dangereuses*, written in 1782 by Pierre Choderlos de Laclos. In it, Annette played a naive nymph manipulated and violated by aristocrats who perceived themselves as sophisticates. Next up for the director/actress duo was a concept Vadim had been considering for some time: The first film version ever of Sheridan Le Fanu's 1872 novella "Carmilla," the story of a beautiful young vampire whose aura of absolute innocence allows her the power to charm and seduce any man or woman she meets, slowly drawing her prey into the desired death—the pleasurable pain of total surrender to the senses. (Note: some sources do argue that Carl Dreyer's early sound film *Vampyre* was inspired by the Le Fanu work, but there is no hint of the original plot in that film and the vampire woman is an old witch). Vadim was, in fact, ahead of his time: A decade later, Hammer and competing companies would seize on Carmilla Karnstein once freedom from censorship was achieved.

BARDOT REBORN?: The similarities between Annete Stroyberg and Roger Vadim's estranged wife caused the director pick the young beauty to play Carmilla Karnstein in *Blood and Roses*; the role had originally been intended for Bebe.

In Vadim's modern retelling, Stroyberg's thin, girlish, sweet yet pro-
foundly evil female-monster attempts to break up the upcoming marriage of her cousin (Mel Ferrer) and a mature beauty (Elsa Martinelli).
At one point, when the two women are alone on a rainy day, a sudden,
unexpected brush of one beauty's lips against the other's allowed for one
of the earliest lesbian exchanges in the history of modern horror. Many
would in time follow, but this sumptuously photographed (by the great

A KISS IS STILL A KISS: The first openly lesbian counter between a succubus and her
victim, albeit brief, had Elsa Martinelli falling under Annette Stroyberg's spell in
Blood and Roses.

A NEW KIND OF HORROR FILM: Roger Vadim was one of those filmmakers who, in the early 1960s, began the significant move away from hoary genre cliches to an arthouse approach to dark material.

A SUCCUBUS MUST SLEEP… BY DAY: Elsa Martinelli's 'normal' girl can't understand why she is so drawn to the strange young beautiful blonde (Stroyberg).

Claude Renoir) phantasmagoria set the pace for sensuality of a highly stylish order to follow. Another remarkable moment occurs as Carmilla slowly, steadily pursues a gorgeous peasant girl who, in the moonlight, desperately runs away, trying in vain to escape her erotic/lethal fate. *Blood and Roses* was alternately known as… *Of Death and Pleasure*.

Danish-born Stroyberg shared several key qualities lauded in Bardot: The "pouty" lips and "kittenish" demeanor, the latter suggesting here was a pussycat who might return a sweet pet of one's hand with a vicious scratch of her claws. Vadim insisted a sense of abiding melancholy was necessary for the female who would incarnate Carmilla, as underneath her quietly classy demeanor and apparently wholesome facade there must exist a sense of morbidity, a quality that Stroyberg neatly delivered. The girl had left Copenhagen, where she and her sister lived, to head for Paris as a Chanel model. She met and became involved with Vadim as early as 1957, while he remained married to Bardot and was shooting her first huge hit,… *And God Created Woman*. Later that year, Annette and Vadim had a child, Nadine. Their relationship might be thought of as parallel to Jimmy Stewart's with the second incarnation of Kim Novak in Alfred Hitchcock's *Vertigo*; like that fictional heroine, Vadim proved unable to accept this fresh beauty for her own unique possibilities, laboring at transforming Annette into a precise replica of the blonde he had loved and lost. This liaison too was doomed to a quick end: By the time that *Blood and Roses* hit theatres, creating quite an intense cult following on the continent and the American arthouse circuit, Vadim was already pursuing Catherine Deneuve.

Though Stroyberg did appear in several nondescript Italian films, her reputation from that point on largely rested on her tempestuous love affairs with guitar great Sacha Distel and actors Vittorio Gassman, Alain Delon, Omar Sharif, and Warren Beatty. Her final years were spent in a marriage to Gregory Callimanopulos, an ultra-wealthy shipping tycoon. But when she passed of cancer in 2005, Stroyberg was back home again in native Denmark.

SELECTED FILMOGRAPHY:

Les Liaisons Dangereuses (Marianne Tourvel, 1959); *(The) Testament of Orpheus* (Orpheus's Lover, 1960); *Blood and Roses* (Carmilla Karnstein, 1960); *Carabiniere* (Letizia, 1961); *Beach Casanova* (Gloria, 1962); *The Eye of the Needle* (Rosaria, 1963); *Agent of Doom* (Florence, 1963); *Lo Scippo* (Luciana, 1965).

Sharon Tate

Birthdate: January 24, 1943; Dallas, TX
Birth name: Sharon Marie Tate
Date of passing: August 9, 1969; Los Angeles, California
Height: 5' 6"
Measurements: N/A

FRISSON **IS A TERM** the French employ to describe a bizarre audience reaction to something onscreen that inspires a sexual turn-on accompanied by an image that evokes horror and death. One such moment occurred when everyday people wandered into a middle-American theatre on a lazy Sunday afternoon in 1973 to catch a Vincent Price horror film, *Scream and Scream Again*. The double-bill also featured the less publicized *Eye of the Devil*, like the superior *The Wicker Man*, a realistic study of the practice of witchcraft (a.k.a., Wicca) in out of the way places in our modern world. An initially blasé audience spotted, in the credits, the name Sharon Tate, playing a black-leather clad virgin witch. Simultaneous gasps merged into heightened excitement as the audience awaited her appearance and a strange silence engulfed the auditorium. Some five years earlier, Sharon Tate would have not elicited such an overpowering reaction while she remained alive and well and working in movies. Everything changed on the night of August 9, 1969, when the pregnant wife of Roman Polanski, he out of the country, along with several friends was slaughtered in the infamous Manson Massacre, named after death-cult leader Charles, a long-haired self-styled guru who bragged about a remote musical attachment to the Beatles. The incident served to turn the American public against the Youth Movement, up until then perceived as starry-eyed innocents. From this point on, the average citizen came to see counter cultural types as a threat, Tate the sacrificial lamb.

'10': Some people may feel that the number signifying female perfection fits Bo Derek; there are those of us who rather apply it to the tragic Sharon Tate.

A self-confessed army brat, Tate was raised in a variety of settings (Italy included) as the family moved whenever her father's assignment changed. In 1959 alone, she won five major beauty pageants. Always intrigued by films, constantly told that she was beautiful enough to be a star, Sharon found extra work. Her first major role hardly prepared her for cult stardom of an edgy order; Sharon played a giggly bank secretary named 'Janet Trego' on CBS' comedy *The Beverly Hillbillies*. She was picked by a dazzled Roman Polanski for the female lead in his *The Fearless Vampire Killers*, an homage to Hammer. Tate incarnates the lovely serving girls at

WITCHCRAFT IN THE MODERN WORLD: In the tradition of Roger Vadim's *Blood and Roses*, J. Lee Thompson's *Eye of the Devil* was designed to play as a serious movie about Wicca, with Tate an alluring witch/huntress replete with bow and arrow.

ONE MORE BEAUTY IN A BATH-TUB: Tate awaits her grim fate in husband
Roman Polanski's *The Fearless Vampire Killers*, aka *Dance of the Dead*.

inns that decorated that studio's projects, now featuring a split-second
moment of nudity when, surprised in a bath-tub by an intruding vampire,
she gasps at his presence. Though an innocent victim throughout, Tate's
character becomes, by film's end, a deadly vampire herself. Such hints of
darkness would cut away her girly-girl mannerisms in *Don't Make Waves*,
a middle-age version of the *Beach Party* films with Tony Curtis falling for
Tate's beach bunny, as well as *The Wrecking Crew*, in which she recycles
the deadly bimbo that Stella Stevens incarnated in the first Matt Helm
movie, *The Silencers*.

THE FACE: Few women have ever come close to Sharon Tate as to beauty and glamour.

Trivia: *Eye of the Devil*, Tate's first starring role, was originally to have been titled *Thirteen*; her final film has sometimes been referred to by that title. At the time of her death, Sharon Tate was reading *Tess of the d'Urbervilles* by Thomas Hardy, in hopes her husband would adapt the novel for her. Ten years after her death, he finally filmed *Tess* with Natassia Kinsky. That film is dedicated to Sharon Tate.

SELECTED FILMOGRAPHY:

Hemingway's Adventures of a Young Man (Stripper, uncredited, 1962); *The Americanization of Emily* (Pretty Girl, uncredited, 1964); *Eye of the Devil* (Odile de Caray, 1966); *The Fearless Vampire Killers* (Sarah Shagal, 1967); *Don't Make Waves* (Malibu, 1967); *The Wrecking Crew* (Freya Carlson, 1968); *Twelve Plus One* aka *Thirteen*, (Pat, 1969).

Dyanne Thorne

aka: DIANE THORN
Birthdate: October 14, 1943; Greenwich, CT
Height: N/A
Measurements: N/A

DIFFICULT AS IT MAY BE to believe, the woman who incarnated the most controversial of all B-movie femme fatales from the 1970s had studied acting on a serious level with no less than Stella Adler and Lee Strasberg, they the greatest avatars of the Method. Yet she would go on to embody Ilsa, She Wolf of the S.S. in an exploitation film derived from the historical tale of a Nazi dominatrix at a World War II concentration camp. Advertising copy on the poster read: "She turned her lovers into lampshades!" (No such thing ever occurs onscreen.) More incredible still, the star who would call herself Dyanne Thorne to enhance her prickly reputation made her premiere at age three when she performed a role at a religious church play. Perhaps most fascinating of all, she would in time return to such devout roots.

At age seventeen, the (to put it mildly) voluptuous young woman won her first movie role in a mainstream comedy, *Who Was That Lady?*, as a college girl. Shortly, she balanced such Hollywood products, including *The President's Analyst* starring James Coburn, with schlock such as *Sin in the Suburbs*, one of Joseph W. Sarno's nudie junk movies. By 1968, with the Ratings System in place, such cheaply turned out items as *The Erotic Adventures of Pinocchio* (Dyanne played an inept if bosomy fairy-godmother) were shown on suburban theatre screens rather than only the groundhouse and Drive-Ins. However controversial these may have initially seemed, such stuff seemed relatively innocent compared to the hardcore porno chic that set in during the early-to-mid 1970s following

NOT ALL VAMPIRES HAVE FANGS: Dyanne Thorne's crazed killers sucked the
life-blood, if not the physical blood, from her victims.

the release of *Deep Throat*. If what had initially been labeled 'X' but now,
in the age of *Behind the Green Door*, barely received an 'R,' was to survive,
such movies had to push into ever more daring territory. Like the *Ginger*
films starring Cherry Caffaro as a female 007 agent (a bad good-girl), Dyanne Thorne's Ilsa vehicles (she a bad bad-girl) offered the most intense
(and downright nasty) sex scenes possible without ever transgressing into
what was now X-territory by including any penetration, this by 1975 the
only dividing-line remaining.

What could possibly have possessed Dyanne to accept the role of
Ilsa? She once told an interviewer: "It was a chance to put my craft to
work. Even so, my Jewish friends were appalled that I would appear in
such a film. My husband is Jewish and he went nuts when he first read
the script. But as an actress I didn't think about that. I was just playing
a role. It was a job to me and I did the best I could with it. I never tried
to glorify Ilsa. I felt she was a character to pity, rather than to emulate."

INTRODUCING ILSA: The surprise success of *She Wolf of the S.S.*
led to several sequels and spin-offs.

ILSA IN ACTION: Supported by her She-Wolves, S.S. officer Ilsa prepares to torture, then kill, a prisoner who only moments before had been her lover.

Still, Dyanne acknowledged the danger of becoming an onscreen femme fatale, particularly in 'fobidden cinema' projects: "If you do too good a job of playing a villain, you will suffer for it. (Ilsa) caused me to lose a good deal of film work. I could no longer get in to see the major studio casting directors and I couldn't even get an agent to represent me. They were scared to handle me." In truth, major players were even more terrified to work with Thorne than with such hardcore performers as Marilyn Chambers. The utter depravity of what Dyanne as Ilsa had performed onscreen (in the first film's opening, she, with fellow Nazi bitches, tortures and then castrates a recent lover) pushed any and all limits as to what was even imaginable. Shortly, VHS tapes, later DVDs, brought Dyanne a far wider (if, again, mostly secretive) fan base.

Trivia: The first Ilsa film was shot on the recently discarded set of the TV series *Hogan's Heroes*.

Adding to Dyanne's cult status is a 1966 *Star Trek* guest shot in the "A Piece of the Action" episode, as well as earlier playing the femme fatale in an episode of *T.H.E. Cat*, a bizarre surrealist-noir series starring Robert Loggia. She also found roles in Hollywood products long after the Ilsa era was over, including James Belushi's transsexual father in the comedy *Real Men*. Dyanne became a Vegas performer, and starred in a series of sketch comedy routines titled "Sex Over 40." Eventually, she retired from show business to create, with her husband Howard Maurer, a wedding chapel in Las Vegas. An ordained minister today, Dyanne co-founded the International Science of Mind Prayer Circle which preaches positivism and peace to all. Also, Dyanne holds a Ph.D. in Comparative Religions.

SELECTED FILMOGRAPHY:

Who Was That Lady? (College Cutie, 1960); *Lash of Lust* (Claudia, 1962); *Love with the Proper Stranger* (Female Musician, 1963); *Sin in the Suburbs* (Yvette Talman, 1964); *The President's Analyst* (Cocktail Waitress, 1967); *Love Me Like I Do* (Sharon Sloane, 1970); *The Erotic Adventures of Pinocchio* (Fairy Godmother, 1971); *Blood Sabbath* (Alotta, Queen of the Witches, 1972); *Point of Terror* (Andrea Hilliard, 1973); *Wham! Bam! Thank You, Spaceman!* (Hooker, 1975); *The Swinging Barmaids* (Boo-Boo, 1975); *Ilsa: She Wolf of the S.S.* (Ilsa, 1975); *Ilsa, Harem Keeper of the Oil Sheiks* (Ilsa, 1976); *Lollipop Palace* (Frenchie, 1976); *Chesty Anderson U.S. Navy* (Nurse, 1976); *Wanda, the Wicked Warden* (Greta, 1977); *Ilsa the Tigress of Siberia* (Ilsa, 1977); *Hellhole* (Crysta, 1985); *Aria* (Bride, 1987); *Real Men* (Father Pirandello, 1987); *House of Forbidden Secrets* (Greta Gristina, 2013).

QUEEN OF THE CAVE GIRLS: A natural brunette, Victoria Vetri reluctantly donned a blonde wig for *When Dinosaurs Ruled the Earth*.

Victoria Vetri

aka: ANGELA DORIAN
Birthdate: September 26, 1944; San Francisco
Birth Name: Victoria Cecilia Vetry
Height: 5' 5"
Measurements: N/A

BORN IN SAN FRANCISCO, raised in Los Angeles, Victoria lived well during her early years, her father a successful restaurateur. In no time, the dark beauty could count herself a TV veteran, playing Native-American heroine Sacajawea on *Death Valley Days*, appearing in Native garb a few years later on the popular Western *Cheyenne*. In one of her best early performances, Vetri enacted a war-scarred Italian girl in an episode of ABC/Warner Bros.' *The Gallant Men*, here revealing a sweet sensitivity that recalled Pier Angeli. In the early 1960s she found herself in the running for the part of Lolita, which went to Sue Lyon. Whether Victoria turned down the opportunity or was passed over is still debated among fans. Likewise, she auditioned for the role in *West Side Story* that went to Natalie Wood. Cult status arrived with roles as 'Charisma Highcloud' on *The Man from U.N.C.L.E.*, 'Isis' on *Star Trek*, and Florence of Arabia in a *Batman* episode starring Victor Buono as King Tut. She and former Bond girl Luciana Paluzzi competed for the hand of rugged Rod Taylor in *Chuka*, one of Hollywood's final old-time Westerns. In *Rosemary's Baby*, she played Terry, a friend of Mia Farrow's title character. Billed as Angela Dorian—Vetri's *Playboy* Monicker (see below), an in-joke—had Farrow and others mistaking neighbor Angela for actress Victoria Vetri. In a TV advertisement, she earned the distinction of being the first girl to appear in hot pants and made-for-walkin' boots in a commercial.

Everything changed when *Playboy* came calling. Uncertain whether her nude layout as the September 1967 Centerfold girl would help or hurt her acting career, Victoria chose to use a fake name. Angela Dorian offered a play on the ill-fated ship the Andrea Doria, though as things turned out, perhaps it was not so great an idea to fuse her identity with such a legendary disaster. Initially, reaction to her stunning looks paved the way for something big. She won the Playmate of the Year (1968). An image of her was carried into space by astronaut Pete Conrad aboard Apollo 12. Shortly, Victoria was able to indulge in such expensive hobbies as car-racing, even owning her own Porsche. For one brief moment, she appeared to be the girl who had everything. Along came two Scream Queen roles. First, for Warner Bros./Seven Arts, she played a blonde (in a wig) cave-girl (wearing a fur bikini) in When *Dinosaurs Ruled the Earth*, a follow-up to Hammer studios' hit *One Million Years B.C.* with Raquel Welch. One charming bit has Vetri's wide-eyed cave girl adopted by a dinosaur mom and riding about on the beast's back. Shortly thereafter she starred in an inventive B-sci-fi film, *Invasion of the Bee Girls*. Victoria

DO YOU THINK THEY INTENDED THAT AS A PHALLIC SYMBOL?: About to slip from a high cliff, Victoria Vetri's Sanna grabs on to anything she can to keep from falling.

WATER, WATER, EVERYWHERE... AGAIN!: Like so many other B-movie babes, posing in the ocean was all but required of Victoria Vetri, aka Angela Dorian.

plays the assistant to a government agent (William Smith) attempting to track down the succubus style beautiful-aliens who love men to death. At one point, Vetri is kidnapped by the girls, stripped and bound, then tortured. If cult-status was assured, this did not lead to any other offers.

In 1980, while in-between husbands and living alone in Hollywood, Vetri was assaulted in her apartment by at least one man. Though she recognized him, the fast fading star was never able to win legal retribution. Unable to find acting jobs, she began waitressing, always telling clients that she was saving her tips to finance a big comeback. Victoria married four times, the first three ending in divorce. The fourth, Bruce Rathgeb, turned out to be unluckier still. On September 7, 2011, during an argument that turned violent, she seized a gun and shot him at close range. Vetri pleaded no contest to the charge of attempted voluntary manslaughter and was sentenced to nine years in prison. At the time of writing, Victoria Vetri remains behind bars at the Central California Women's Facility in Chowchilla.

SELECTED FILMOGRAPHY:

The Pigeon That Took Rome (bit, uncredited, 1962); *Chuka* (Helena Chavez, 1967); *When Dinosaurs Ruled the Earth* (Sanna, 1970); *Group Marriage* (Jan, 1973); *Invasion of the Bee Girls* (Julie Zorn, 1973).

Tuesday Weld

Birthdate: August 27, 1943; New York, NY
Birth name: Susan Ker Weld
Height: 5' 4"
Measurements: 36C – 23 - 35

TRIVIA QUESTION: Who turned down the female leading roles in *Lolita* (Sue Lyon, 1962), *Bonnie and Clyde* (Faye Dunaway), *Rosemary's Baby* (Mia Farrow, 1968), *Cactus Flower* (Goldie Hawn, 1968), *True Grit* (Kim Darby, 1969), *Bob & Carol & Ted & Alice* (Dyan Cannon, 1969), and Roman Polanski's *Macbeth* (Francesca Annis, 1971)? Tuesday Weld, *that's* who! Had she deigned to do them (and passed on the bizarre projects Tuesday accepted in their stead) she might well be remembered alongside Katharine Hepburn, Carole Lombard, and Marilyn Monroe. Possibly, Sue Weld could have been the greatest of all such stars. Apparently, she had a deep-seated fear of success, avoiding quality films unless they were of an indie order, unlikely to prove popular. So instead of Uber-actress/star status, Tuesday Weld exists in Hollywood history as the greatest cult star of all time.

As to her passing on Kubrick's offer for immediate iconic status, Tuesday has reflected: "I didn't need to play Lolita. I *was* Lolita!" Among the numerous older men she is rumored to have enjoyed affairs with somewhere between the ages of 12 and 15 was the great character actor John Ireland, then old enough to be her grandfather. Apparently, young boys were too immature, though she did enjoy a fling with Elvis while working with him on *Wild in the County*. Tuesday also appeared with Fabian twice, once in a movie (*High Time*, though reports are that she found top-billed Bing Crosby more to her liking) and again on a 1963 episode of NBC's *The Dick Powell Theatre*, one of the finest dramatic filmed show-

IF BARDOT HAD BEEN BORN AMERICAN...: Tuesday Weld may well have been the greatest actress of her generation; yet she turned down Roman Polanski's *Macbeth* and said yes to Albert Zugsmith's *Sex Kittens Go to College*????

cases to appear after the golden age of live drama was over. Frankie Avalon was also a co-star in the glitzy escapist fare *I'll Take Sweden*. Tuesday joined Mamie Van Doren in a pair of her infamously sleazy junk movies (*Sex Kittens Go to College* and *The Private Lives of Adam and Eve*) for exploitation producer Albert Zugsmith. The blonde nymphet, who made her debut as a bit player in a Hitchcock film, might well have made for a

"I DIDN'T NEED TO PLAY LOLITA; I WAS LOLITA!": That famous quote from the young Tuesday Weld pretty much says it all for the most remarkably beautiful teenage star of the late 1950s/early 1960s.

great Hitchcock blonde had he cast her in *The Birds* and *Marnie* instead of the pneumatic Tippi Hedren, though it's likely that Tuesday would have turned those roles down.

After all, why work with genius when you can appear in two of the most dizzyingly pretentious (and all but unseen) films of the hippie era, *A Safe Place* and *Play It as It Lays*? (Maybe the term Crazy/Beautiful explains everything). Following the release of those bombs, the *New York Times* printed an editorial in their Sunday Theatre Section begging Tuesday Weld to please pick decent projects and become the superstar she so clearly had the potential to be. No way! In truth, though, she did accept some challenging TV work that reveals her true/natural genius as a performer: Cherie (The Marilyn Monroe role) in *Bus Stop* (1961) and Abigail (opposite George C. Scott) in Arthur Miller's *The Crucible* (1966). Also, leads in *Madame X* (1980), *The Rainmaker* (Hepburn's role, 1982), and *The Winter of our Discontent* (1983) from a John Steinbeck novel. She would have played Daisy Buchanan in *The Great Gatsby*, though the producers unwisely cast Mia Farrow (all wrong for the role) when Weld refused to go through the rigors of a screen test.

Early on, Tuesday played roles similar to those in which Sandra Dee was cast: The girl next door, Thalia Meninger, on TV's *(The Many Loves of) Dobie Gillis* (1959) and a gentle charmer so sweet she's named Christian in *The Cincinnati Kid* opposite Steve McQueen. Gradually, she would embrace the Lolita underage-girl-child-as-femme-fatale role, playing such parts with perfection in *Lord Love a Duck*, an off-the-wall mini-masterpiece (and the only directorial work by George Axelrod, author of *The Seven Year Itch*), and as a moonshiner's daughter whose seductiveness cannot be ignored by stalwart Gregory Peck in *I Walk the Line*. Perhaps most memorable of all was *Pretty Poison* (aka *She Let Him Continue*), a cult classic in which her all-American teenager convinces a gawky boy (Tony Perkins) to join her on a crime spree. The sequence in which she licks her lips while squinting as she shoots her mom (Beverly Garland) dead ranks among the greatest moments in cult movie history. Pundits referred to that film as "Lolita meets Psycho!"

The only reason that Tuesday gave for turning down Roman Polanski's offer to play Lady Macbeth was that the character would have to perform a brief (though mild and tasteful) nude sleepwalking scene. However scandalous Tuesday's private life might have been (she did keep the

LOLITA IN THE BIBLE BELT: Even so stalwart a chap as Gregory Peck falls victim to Tuesday Weld's deadly allure in the under-appreciated *I Walk the Line*.

WELD'S BEST REMEMBERED MOMENT: In the cult film *Pretty Poison*, Tuesday's latest deadly Lolita licks her lips as she blows her mother (Beverly Garland) away.

affairs secret) she was too old-fashioned a girl to ever strip down for the camera, even to do Shakespeare. Unaccountably, though, she eventually went nude for a grotesquely graphic rape scene in Sergio Leone's *Once Upon a Time in America* and participated in a wild orgy sequence in *Looking for Mr. Goodbar*. Check it off to the remarkable enigma that always has been, still is, and always will be Tuesday Weld.

Trivia: The Lynard Skynrd song "Tuesday's Gone" does not refer to the day of the week but to the girl born Suzanne.

SELECTED FILMOGRAPHY:

The Wrong Man (Blonde Girl, 1955); *Rock, Rock, Rock* (Dori Graham, 1956); *Rally 'Round the Flag, Boys!* (Comfort Goodpasture, 1958); *The Five Pennies* (Dorothy Nichols, 1959); *Because They're Young* (Anne Gregor, 1959); *Sex Kittens Go to College* (Jody, 1960); *High Time* (Joy Elder, 1960); *The Private Lives of Adam and Eve* (Vangie Harper, 1960); *Return to Peyton Place* (Selena, 1961); *Wild in the Country* (Noreen, 1961); *Bachelor Flat* (Libby, 1962); *Soldier in the Rain* (Bobby Jo Pepperdine, 1963); *I'll Take Sweden* (JoJo, 1965); *The Cincinnati Kid* (Christian, 1965); *Lord Love a Duck* (Barbara Ann Greene, 1966); *Pretty Poison* (Sue Ann, 1968); *I Walk the Line* (Alma McCain, 1970); *A Safe Place* (Susan/Noah, 1971); *Play It As it Lays* (Maria, 1972); *Looking for Mr. Goodbar* (Katherine, 1977); *Who'll Stop the Rain* (Marge, 1978); *Serial* (Kate Linville, 1980); *Thief* (Jessie, 1981); *Author! Author!* (Gloria, 1981); *Once Upon a Time in America* (Carol, 1984); *Heartbreak Hotel* (Marie Wolfe, 1988); *Falling Down* (Amanda Prendergast, 1993); *Feeling Minnesota* (Nora, 1996); *Chelsea Walls* (Greta, 2001).

Celeste Yarnall

Birthdate: July 26, 1944; Long Beach, CA
Height: N/A
Measurements: N/A

HAD YOU STROLLED THROUGH Beverly Hills and its surrounding Chi-Chi locations during the 1980s, you'd have been overwhelmed by large signs on commercial properties reading: "For Sale: Celeste Yarnall Real Estate." If you happened to be a fan of forbidden cinema, you could not help but pause and wonder: Is that the same 'Celeste Yarnall' who starred in *The Velvet Vampire*? Yes, it was. Unlike so many statuesque beauties who briefly decorated films only to find themselves unemployed as newer, younger girls happened along, Yarnall recreated herself— several times, in fact—ultimately becoming a successful businesswoman. And, better yet, one with a cause: Animal Rights Activism.

Back in 1964, a once-beloved, now quaint custom held over from the Fifties remained alive if not necessarily well: The Miss Rheingold (beer) Competition. Eighteen-year-old Celeste was the final winner (Number 25) before that beauty contest expired. She garnered a whopping 20,000,000 votes from enamored (mostly male) fans who'd fallen in love with that perfectly modulated face as they reached for a six pack at the corner (family-owned) neighborhood Deli. Celeste embarked on a series of personal appearances and TV, radio, and print spots that made her if not a household name then certainly a nationally-known glamour girl to be reckoned with. Among the opportunities that arose: Appearing with Elvis Presley (though Michele Carey was the top-billed female lead) in what, unfortunately, rates of one of The King's lesser vehicles, *Live a Little, Love a Little*. Hardly a Big Beat classic on the order of *Jailhouse Rock*, this

SHEENA BY ANY OTHER NAME IS STILL SHEENA!: Celeste Yarnell as a jungle goddess in *Eve*.

ONCE IN LOVE WITH ELVIS: Though not the female lead, Celeste had a most impressive
moment with The King in *Live a Little, Love a Little*.

MR. CHEKOV'S GREAT LOVE: The *Star Trek* scene-stealer had a memorably
close encounter with crew-mate Celeste Yarnall.

mini-musical at least allowed Charlene to listen adoringly while The King sang a hard-driving love ballad ("A Little Less Conversation") to her.

Earlier, she'd appeared in two mid-1960s TV series that relied heavily on glamorous femme fatales: *The Man from U.N.C.L.E.* (10/14/1966), as sleek spy Andrea Fouchet and, more memorably still, *Star Trek* (10/13/1967). In "The Apple" she played Yoeman Martha Landon, pro-

THE SPY WITH GREAT THIGHS: Celeste Yarnell was one of the many deadly female agents to appear on *The Man from U.N.C.L.E.*

viding a love interest for Chekhov. Despite being named a top Deb Star in 1967, Yarnall's career went nowhere. There were quickie films for producers well known for such stuff: Harry Allan Towers' *Eve*, about a Sheena-like jungle goddess in which she wore the skimpiest bikini yet to appear in a mainstream film (this shortly before The String was unveiled) and Roger Corman's *The Velvet Vampire*. The latter was, intriguingly, directed by a woman, Stephanie Rothman, she attempting to depict the traditional succubus-beauty (Celeste's character's name is Diane LeFanu) less as a cold and calculating beautiful-monster than a strong, smart woman who has empowered herself, if in a less than socially-acceptable manner. Meanwhile, Celeste set out to conquer the upscale real-estate world (and did) and penned the world's first holistic healthcare book... for cats! She bred felines as well, shortly moving on to proper care for dogs. Eventually Yarnall earned a Ph.D. in Nutrition and set about lecturing in various venues.

SELECTED FILMOGRAPHY:

Under the Yum Yum Tree (The New Girl, 1963); *Eve* (Eve, 1968); *Live a Little, Love a Little* (Ellen, 1968); *Bob & Carol & Ted & Alice* (Susan, 1969); *Beast of Blood* (Myra, 1971); *The Velvet Vampire* (Diane LeFanu, 1971); *The Mechanic* (The Mark's Girl, 1972); *Scorpio* (Helen Thomas, 1973); *Midnight Kiss* (Sheila, 1993); *Born Yesterday* (Mrs. Hedges, 1993).

AN ERA TO REMEMBER: However much edgy fun the movies supplied, some of the advertising posters are, in truth, more memorable than the films themselves!

EL MILLON DE OJOS DE SU-MURU

TECHNICOLOR® TECHNISCOPE®

FRANKIE AVALON · GEORGE NADER
SHIRLEY EATON · WILFRID HYDE-WHITE

DIRECTOR: LINDSAY SHONTEFF

CPSIA information can be obtained at www.ICGtesting.com
Printed in the USA
BVOW06*0641240216

437873BV00009B/175/P